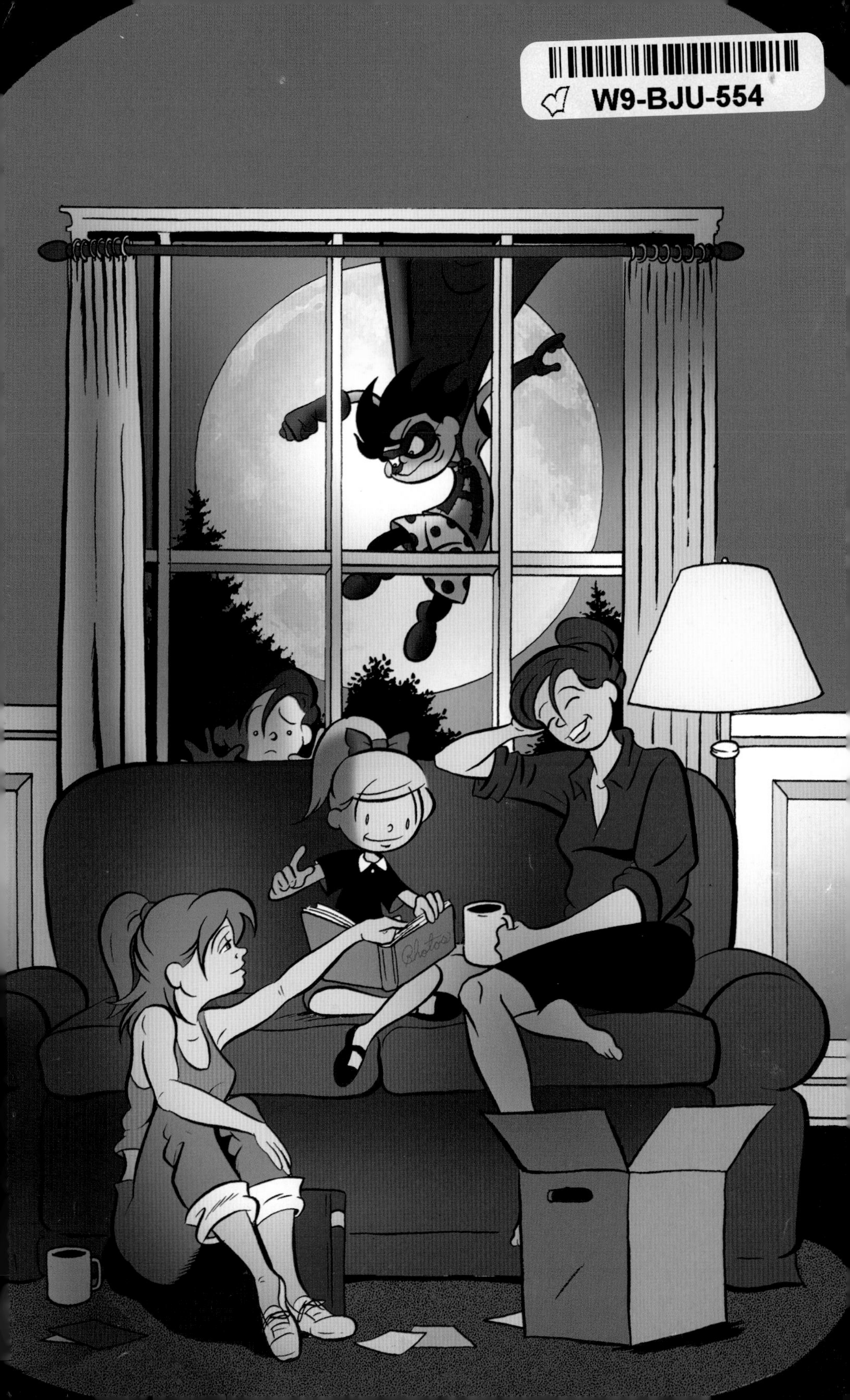
Photos

A Publication of **Renaissance Press**

Amelia Rules! Volume Four:
When the Past Is a Present

TM and Copyright © 2008 Jimmy Gownley
All Rights Reserved

Introduction Copyright © David Fury

Cover art and design
Copyright © Jimmy Gownley

A Renaissance Press Book

Renaissance Press
PO Box 5060
Harrisburg, PA 17110

www.ameliarules.com

ISBN 978-09712169-9-0 (softcover)
ISBN 978-09712169-8-3 (hardcover)

First Renaissance Press edition 2008
10 9 8 7 6 5 4 3 2 1

Editor: Michael Cohen
Marketing and Promotion: Karen Gownley
Director of Publishing and Operations: Harold Buchholz
Brand Manager: Ben Haber

Printed in Korea

Other Books in This Series:

Amelia Rules! The Whole World's Crazy
ISBN 978-0-9712169-2-1 (softcover)
ISBN 978-0-9712169-3-8 (hardcover)
Amelia Rules! What Makes You Happy
ISBN 978-0-9712169-4-5 (softcover)
ISBN 978-0-9712169-5-2 (hardcover)
Amelia Rules! Superheroes
ISBN 978-0-9712169-6-9 (softcover)
ISBN 978-0-9712169-7-6 (hardcover)

To order additional volumes from Renaissance Press, visit us at ameliarules.com
Also available in fine bookstores and comic shops everywhere
To find the comic shop nearest you call 1-888-comicbook

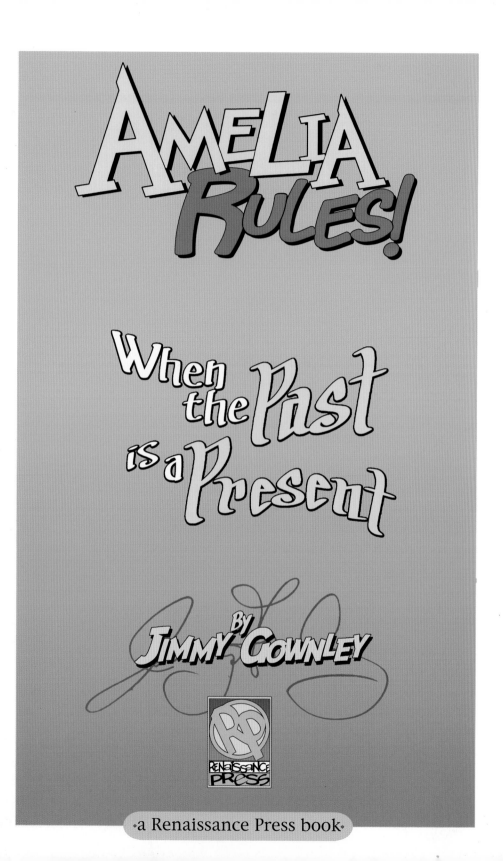

AMELIA RULES!

When the Past is a Present

By JIMMY GOWNLEY

Renaissance Press

a Renaissance Press book

DEDICATION

This book is dedicated to:

Kerensa Bartlett, Hailey Cook, Ethan Gourlay,
James Elmour, Frances Cooke, and everyone at
Small Pond Productions. And especially to
Kasey Perkins who brought Amelia McBride
to life before my very eyes.

That's what magic is.

INTRODUCTION

A few years ago I was appearing at my first convention panel at San Diego's Comic-Con. As enjoyable as it was to wander the cavernous aisles of my comic book heroes, I couldn't help but wish my kids were there to enjoy it with me. Being the good geek father that I am, I tried to raise my children with a healthy dose of Batman, Superman, Spider-Man, etc. My five year-old twin sons were hooked. But, alas, my eight year-old daughter Eden never quite warmed to the exploits of these "-men." She couldn't relate. They weren't real.

And then I met Amelia. Or more accurately, I met Jimmy Gownley and his wife Karen when I stumbled upon and flipped through issues of *Amelia Rules!* at their Comic-Con booth. The artwork was clean and pleasurable, the writing was smart and genuine. And most importantly, Amelia was a girl after my daughter's own heart: a girl roughly the same age, a transplanted New Yorker. And while Eden didn't come from a broken home, she had many friends who did. Amelia was real.

Jimmy and Karen, being fans of my work, generously gave me several issues to take home with me. Eden lapped them up, loving every one of them, hungry for more. So thank you, Amelia, and congratulations, Jimmy. Because of you, my daughter and I now have a comic book we can geek out over together.

David Fury
Writer, Producer
Buffy the Vampire Slayer, Lost, Angel, 24

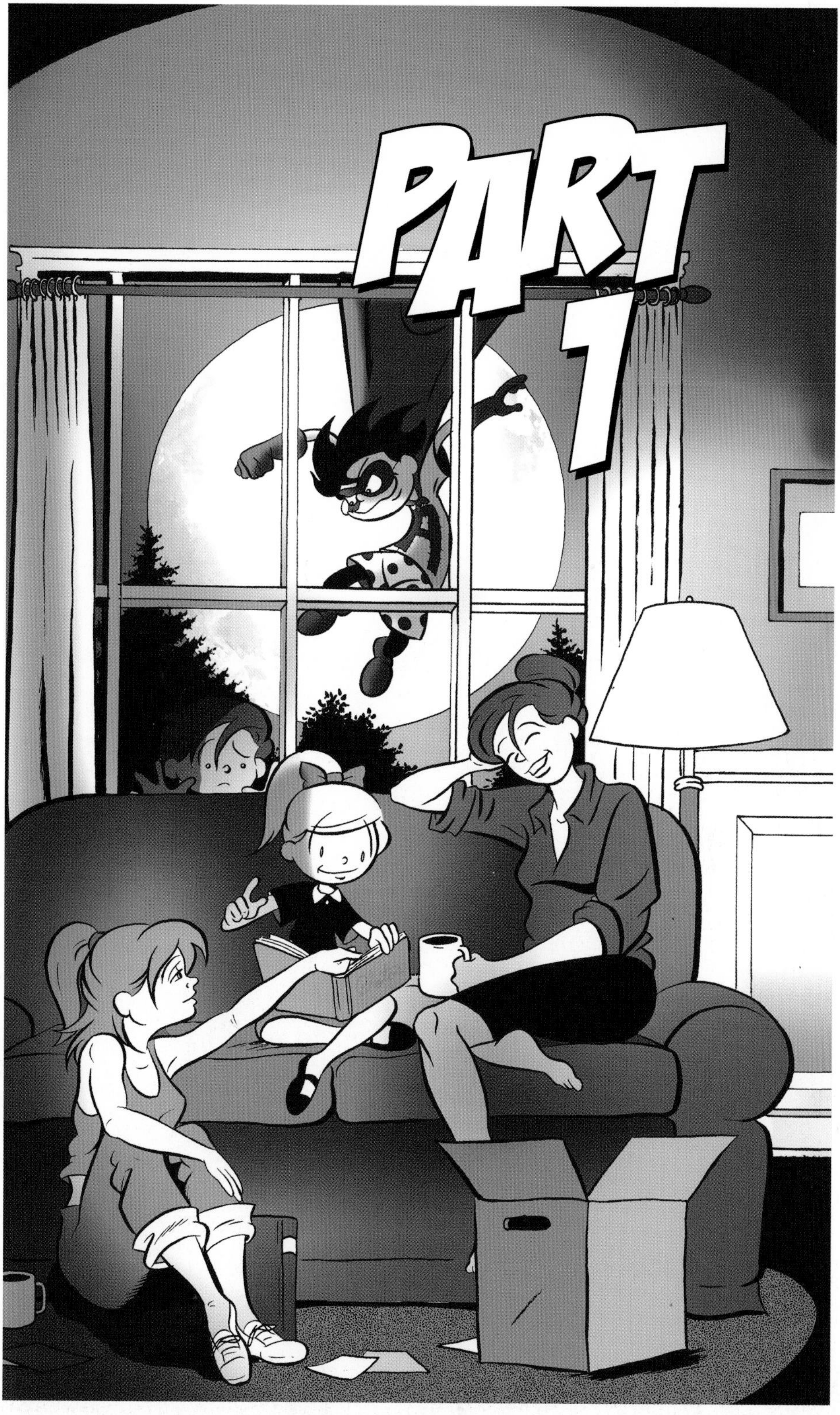
PART
1

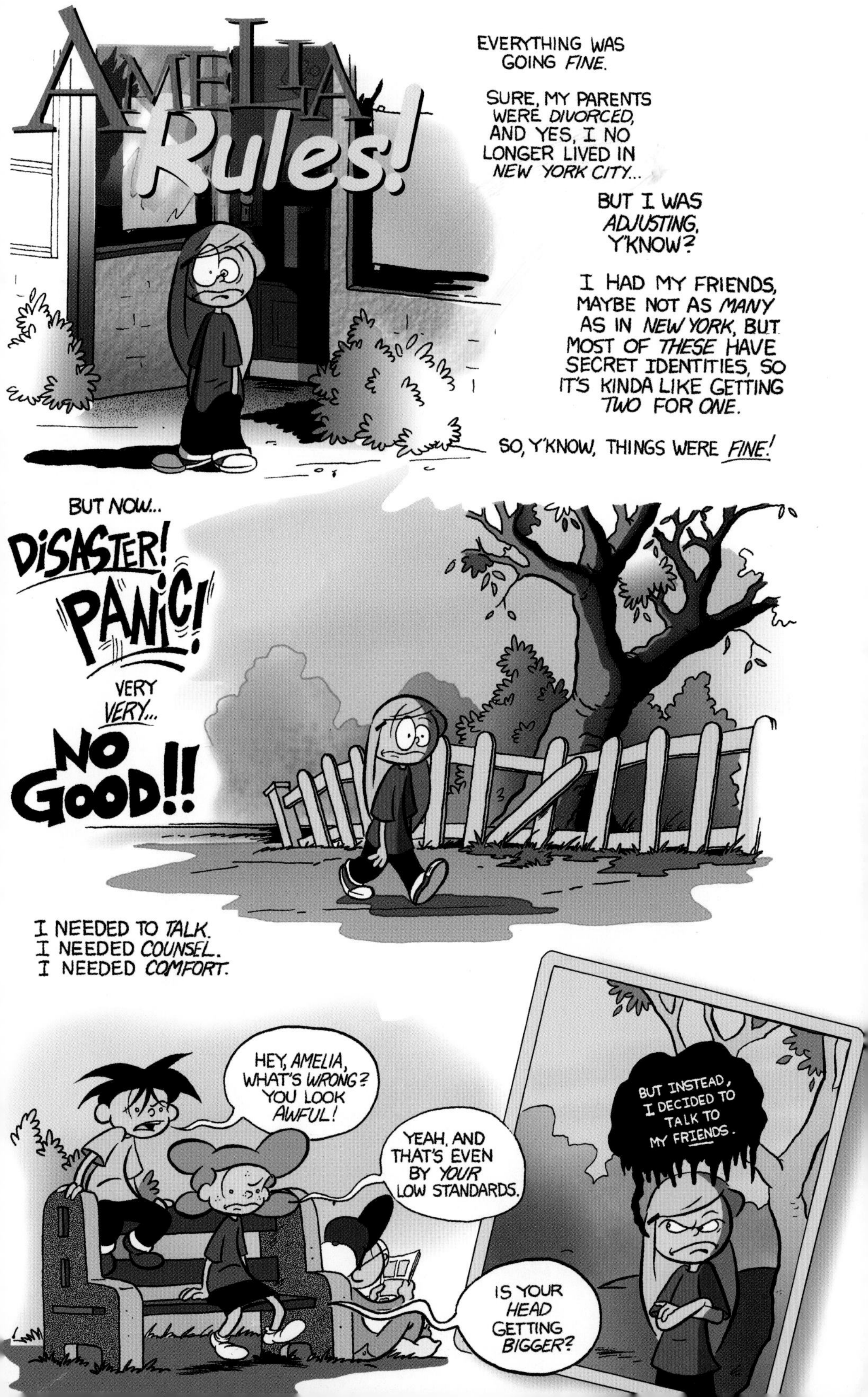
AMELIA Rules!
EVERYTHING WAS GOING FINE.
SURE, MY PARENTS WERE DIVORCED, AND YES, I NO LONGER LIVED IN NEW YORK CITY...
BUT I WAS ADJUSTING, Y'KNOW?
I HAD MY FRIENDS, MAYBE NOT AS MANY AS IN NEW YORK, BUT MOST OF THESE HAVE SECRET IDENTITIES, SO IT'S KINDA LIKE GETTING TWO FOR ONE.
SO, Y'KNOW, THINGS WERE FINE!
BUT NOW...
DISASTER!
PANIC!
VERY VERY...
NO GOOD!!
I NEEDED TO TALK.
I NEEDED COUNSEL.
I NEEDED COMFORT.
BUT INSTEAD, I DECIDED TO TALK TO MY FRIENDS.
HEY, AMELIA, WHAT'S WRONG? YOU LOOK AWFUL!
YEAH, AND THAT'S EVEN BY YOUR LOW STANDARDS.
IS YOUR HEAD GETTING BIGGER?

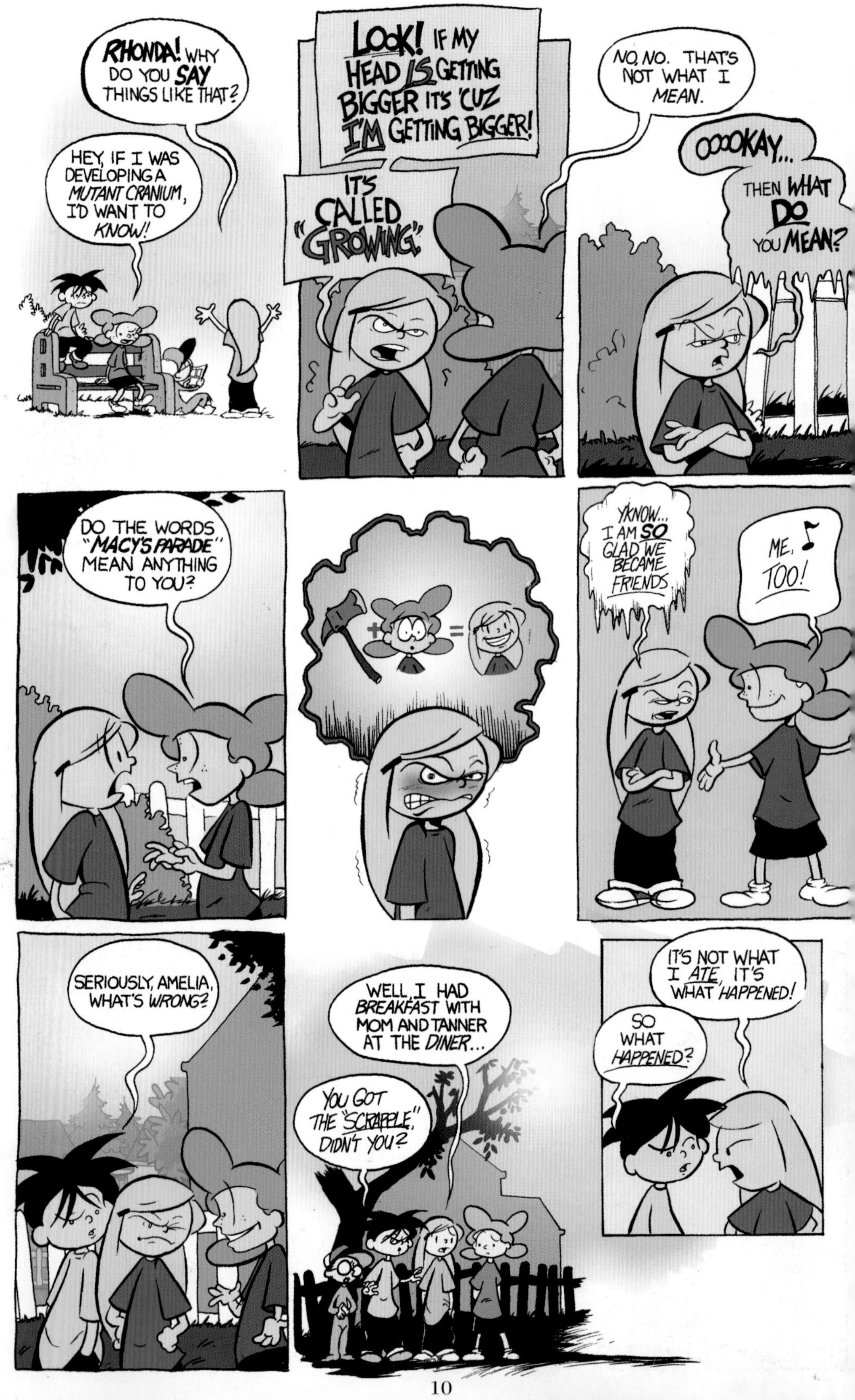
RHONDA! WHY DO YOU SAY THINGS LIKE THAT?
HEY, IF I WAS DEVELOPING A MUTANT CRANIUM, I'D WANT TO KNOW!
LOOK! IF MY HEAD IS GETTING BIGGER IT'S 'CUZ I'M GETTING BIGGER!
IT'S CALLED "GROWING."
NO, NO. THAT'S NOT WHAT I MEAN.
OOOOKAY... THEN WHAT DO YOU MEAN?
DO THE WORDS "MACY'S PARADE" MEAN ANYTHING TO YOU?
Y'KNOW... I AM SO GLAD WE BECAME FRIENDS
ME, TOO!
SERIOUSLY, AMELIA, WHAT'S WRONG?
WELL, I HAD BREAKFAST WITH MOM AND TANNER AT THE DINER...
YOU GOT THE "SCRAPPLE," DIDN'T YOU?
IT'S NOT WHAT I ATE, IT'S WHAT HAPPENED!
SO WHAT HAPPENED?

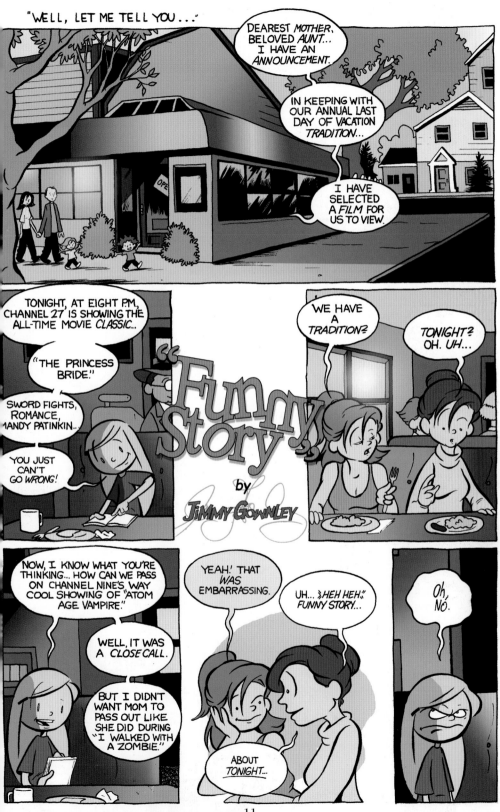

"WELL, LET ME TELL YOU..."

DEAREST *MOTHER*, BELOVED *AUNT*... I HAVE AN *ANNOUNCEMENT*.

IN KEEPING WITH OUR ANNUAL LAST DAY OF VACATION *TRADITION*...

I HAVE SELECTED A *FILM* FOR US TO VIEW.

TONIGHT, AT EIGHT PM, CHANNEL 27 IS SHOWING THE ALL-TIME MOVIE *CLASSIC*...

"THE PRINCESS BRIDE."

SWORD FIGHTS, ROMANCE, MANDY PATINKIN...

YOU JUST CAN'T GO *WRONG*!

Funny Story
by
Jimmy Gownley

WE HAVE A *TRADITION*?

TONIGHT? OH. UH...

NOW, I KNOW WHAT YOU'RE THINKING... HOW CAN WE PASS ON CHANNEL NINE'S WAY COOL SHOWING OF "ATOM AGE VAMPIRE."

WELL, IT WAS A *CLOSE CALL*.

BUT I DIDN'T WANT MOM TO PASS OUT LIKE SHE DID DURING "I WALKED WITH A ZOMBIE."

YEAH! THAT *WAS* EMBARRASSING.

UH... ⟩HEH HEH.⟨ FUNNY STORY...

ABOUT *TONIGHT*...

Oh, NO.

11

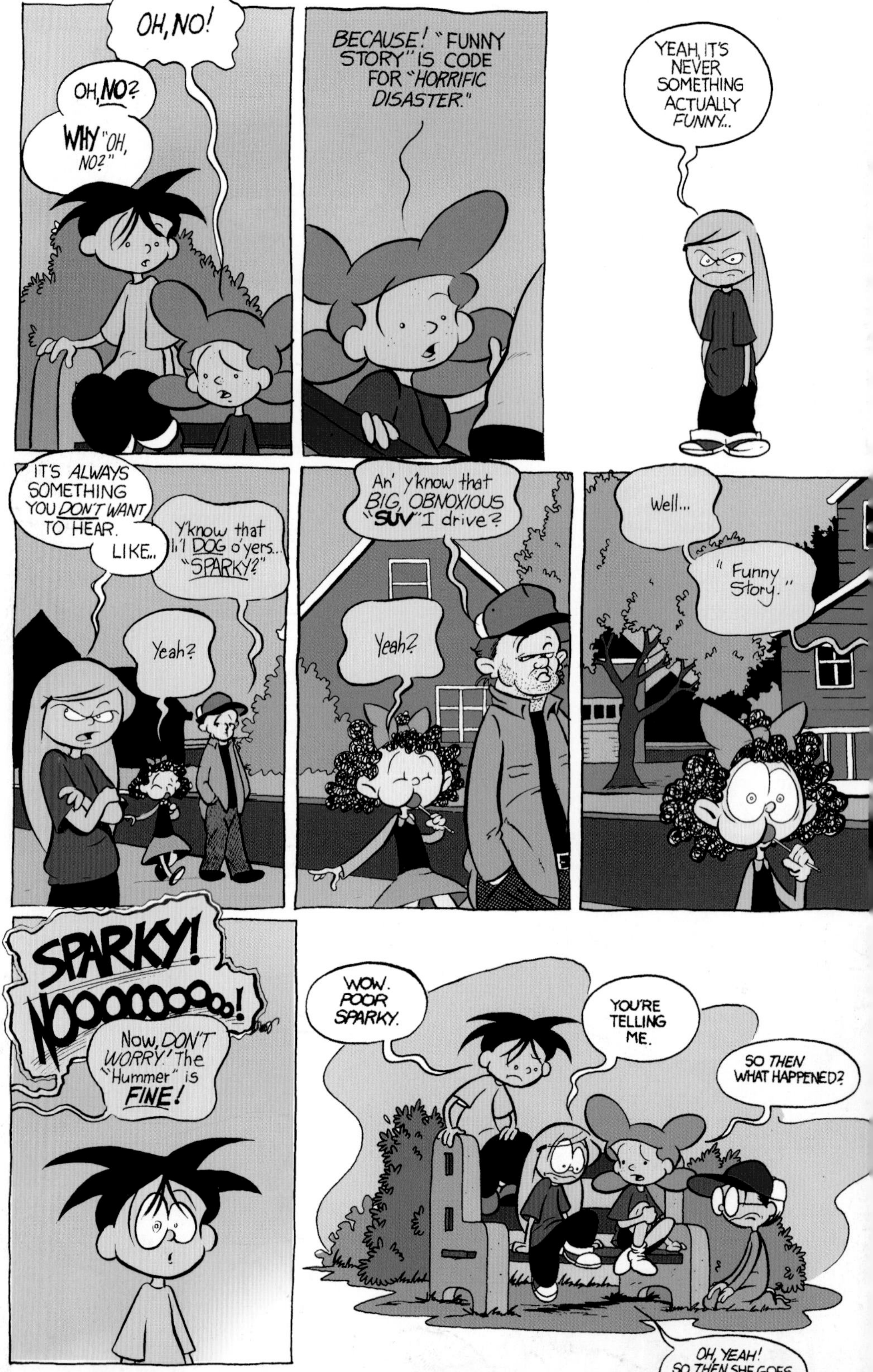
OH, NO!
OH, NO?
WHY "OH, NO?"
BECAUSE! "FUNNY STORY" IS CODE FOR "HORRIFIC DISASTER."
YEAH, IT'S NEVER SOMETHING ACTUALLY FUNNY...
IT'S ALWAYS SOMETHING YOU DON'T WANT TO HEAR.
LIKE...
Y'know that li'l DOG o'yers... "SPARKY?"
Yeah?
An' y'know that BIG, OBNOXIOUS "SUV" I drive?
Yeah?
Well...
" Funny Story."
SPARKY! NOOOOOOOOoo!
Now, DON'T WORRY! The "Hummer" is FINE!
WOW. POOR SPARKY.
YOU'RE TELLING ME.
SO THEN WHAT HAPPENED?
OH, YEAH! SO THEN SHE GOES.

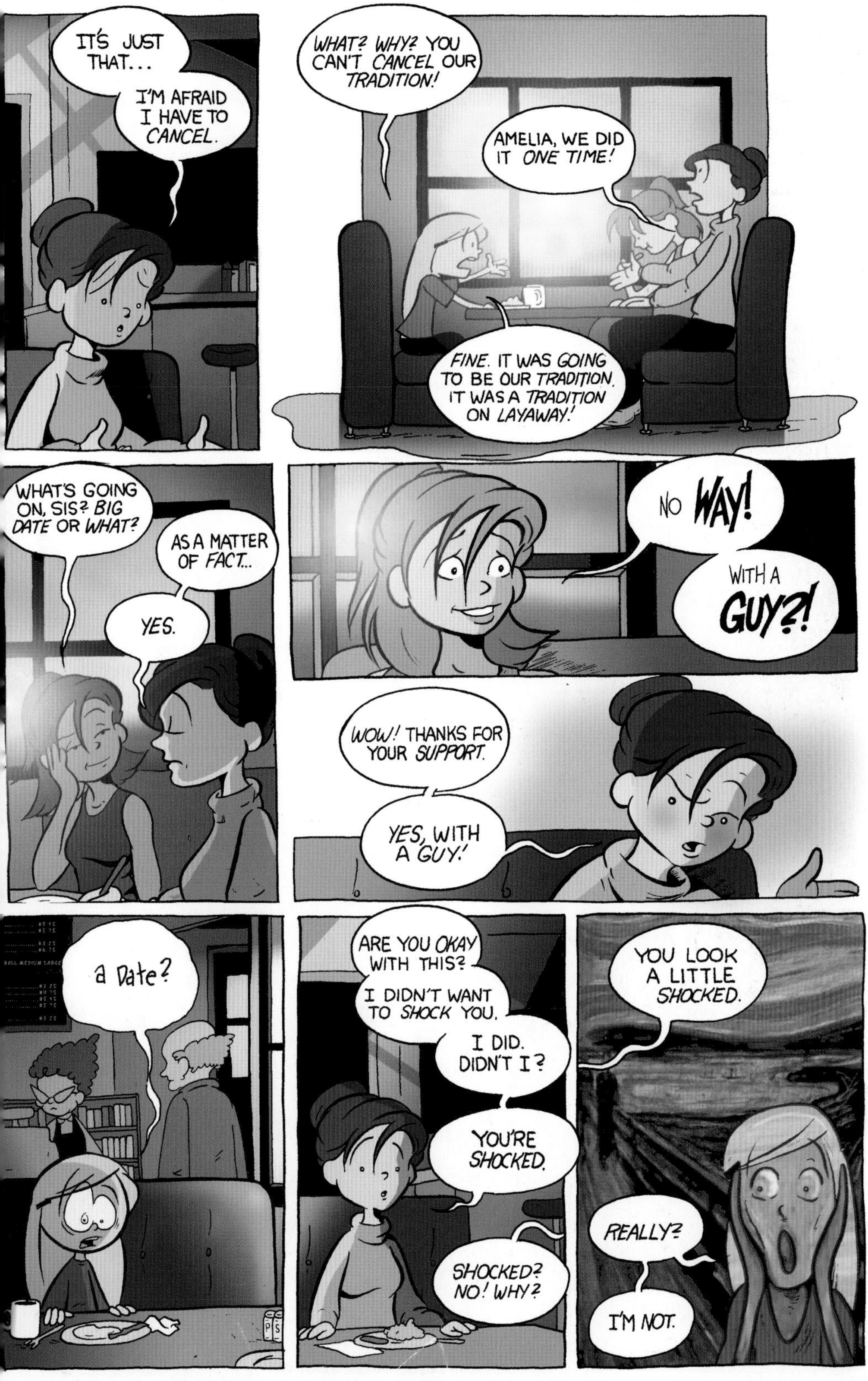
IT'S JUST THAT...
I'M AFRAID I HAVE TO CANCEL.
WHAT? WHY? YOU CAN'T CANCEL OUR TRADITION!
AMELIA, WE DID IT ONE TIME!
FINE. IT WAS GOING TO BE OUR TRADITION. IT WAS A TRADITION ON LAYAWAY!
WHAT'S GOING ON, SIS? BIG DATE OR WHAT?
AS A MATTER OF FACT...
YES.
NO WAY!
WITH A GUY?!
WOW! THANKS FOR YOUR SUPPORT.
YES, WITH A GUY!
a Date?
ARE YOU OKAY WITH THIS?
I DIDN'T WANT TO SHOCK YOU.
I DID. DIDN'T I?
YOU'RE SHOCKED.
SHOCKED? NO! WHY?
YOU LOOK A LITTLE SHOCKED.
REALLY?
I'M NOT.

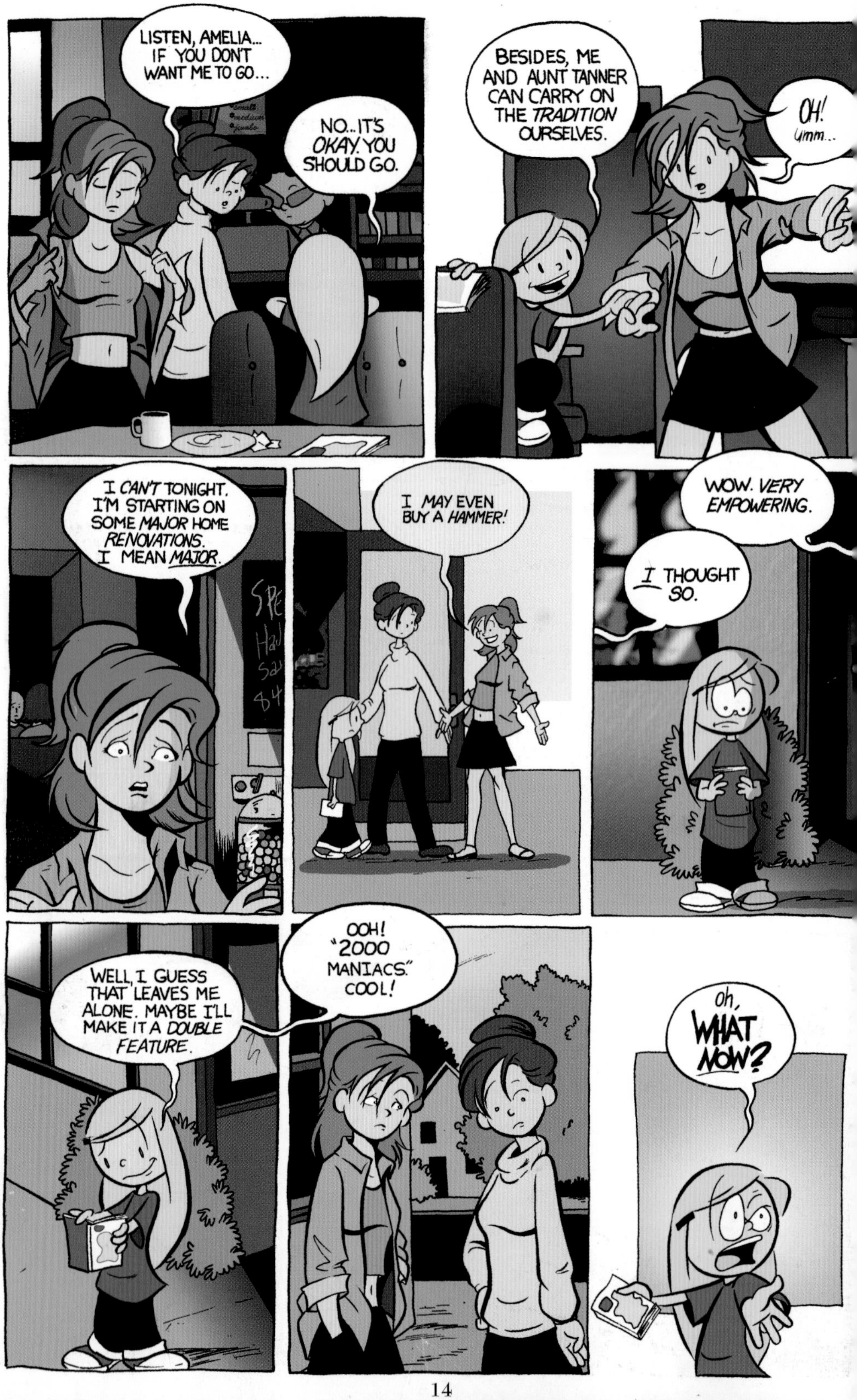
LISTEN, AMELIA... IF YOU DON'T WANT ME TO GO...
small medium jumbo
NO...IT'S OKAY. YOU SHOULD GO.
BESIDES, ME AND AUNT TANNER CAN CARRY ON THE TRADITION OURSELVES.
OH! umm...
I CAN'T TONIGHT. I'M STARTING ON SOME MAJOR HOME RENOVATIONS. I MEAN MAJOR.
I MAY EVEN BUY A HAMMER!
WOW. VERY EMPOWERING.
I THOUGHT SO.
WELL, I GUESS THAT LEAVES ME ALONE. MAYBE I'LL MAKE IT A DOUBLE FEATURE.
OOH! "2000 MANIACS." COOL!
oh, WHAT NOW?

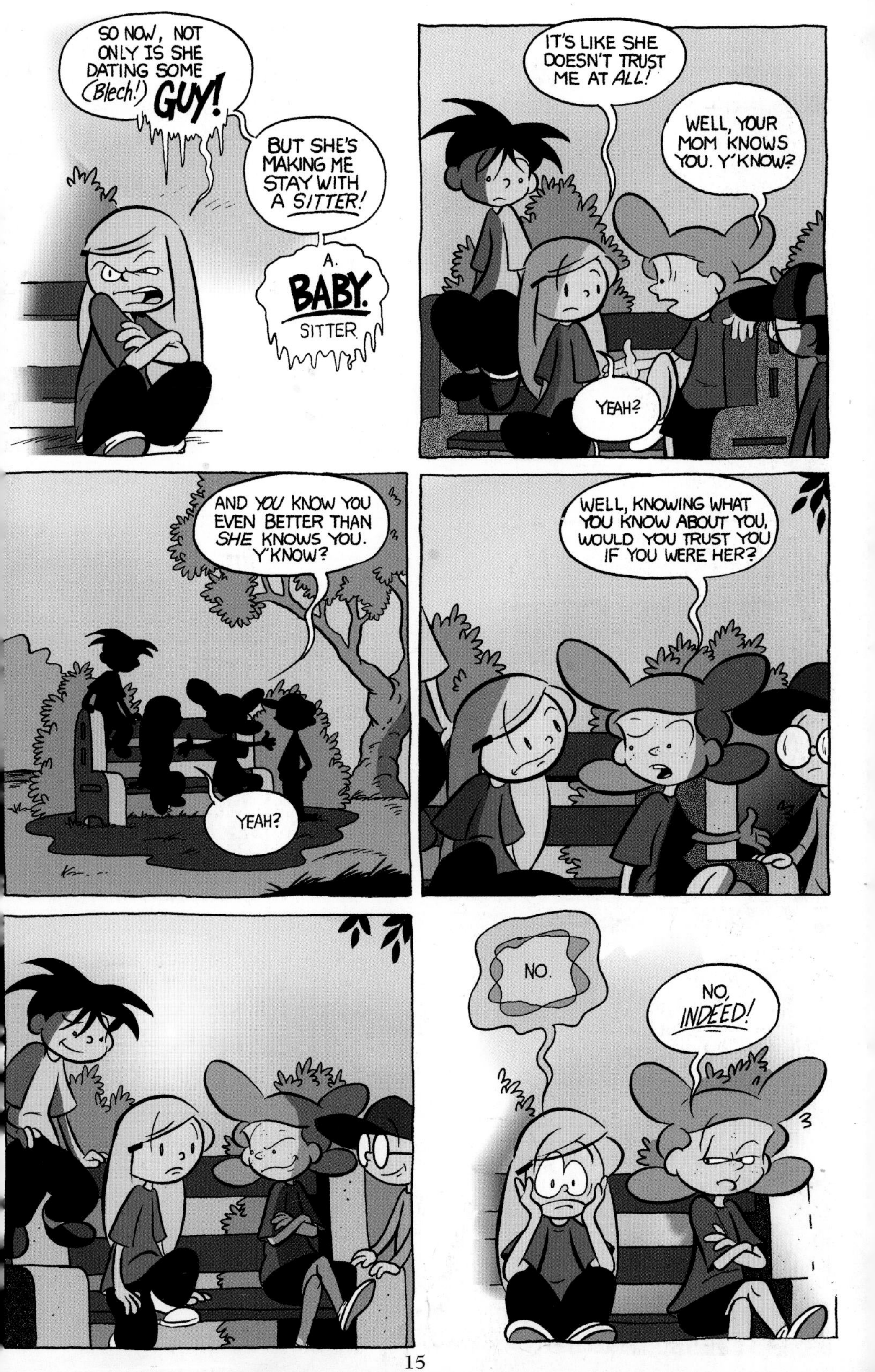
SO NOW, NOT ONLY IS SHE DATING SOME (Blech!) GUY!
BUT SHE'S MAKING ME STAY WITH A SITTER!
A. BABY. SITTER
IT'S LIKE SHE DOESN'T TRUST ME AT ALL!
WELL, YOUR MOM KNOWS YOU. Y'KNOW?
YEAH?
AND YOU KNOW YOU EVEN BETTER THAN SHE KNOWS YOU. Y'KNOW?
YEAH?
WELL, KNOWING WHAT YOU KNOW ABOUT YOU, WOULD YOU TRUST YOU IF YOU WERE HER?
NO.
NO, INDEED!

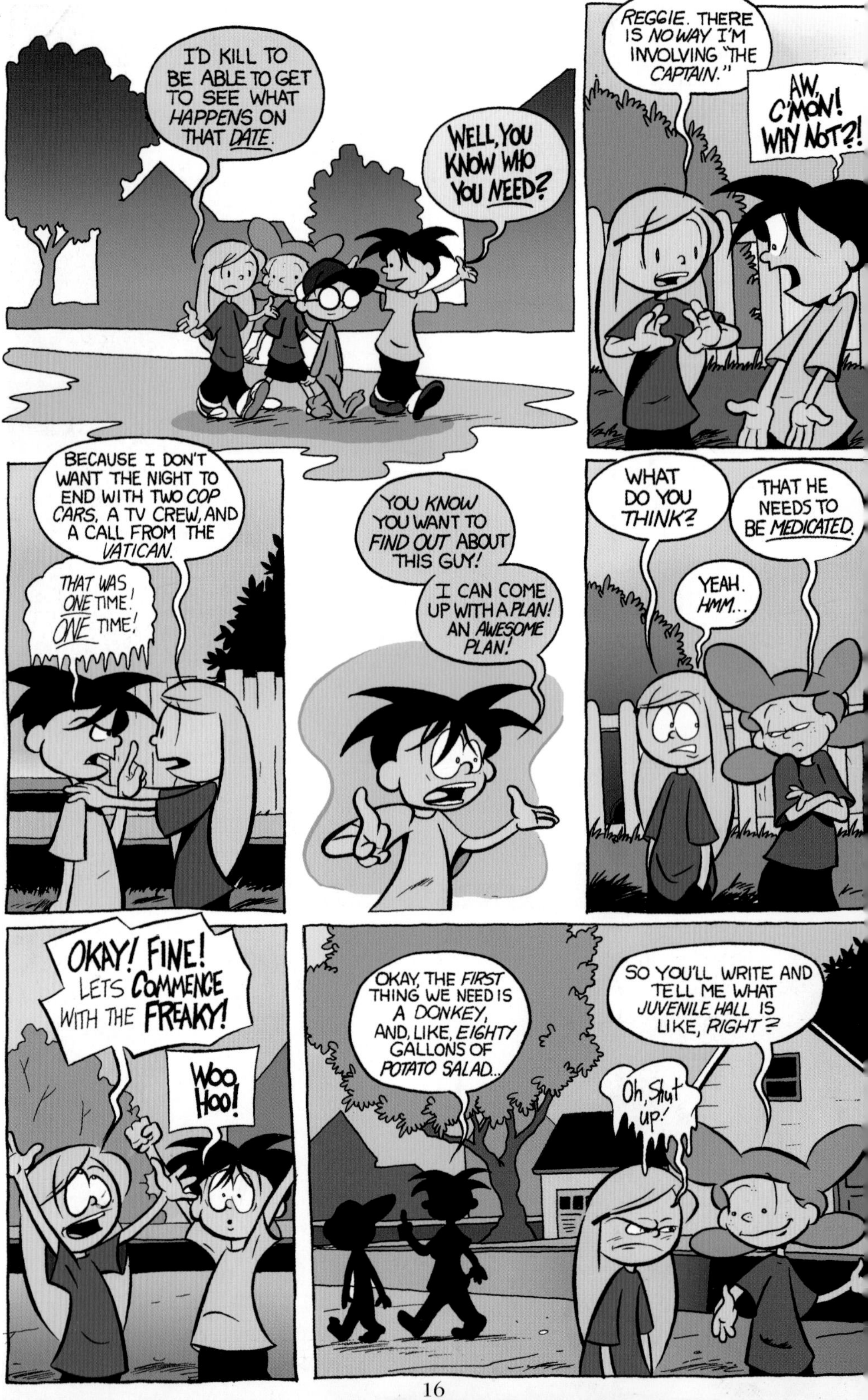
I'D KILL TO BE ABLE TO GET TO SEE WHAT HAPPENS ON THAT DATE.
WELL, YOU KNOW WHO YOU NEED?
REGGIE. THERE IS NO WAY I'M INVOLVING "THE CAPTAIN."
AW, C'MON! WHY NOT?!
BECAUSE I DON'T WANT THE NIGHT TO END WITH TWO COP CARS, A TV CREW, AND A CALL FROM THE VATICAN.
THAT WAS ONE TIME! ONE TIME!
YOU KNOW YOU WANT TO FIND OUT ABOUT THIS GUY!
I CAN COME UP WITH A PLAN! AN AWESOME PLAN!
WHAT DO YOU THINK?
THAT HE NEEDS TO BE MEDICATED.
YEAH. HMM...
OKAY! FINE! LETS COMMENCE WITH THE FREAKY!
WOO HOO!
OKAY, THE FIRST THING WE NEED IS A DONKEY, AND, LIKE, EIGHTY GALLONS OF POTATO SALAD...
SO YOU'LL WRITE AND TELL ME WHAT JUVENILE HALL IS LIKE, RIGHT?
Oh, Shut up!

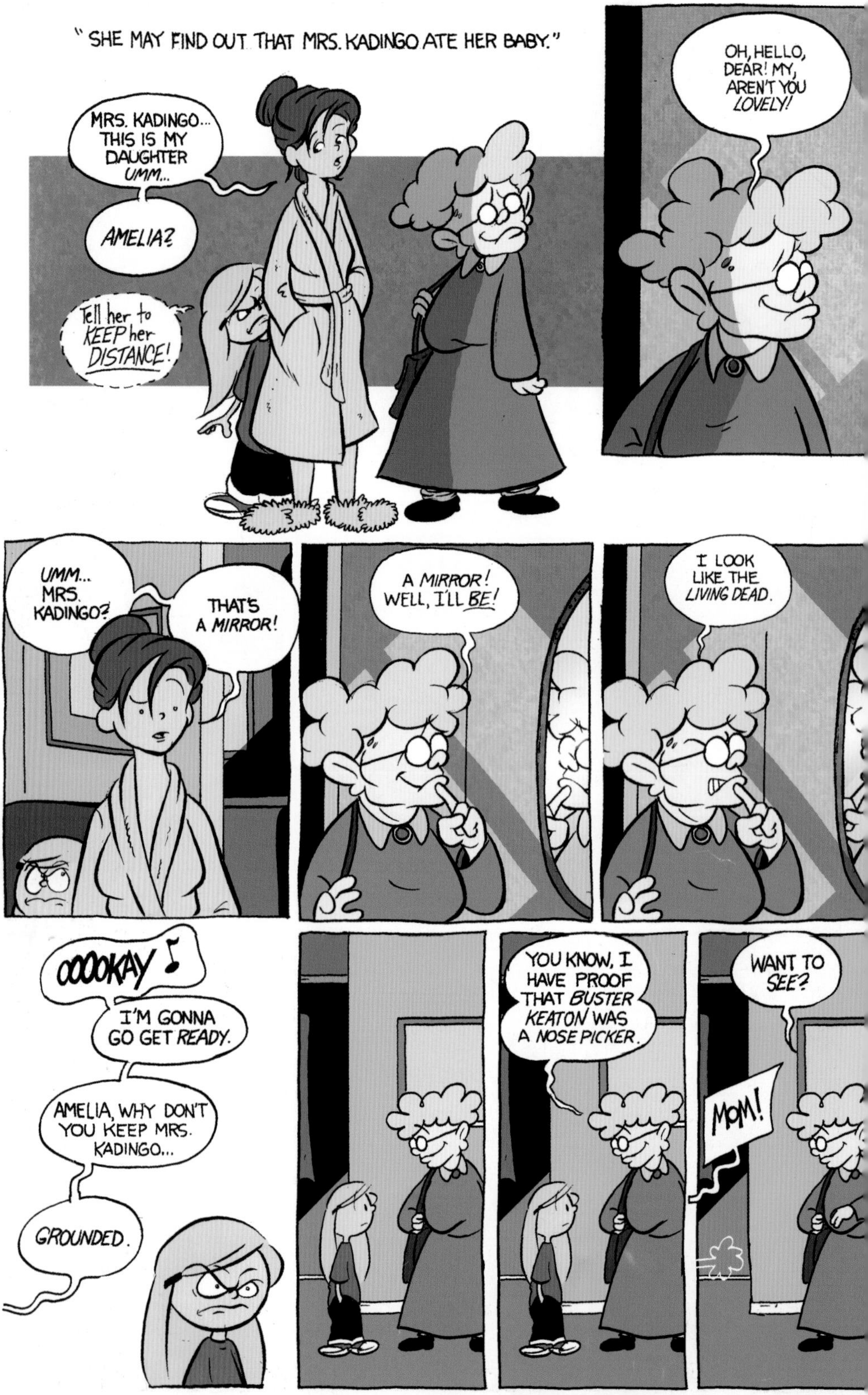
"SHE MAY FIND OUT THAT MRS. KADINGO ATE HER BABY."
MRS. KADINGO... THIS IS MY DAUGHTER UMM...
AMELIA?
Tell her to KEEP her DISTANCE!
OH, HELLO, DEAR! MY, AREN'T YOU LOVELY!
UMM... MRS. KADINGO?
THAT'S A MIRROR!
A MIRROR! WELL, I'LL BE!
I LOOK LIKE THE LIVING DEAD.
OOOOKAY
I'M GONNA GO GET READY.
AMELIA, WHY DON'T YOU KEEP MRS. KADINGO...
GROUNDED.
YOU KNOW, I HAVE PROOF THAT BUSTER KEATON WAS A NOSE PICKER.
WANT TO SEE?
MOM!

SO, BEING TOTALLY ***GROSSED OUT***, I WENT UPSTAIRS TO WATCH MOM GET READY. LOOKING IN THE MIRROR, I DIDN'T SEE THE ***LIVING DEAD***, BUT I FELT LIKE THE ***WALKING WOUNDED***.

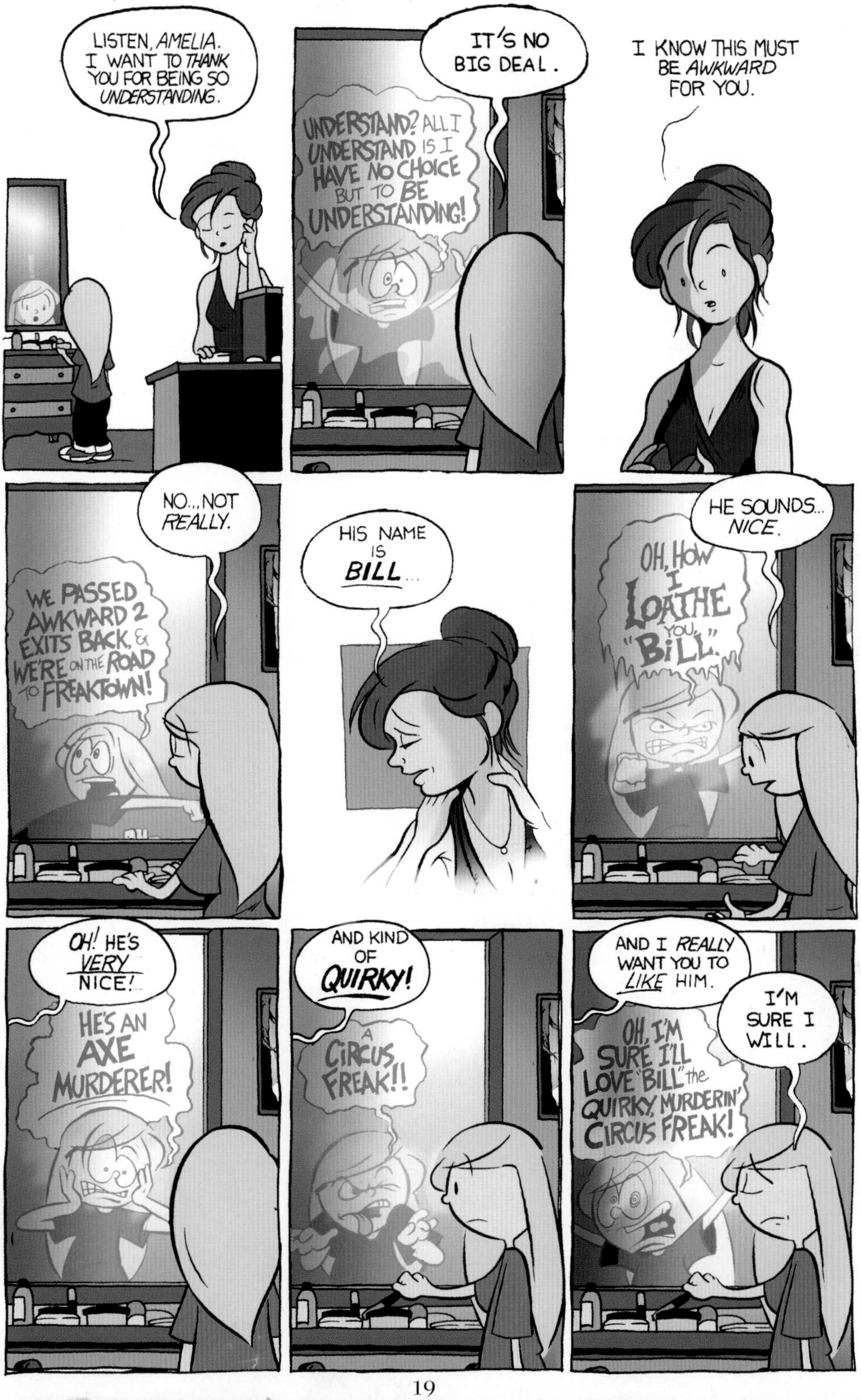
LISTEN, AMELIA. I WANT TO THANK YOU FOR BEING SO UNDERSTANDING.
IT'S NO BIG DEAL.
UNDERSTAND? ALL I UNDERSTAND IS I HAVE NO CHOICE BUT TO BE UNDERSTANDING!
I KNOW THIS MUST BE AWKWARD FOR YOU.
NO... NOT REALLY.
WE PASSED AWKWARD 2 EXITS BACK, & WE'RE ON THE ROAD TO FREAKTOWN!
HIS NAME IS BILL...
HE SOUNDS... NICE.
OH, HOW I LOATHE YOU, "BILL."
OH! HE'S VERY NICE!
HE'S AN AXE MURDERER!
AND KIND OF QUIRKY!
A CIRCUS FREAK!!
AND I REALLY WANT YOU TO LIKE HIM.
I'M SURE I WILL.
OH, I'M SURE I'LL LOVE "BILL" the QUIRKY, MURDERIN' CIRCUS FREAK!

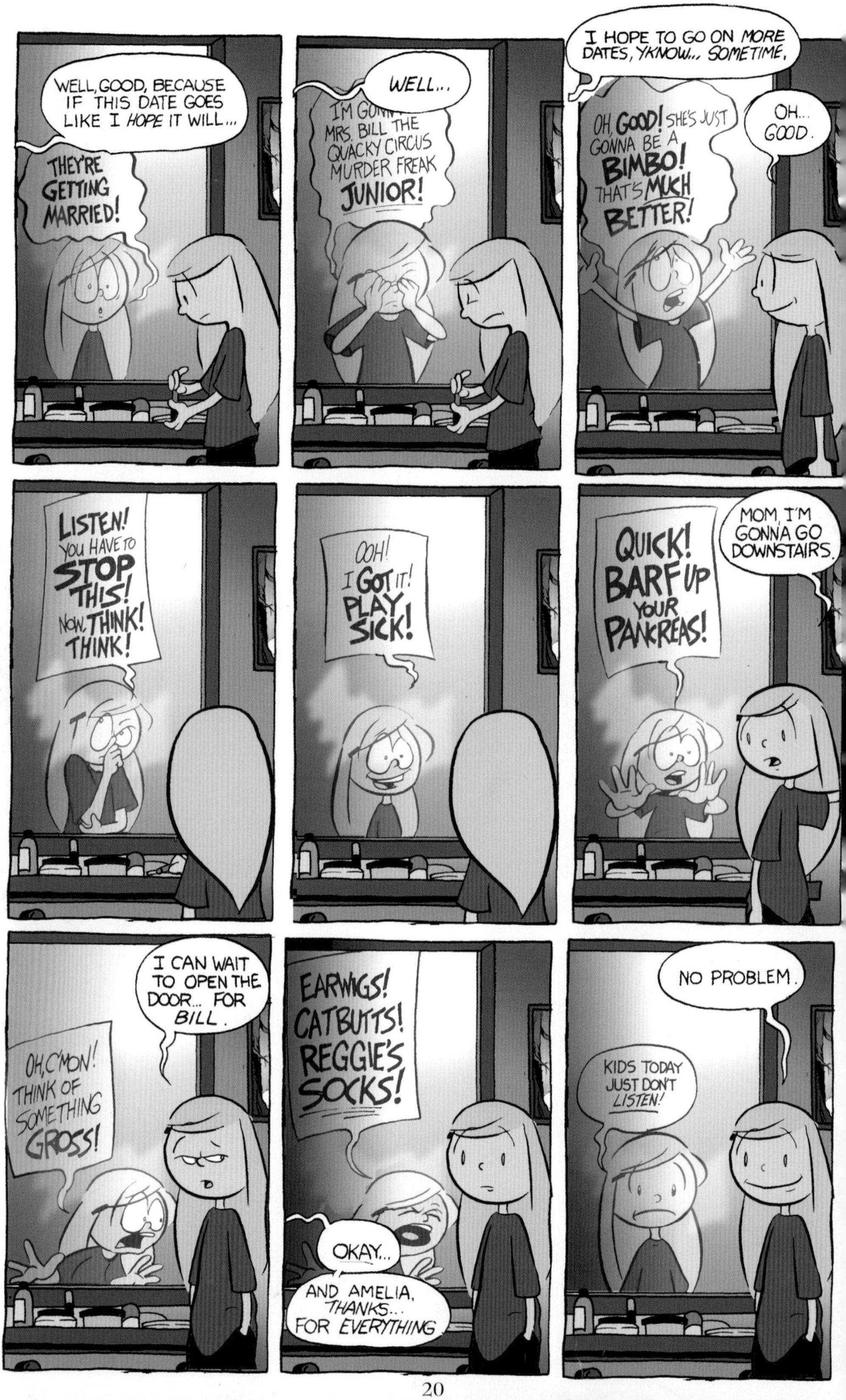
WELL, GOOD, BECAUSE IF THIS DATE GOES LIKE I *HOPE* IT WILL...
THEY'RE GETTING MARRIED!
WELL...
MRS. BILL THE QUACKY CIRCUS MURDER FREAK JUNIOR!
I HOPE TO GO ON *MORE* DATES, Y'KNOW... *SOMETIME*.
OH, GOOD! SHE'S JUST GONNA BE A BIMBO! THAT'S MUCH BETTER!
OH... GOOD.
LISTEN! YOU HAVE TO STOP THIS! NOW, THINK! THINK!
OOH! I GOT IT! PLAY SICK!
QUICK! BARF UP YOUR PANCREAS!
MOM, I'M GONNA GO DOWNSTAIRS.
I CAN WAIT TO OPEN THE DOOR... FOR *BILL*.
OH, C'MON! THINK OF SOMETHING GROSS!
EARWIGS! CATBUTTS! REGGIE'S SOCKS!
OKAY...
AND AMELIA, *THANKS*... FOR *EVERYTHING*.
NO PROBLEM.
KIDS TODAY JUST DON'T *LISTEN*!

23

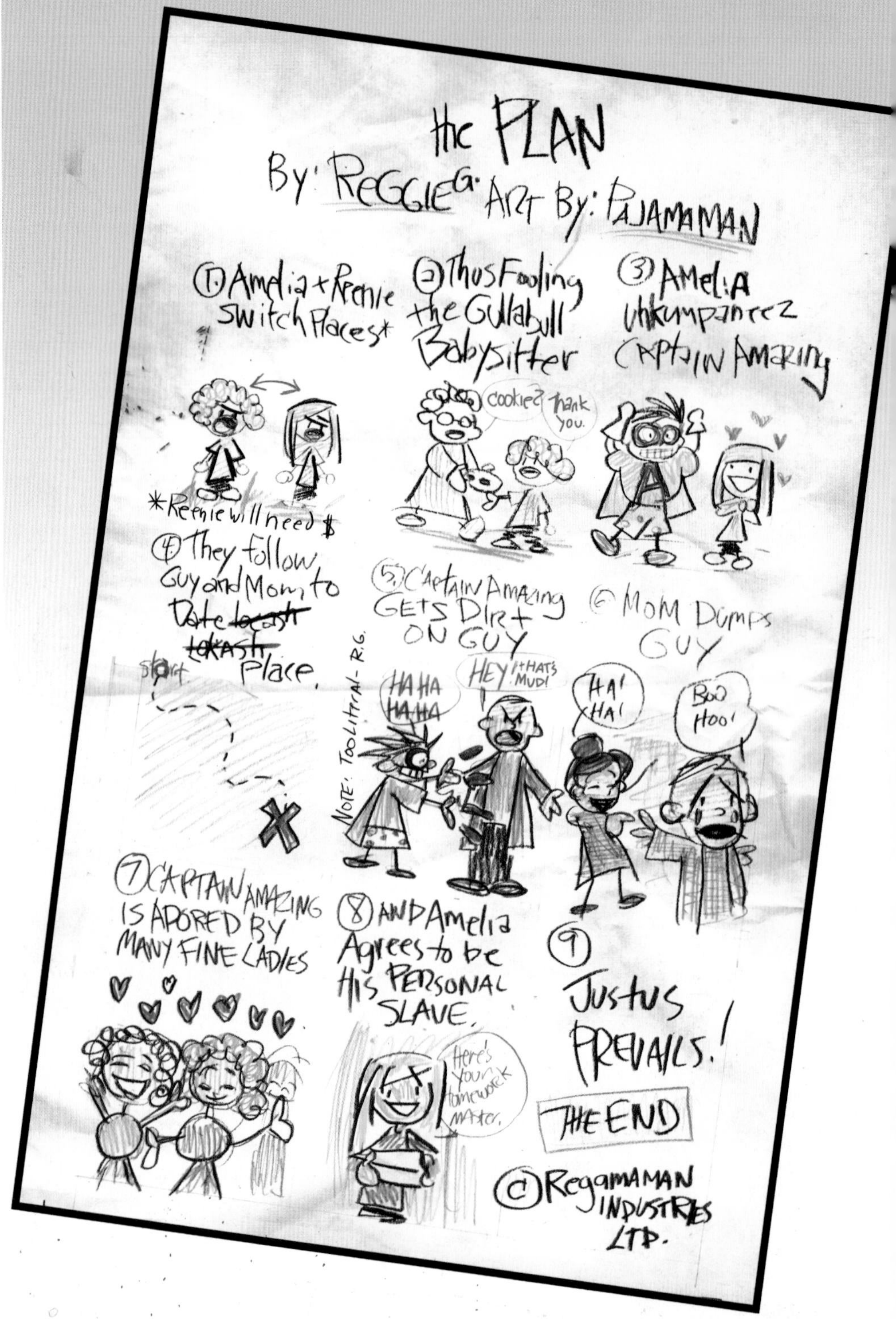
the PLAN
By: ReGGIE G. Art By: PAJAMAMAN
1. Amelia + Reenie switch Places*
2. Thus Fooling the Gullabull Babysitter
3. AMeliA ukumpaneez Captain Amazing
cookie?
thank you.
*Reenie will need $
4. They follow Guy and Mom to Date lokash lokash Place.
start
5. Captain Amazing Gets Dirt on Guy
6. Mom Dumps Guy
NOTE: TOO LITERAL - R.G.
HA HA HA HA
HEY! THAT'S MUD!
HA! HA!
Boo Hoo!
7. CAPTAIN AMAZING IS ADORED BY MANY FINE LADIES
8. AND Amelia Agrees to be His PERSONAL SLAVE.
Here's your homework master.
9. Justus PREVAILS!
THE END
© Regamaman INDUSTRIES LTD.

OKAY, SO MAYBE IT WAS A DUMB PLAN, BUT SINCE I HAD NO DESIRE TO BE "SAT" BY "KRAZY KATE," I TRADED SHIRTS WITH RHONDA'S SISTER AND SENT HER INSIDE, LEAVING ME FREE TO CAVORT WITH THE INFAMOUS CAPTAIN AMAZING.

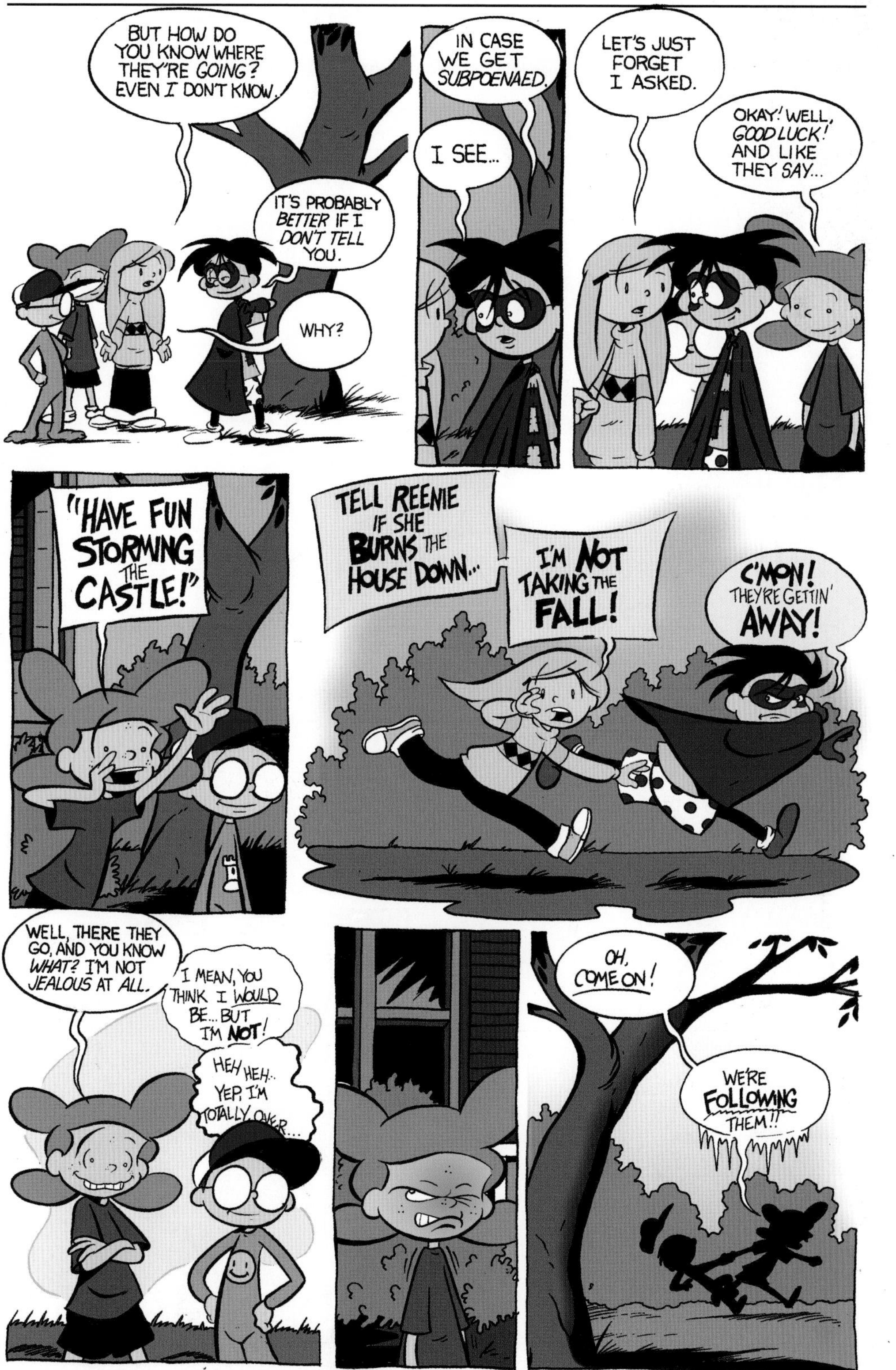

BUT HOW DO YOU KNOW WHERE THEY'RE *GOING*? EVEN *I* DON'T KNOW.
IT'S PROBABLY *BETTER* IF I *DON'T TELL* YOU.
WHY?
IN CASE WE GET *SUBPOENAED*.
I SEE...
LET'S JUST FORGET I ASKED.
OKAY! WELL, *GOOD LUCK!* AND LIKE THEY *SAY*...
"HAVE FUN STORMING THE CASTLE!"
TELL REENIE IF SHE BURNS THE HOUSE DOWN...
I'M NOT TAKING THE FALL!
C'MON! THEY'RE GETTIN' AWAY!
WELL, THERE THEY GO, AND YOU KNOW *WHAT?* I'M NOT *JEALOUS AT ALL*.
I MEAN, YOU THINK I WOULD BE... BUT I'M NOT!
HEH HEH.. YEP, I'M TOTALLY OVER...
OH, COME ON!
WE'RE FOLLOWING THEM!!

26

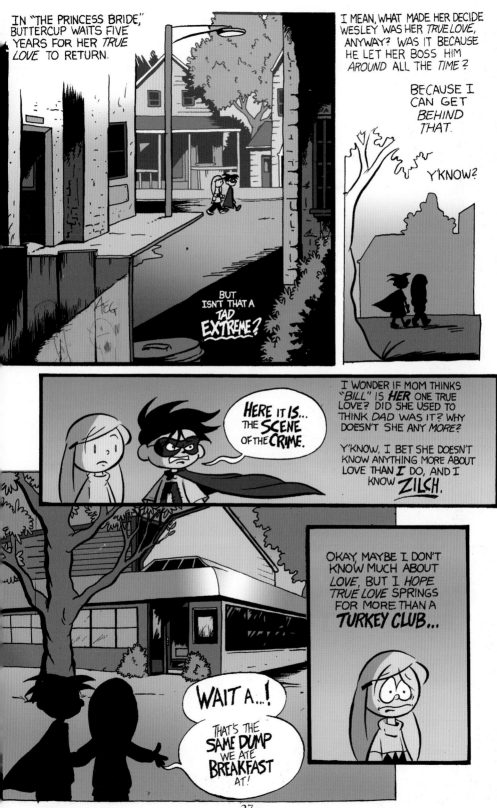

IN "THE PRINCESS BRIDE," BUTTERCUP WAITS FIVE YEARS FOR HER *TRUE LOVE* TO RETURN.

BUT ISN'T THAT A *TAD EXTREME?*

I MEAN, WHAT MADE HER DECIDE WESLEY WAS HER *TRUE LOVE*, ANYWAY? WAS IT BECAUSE HE LET HER BOSS HIM *AROUND* ALL THE *TIME?*

BECAUSE I CAN GET *BEHIND THAT.*

Y'KNOW?

HERE IT *IS...* THE *SCENE* OF THE *CRIME.*

I WONDER IF MOM THINKS "*BILL*" IS *HER* ONE TRUE LOVE? DID SHE USED TO THINK *DAD* WAS IT? WHY DOESN'T SHE ANY *MORE?*

Y'KNOW, I BET SHE DOESN'T KNOW ANYTHING MORE ABOUT LOVE THAN *I* DO, AND I KNOW *ZILCH.*

OKAY, MAYBE I DON'T KNOW MUCH ABOUT *LOVE,* BUT I *HOPE TRUE LOVE* SPRINGS FOR MORE THAN A *TURKEY CLUB...*

WAIT A...!

THAT'S THE *SAME DUMP* WE ATE *BREAKFAST* AT!

27

OTHERWISE, WHY IS EVERYBODY TRYING SO HARD TO FIND IT?

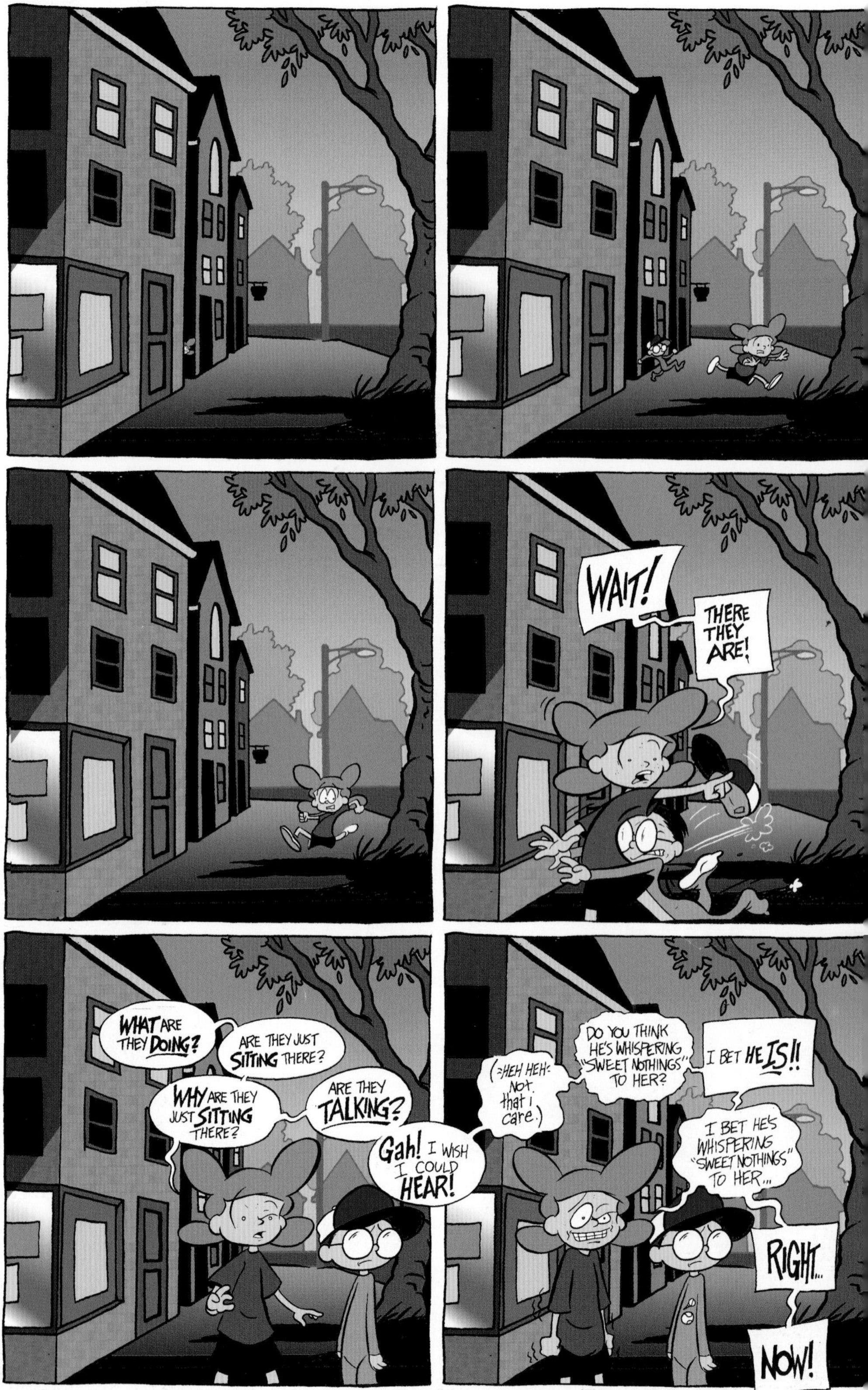

WAIT!
THERE THEY ARE!
WHAT ARE THEY DOING?
ARE THEY JUST SITTING THERE?
WHY ARE THEY JUST SITTING THERE?
ARE THEY TALKING?
Gah! I WISH I COULD HEAR!
(HEH HEH Not that i care.)
DO YOU THINK HE'S WHISPERING "SWEET NOTHINGS" TO HER?
I BET HE IS!!
I BET HE'S WHISPERING "SWEET NOTHINGS" TO HER...
RIGHT...
NOW!

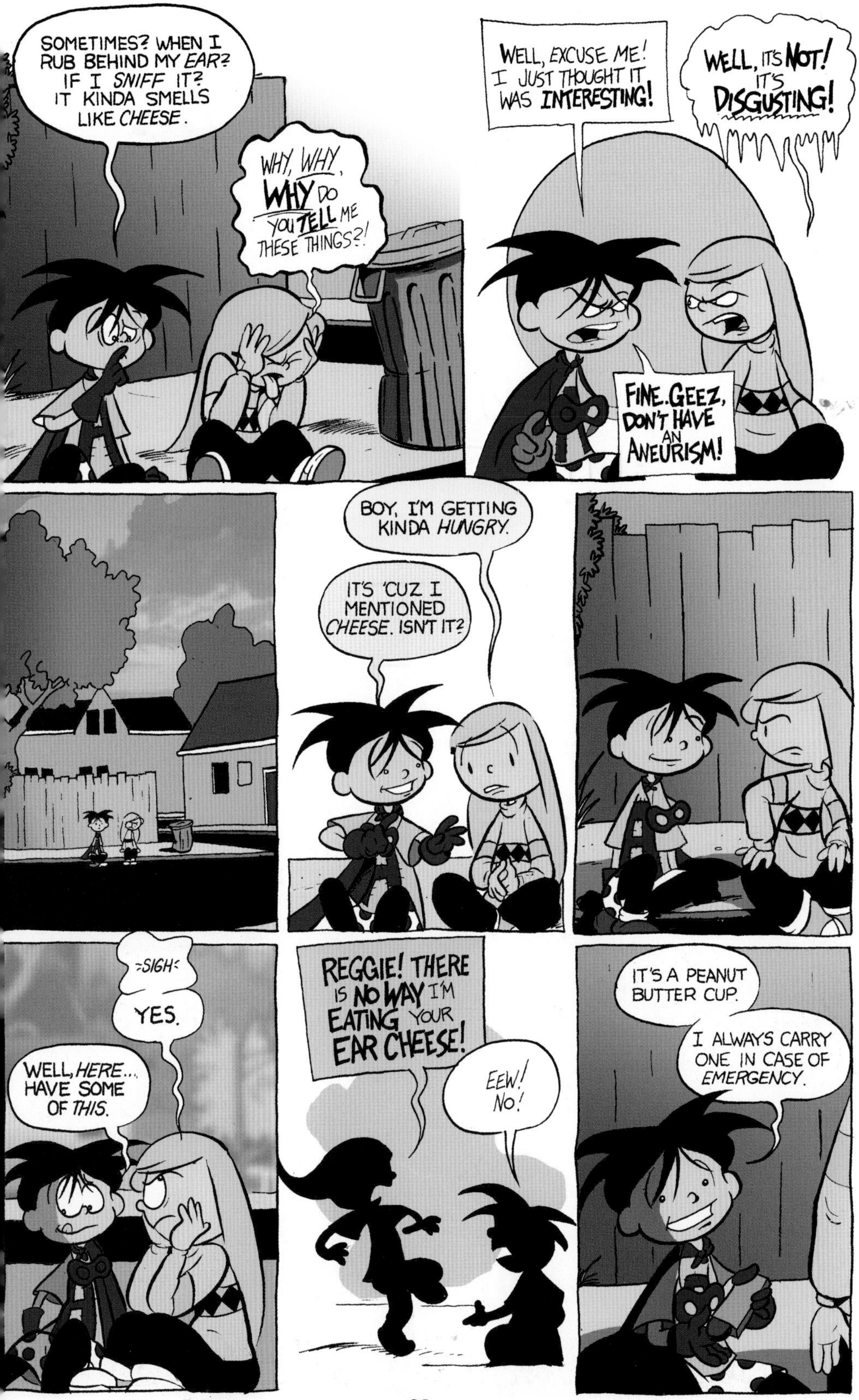
SOMETIMES? WHEN I RUB BEHIND MY EAR? IF I SNIFF IT? IT KINDA SMELLS LIKE CHEESE.
WHY, WHY, WHY DO YOU TELL ME THESE THINGS?!
WELL, EXCUSE ME! I JUST THOUGHT IT WAS INTERESTING!
WELL, IT'S NOT! IT'S DISGUSTING!
FINE. GEEZ, DON'T HAVE AN ANEURISM!
BOY, I'M GETTING KINDA HUNGRY.
IT'S 'CUZ I MENTIONED CHEESE. ISN'T IT?
=SIGH=
YES.
WELL, HERE... HAVE SOME OF THIS.
REGGIE! THERE IS NO WAY I'M EATING YOUR EAR CHEESE!
EEW! NO!
IT'S A PEANUT BUTTER CUP.
I ALWAYS CARRY ONE IN CASE OF EMERGENCY.

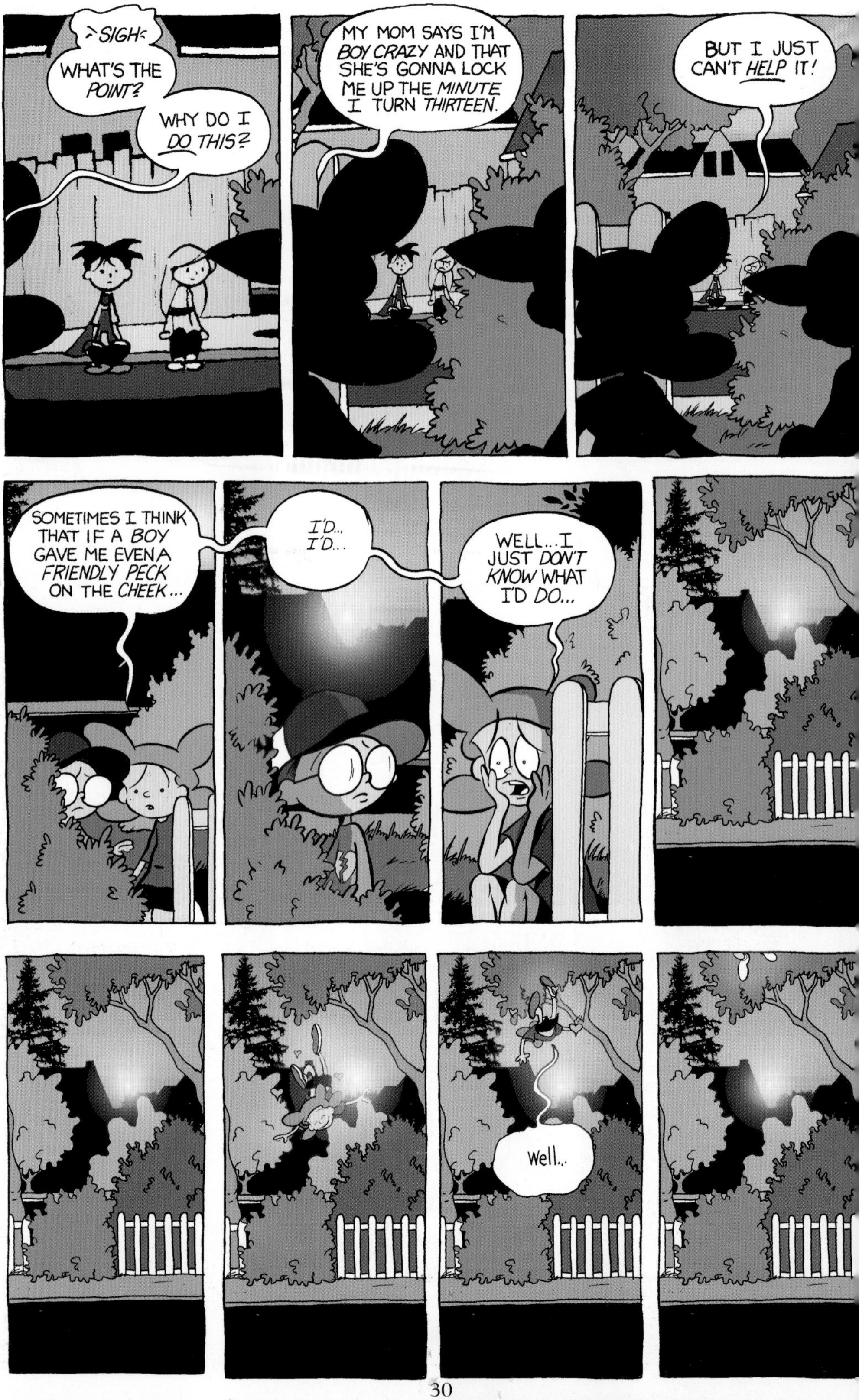

SIGH
WHAT'S THE POINT?
WHY DO I DO THIS?
MY MOM SAYS I'M BOY CRAZY AND THAT SHE'S GONNA LOCK ME UP THE MINUTE I TURN THIRTEEN.
BUT I JUST CAN'T HELP IT!
SOMETIMES I THINK THAT IF A BOY GAVE ME EVEN A FRIENDLY PECK ON THE CHEEK...
I'D... I'D...
WELL... I JUST DON'T KNOW WHAT I'D DO...
Well..

THAT ANSWERS *THAT* QUESTION.

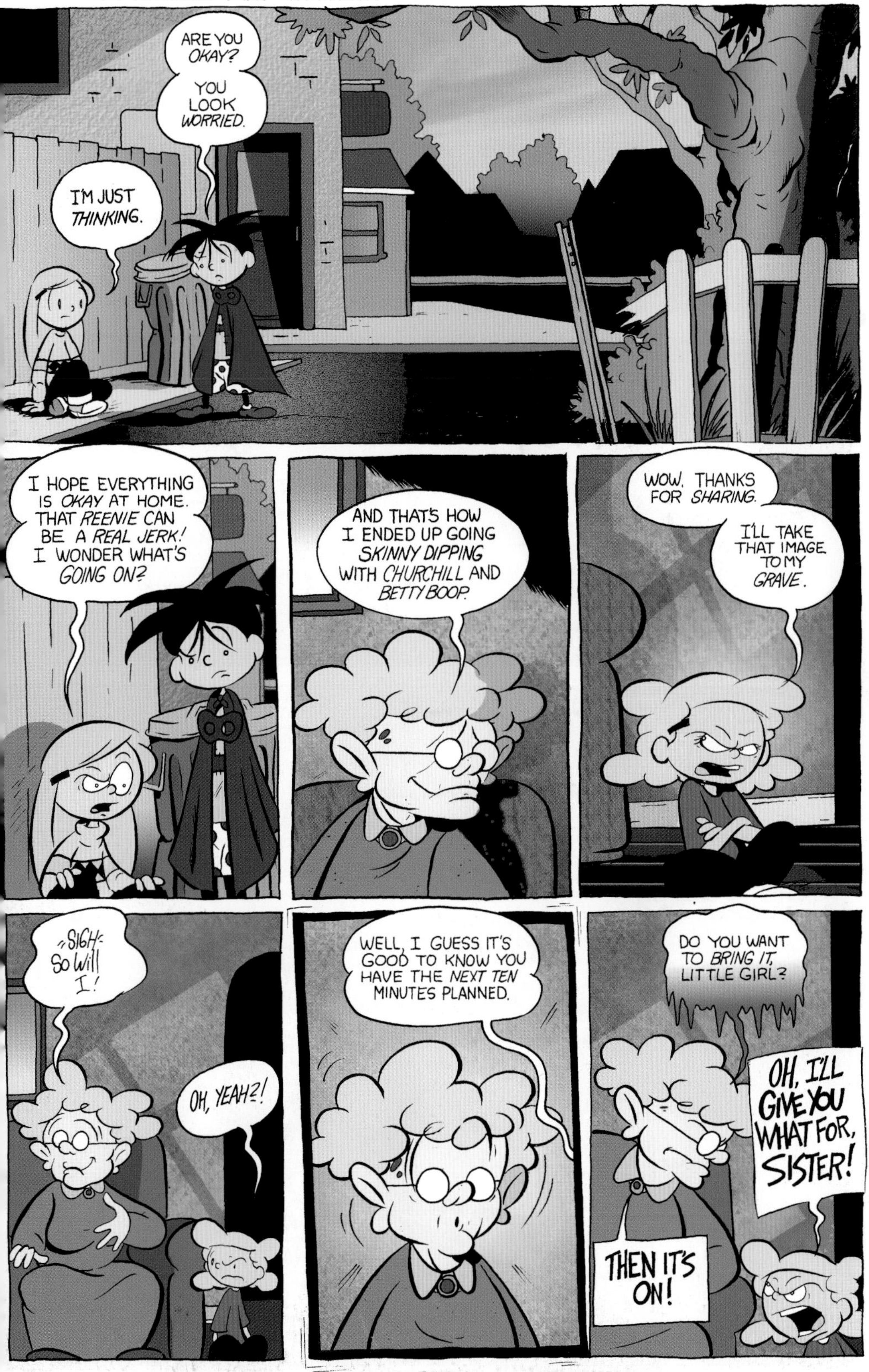
ARE YOU OKAY?
YOU LOOK WORRIED.
I'M JUST THINKING.
I HOPE EVERYTHING IS OKAY AT HOME. THAT REENIE CAN BE A REAL JERK! I WONDER WHAT'S GOING ON?
AND THAT'S HOW I ENDED UP GOING SKINNY DIPPING WITH CHURCHILL AND BETTY BOOP.
WOW. THANKS FOR SHARING.
I'LL TAKE THAT IMAGE TO MY GRAVE.
SIGH
So Will I!
OH, YEAH?!
WELL, I GUESS IT'S GOOD TO KNOW YOU HAVE THE NEXT TEN MINUTES PLANNED.
DO YOU WANT TO BRING IT, LITTLE GIRL?
OH, I'LL GIVE YOU WHAT FOR, SISTER!
THEN IT'S ON!

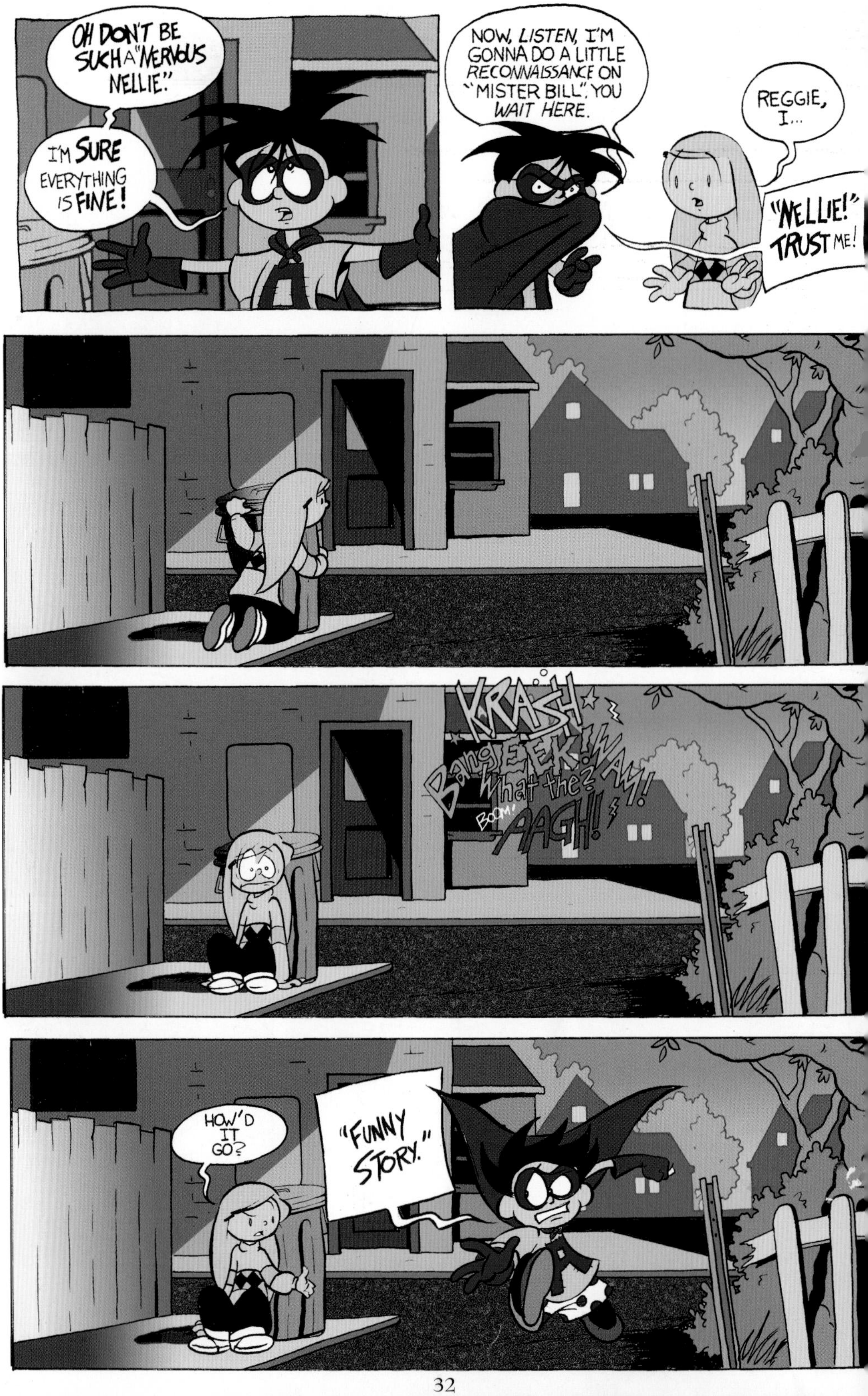
OH DON'T BE SUCH A "NERVOUS NELLIE."
I'M SURE EVERYTHING IS FINE!
NOW, LISTEN, I'M GONNA DO A LITTLE RECONNAISSANCE ON "MISTER BILL". YOU WAIT HERE.
REGGIE, I...
"NELLIE!" TRUST ME!
KRASH
Bang
EEK!
WAM!
What the?
BOOM!
AAGH!
HOW'D IT GO?
"FUNNY STORY."

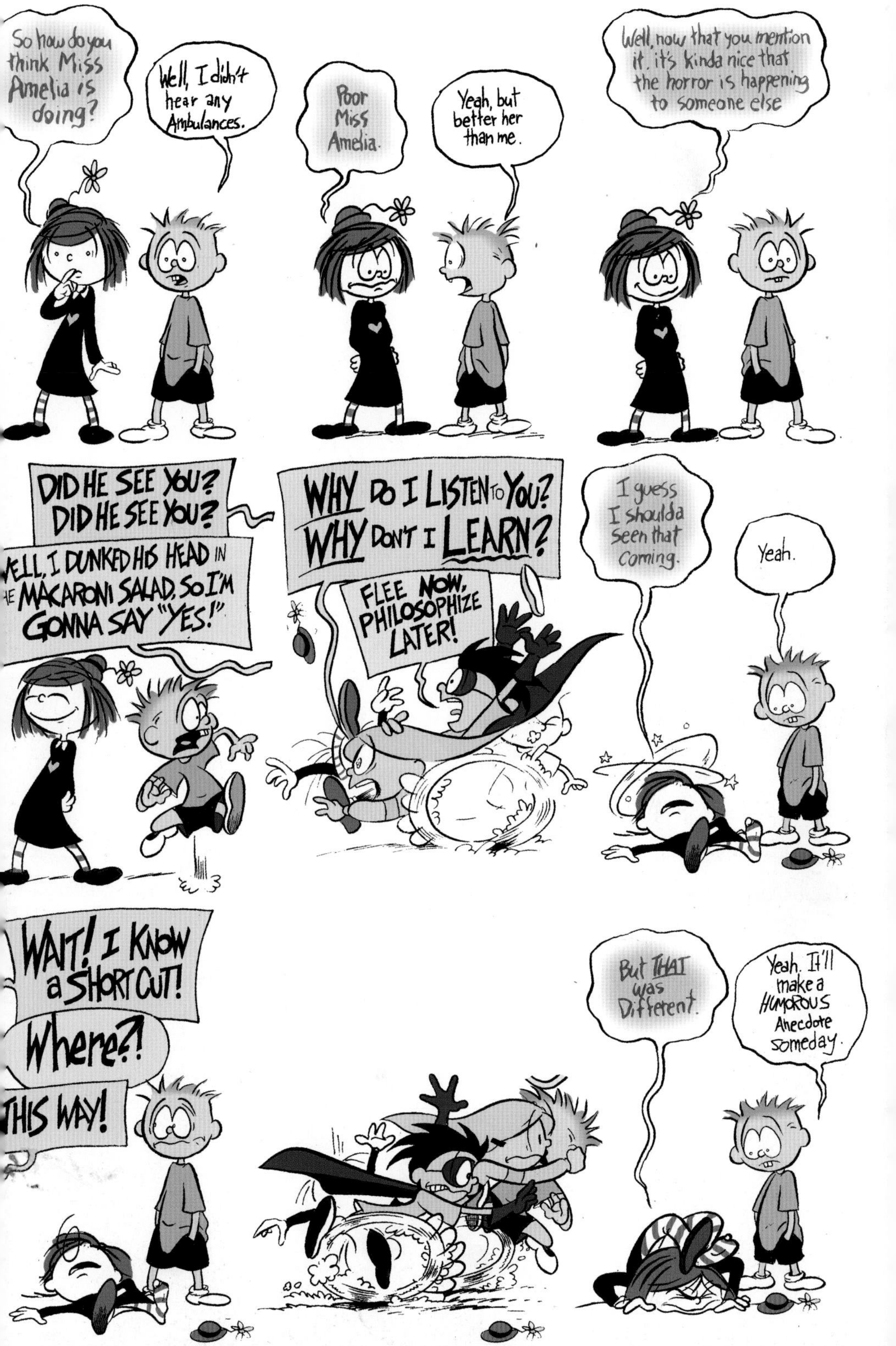
So how do you think Miss Amelia is doing?
Well, I didn't hear any Ambulances.
Poor Miss Amelia.
Yeah, but better her than me.
Well, now that you mention it, it's kinda nice that the horror is happening to someone else
DID HE SEE YOU? DID HE SEE YOU?
WELL, I DUNKED HIS HEAD IN THE MACARONI SALAD, SO I'M GONNA SAY "YES!"
WHY DO I LISTEN TO YOU? WHY DON'T I LEARN?
FLEE NOW, PHILOSOPHIZE LATER!
I guess I shoulda seen that coming.
Yeah.
WAIT! I KNOW a SHORT CUT!
Where?!
THIS WAY!
But THAT was Different.
Yeah. It'll make a HUMOROUS Anecdote someday.

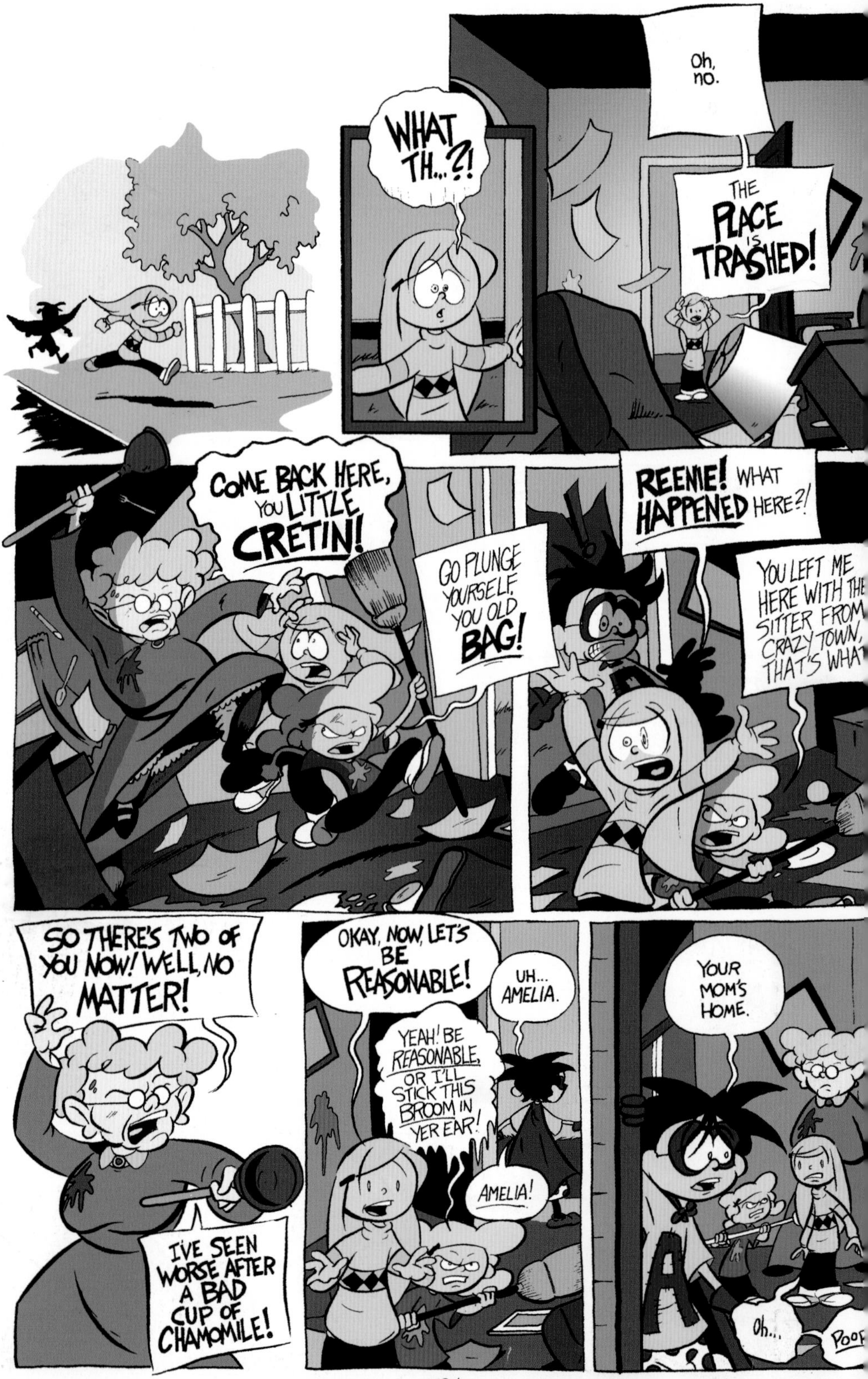
WHAT TH...?!
Oh, no.
THE PLACE IS TRASHED!
COME BACK HERE, YOU LITTLE CRETIN!
GO PLUNGE YOURSELF, YOU OLD BAG!
REENIE! WHAT HAPPENED HERE?!
YOU LEFT ME HERE WITH THE SITTER FROM CRAZY TOWN, THAT'S WHAT
SO THERE'S TWO OF YOU NOW! WELL, NO MATTER!
I'VE SEEN WORSE AFTER A BAD CUP OF CHAMOMILE!
OKAY, NOW, LET'S BE REASONABLE!
YEAH! BE REASONABLE, OR I'LL STICK THIS BROOM IN YER EAR!
UH... AMELIA.
AMELIA!
YOUR MOM'S HOME.
Oh...
POOF

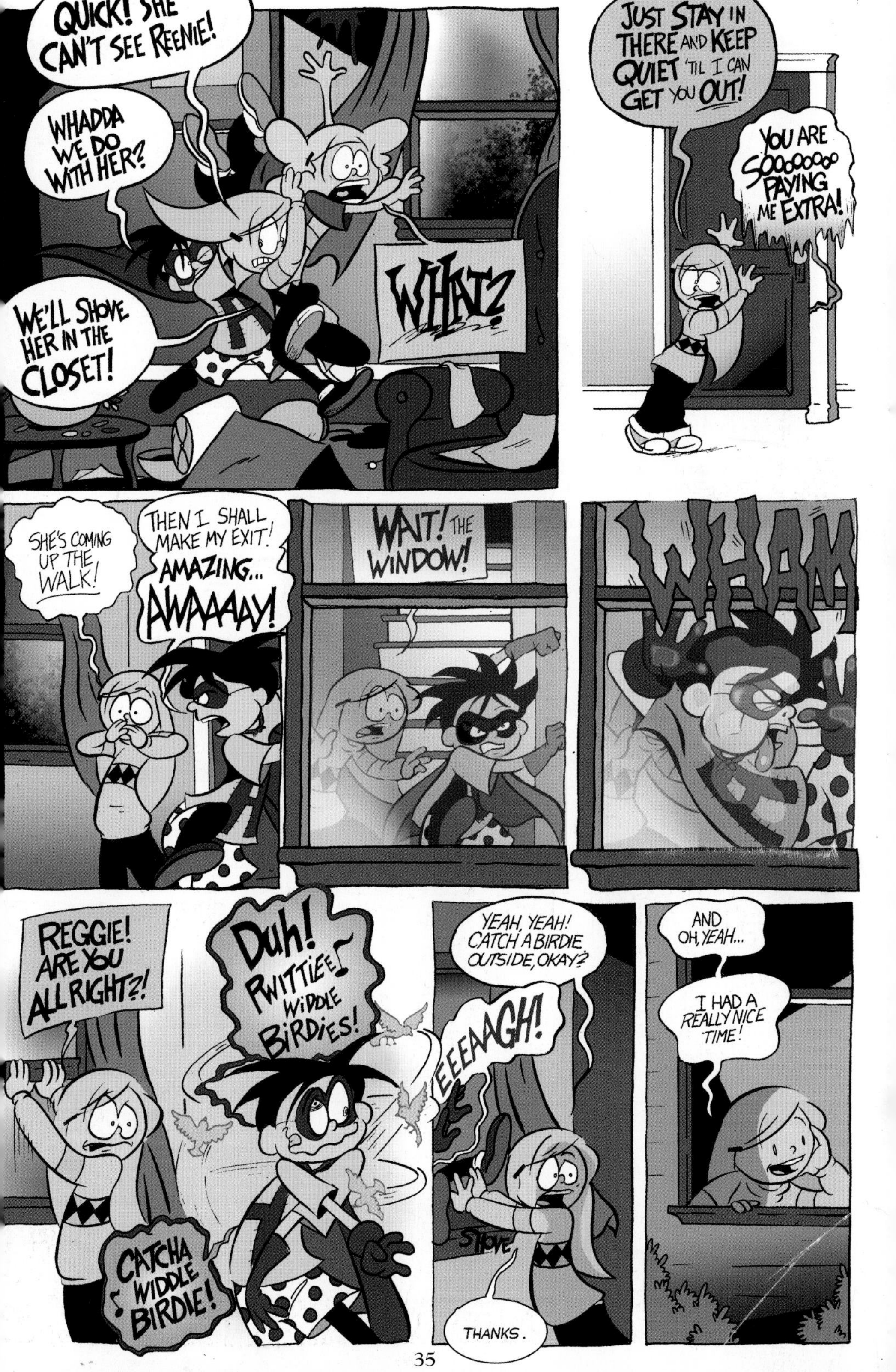
QUICK! SHE CAN'T SEE REENIE!
WHADDA WE DO WITH HER?
WE'LL SHOVE HER IN THE CLOSET!
WHAT?
JUST STAY IN THERE AND KEEP QUIET 'TIL I CAN GET YOU OUT!
YOU ARE SOOOOOOOO PAYING ME EXTRA!
SHE'S COMING UP THE WALK!
THEN I SHALL MAKE MY EXIT! AMAZING... AWAAAAY!
WAIT! THE WINDOW!
WHAM
REGGIE! ARE YOU ALL RIGHT?!
Duh! PWITTIEEE! WIDDLE BIRDIES!
CATCHA WIDDLE BIRDIE!
YEAH, YEAH! CATCH A BIRDIE OUTSIDE, OKAY?
EEEAAGH!
SHOVE
THANKS.
AND OH, YEAH...
I HAD A REALLY NICE TIME!

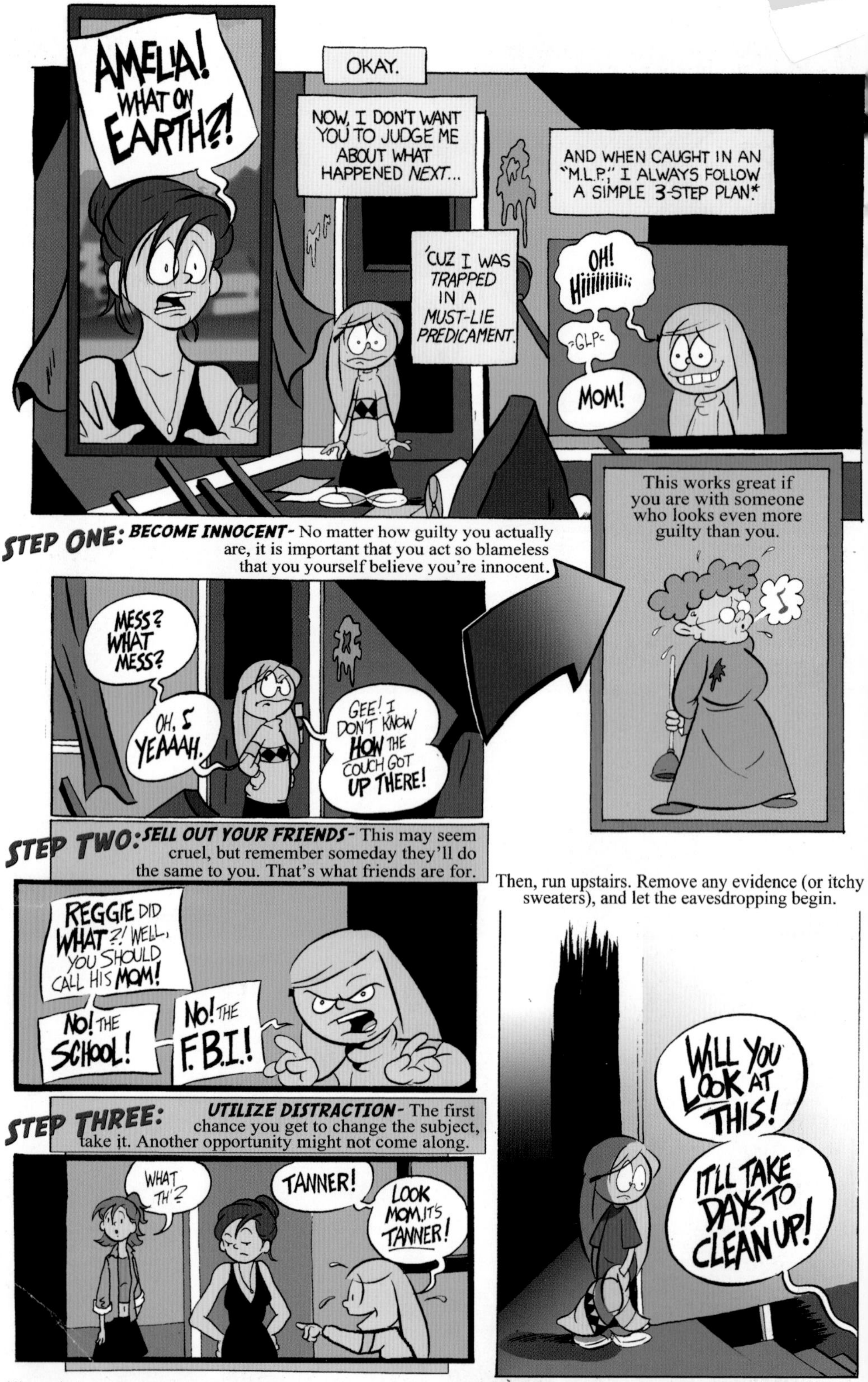
AMELIA! WHAT ON EARTH?!
OKAY.
NOW, I DON'T WANT YOU TO JUDGE ME ABOUT WHAT HAPPENED NEXT...
'CUZ I WAS TRAPPED IN A MUST-LIE PREDICAMENT.
AND WHEN CAUGHT IN AN "M.L.P.," I ALWAYS FOLLOW A SIMPLE 3-STEP PLAN.*
OH! Hiiiiiiii
GLP
MOM!
STEP ONE: BECOME INNOCENT- No matter how guilty you actually are, it is important that you act so blameless that you yourself believe you're innocent.
MESS? WHAT MESS?
OH, YEAAAH.
GEE! I DON'T KNOW HOW THE COUCH GOT UP THERE!
This works great if you are with someone who looks even more guilty than you.
STEP TWO: SELL OUT YOUR FRIENDS- This may seem cruel, but remember someday they'll do the same to you. That's what friends are for.
REGGIE DID WHAT?! WELL, YOU SHOULD CALL HIS MOM!
NO! THE SCHOOL!
NO! THE F.B.I.!
STEP THREE: UTILIZE DISTRACTION- The first chance you get to change the subject, take it. Another opportunity might not come along.
WHAT TH'?
TANNER!
LOOK MOM, IT'S TANNER!
Then, run upstairs. Remove any evidence (or itchy sweaters), and let the eavesdropping begin.
WILL YOU LOOK AT THIS!
IT'LL TAKE DAYS TO CLEAN UP!

*Please don't try this plan at home, and when you do try this plan at home, please leave my name out of it - Amelia Louise McBride

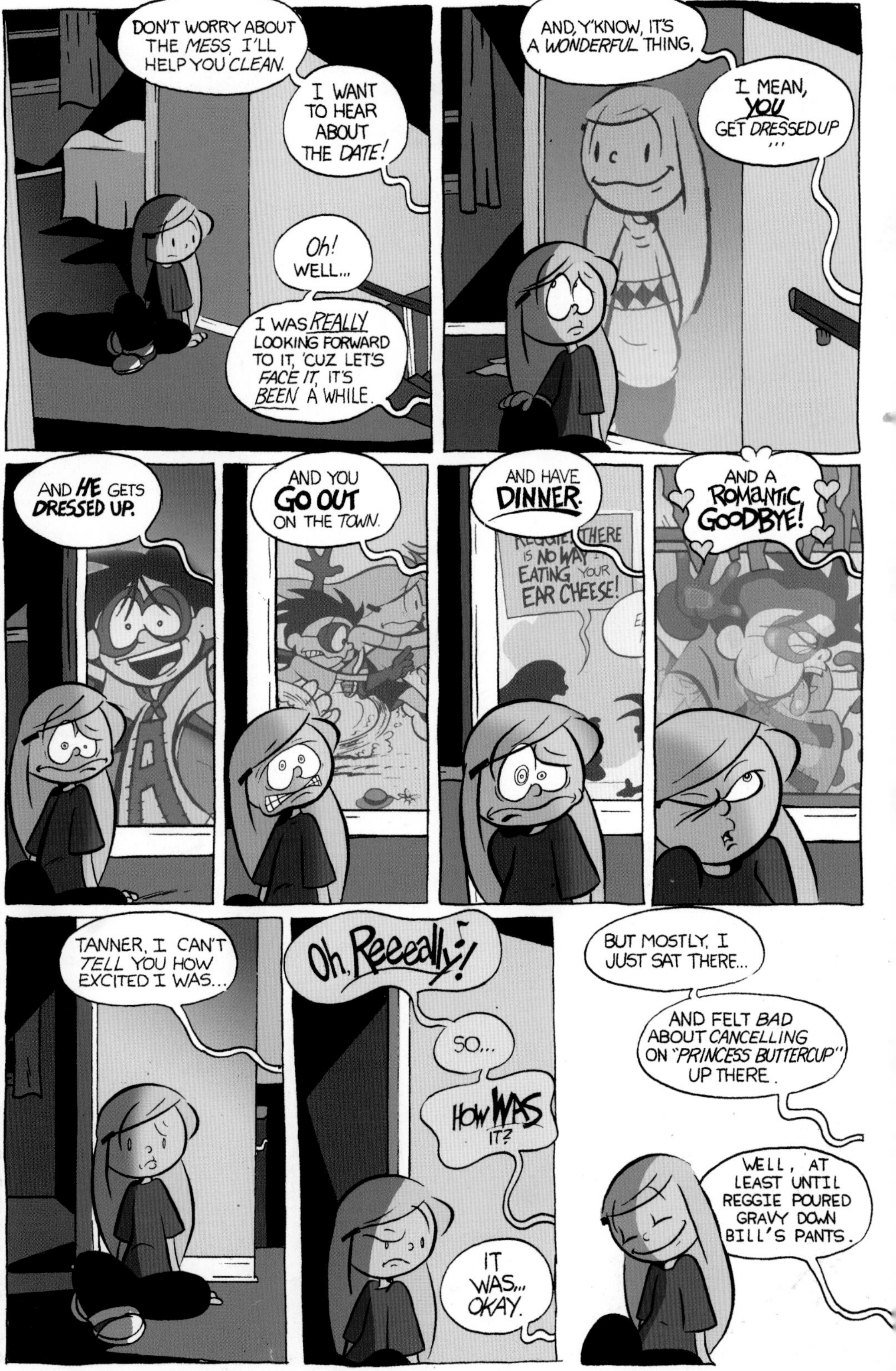
DON'T WORRY ABOUT THE *MESS*, I'LL HELP YOU *CLEAN*.
I WANT TO HEAR ABOUT THE *DATE*!
Oh! WELL...
I WAS *REALLY* LOOKING FORWARD TO IT, 'CUZ LET'S *FACE IT*, IT'S *BEEN* A WHILE.
AND, Y'KNOW, IT'S A *WONDERFUL* THING,
I MEAN, **YOU** GET *DRESSED UP*...
AND **HE** GETS **DRESSED UP**.
AND YOU **GO OUT** ON THE *TOWN*.
AND HAVE **DINNER**.
THERE
IS NO WAY
EATING YOUR
EAR CHEESE!
AND A ROMANTIC GOODBYE!
TANNER, I CAN'T *TELL* YOU HOW EXCITED I WAS...
Oh, Reeeally!
SO...
HOW WAS IT?
IT WAS... OKAY.
BUT MOSTLY, I JUST SAT THERE...
AND FELT *BAD* ABOUT *CANCELLING* ON "*PRINCESS BUTTERCUP*" UP THERE.
WELL, AT LEAST UNTIL REGGIE POURED GRAVY DOWN BILL'S PANTS.

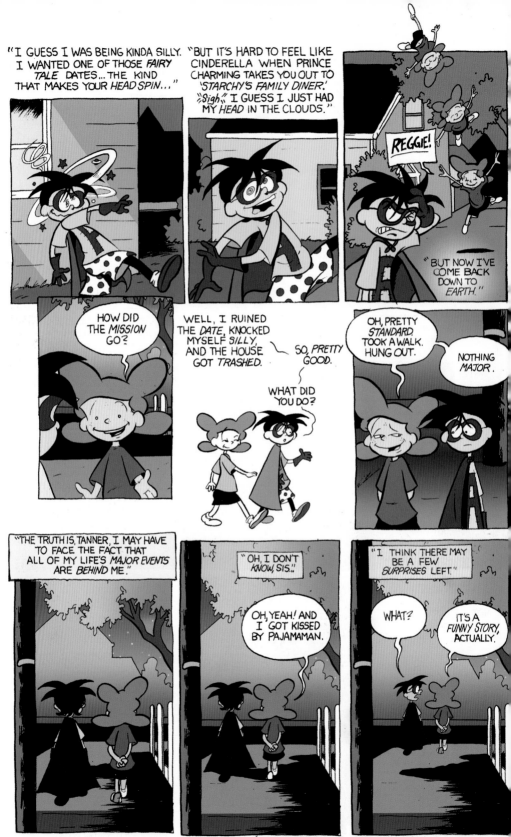

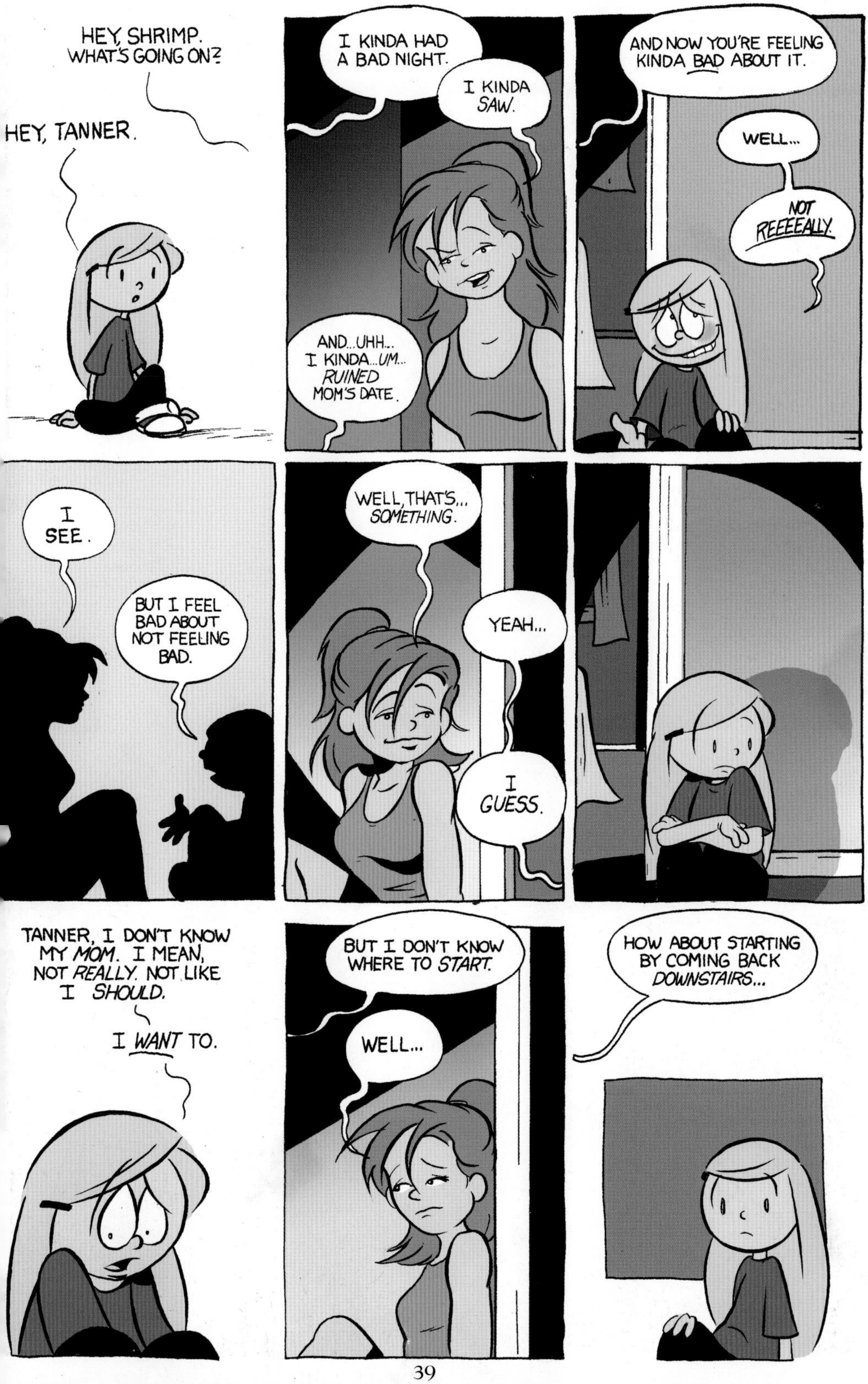
HEY, SHRIMP. WHAT'S GOING ON?
HEY, TANNER.
I KINDA HAD A BAD NIGHT.
I KINDA SAW.
AND...UHH... I KINDA...UM... RUINED MOM'S DATE.
AND NOW YOU'RE FEELING KINDA BAD ABOUT IT.
WELL...
NOT REEEEALLY.
I SEE.
BUT I FEEL BAD ABOUT NOT FEELING BAD.
WELL, THAT'S... SOMETHING.
YEAH...
I GUESS.
TANNER, I DON'T KNOW MY MOM. I MEAN, NOT REALLY. NOT LIKE I SHOULD.
I WANT TO.
BUT I DON'T KNOW WHERE TO START.
WELL...
HOW ABOUT STARTING BY COMING BACK DOWNSTAIRS...

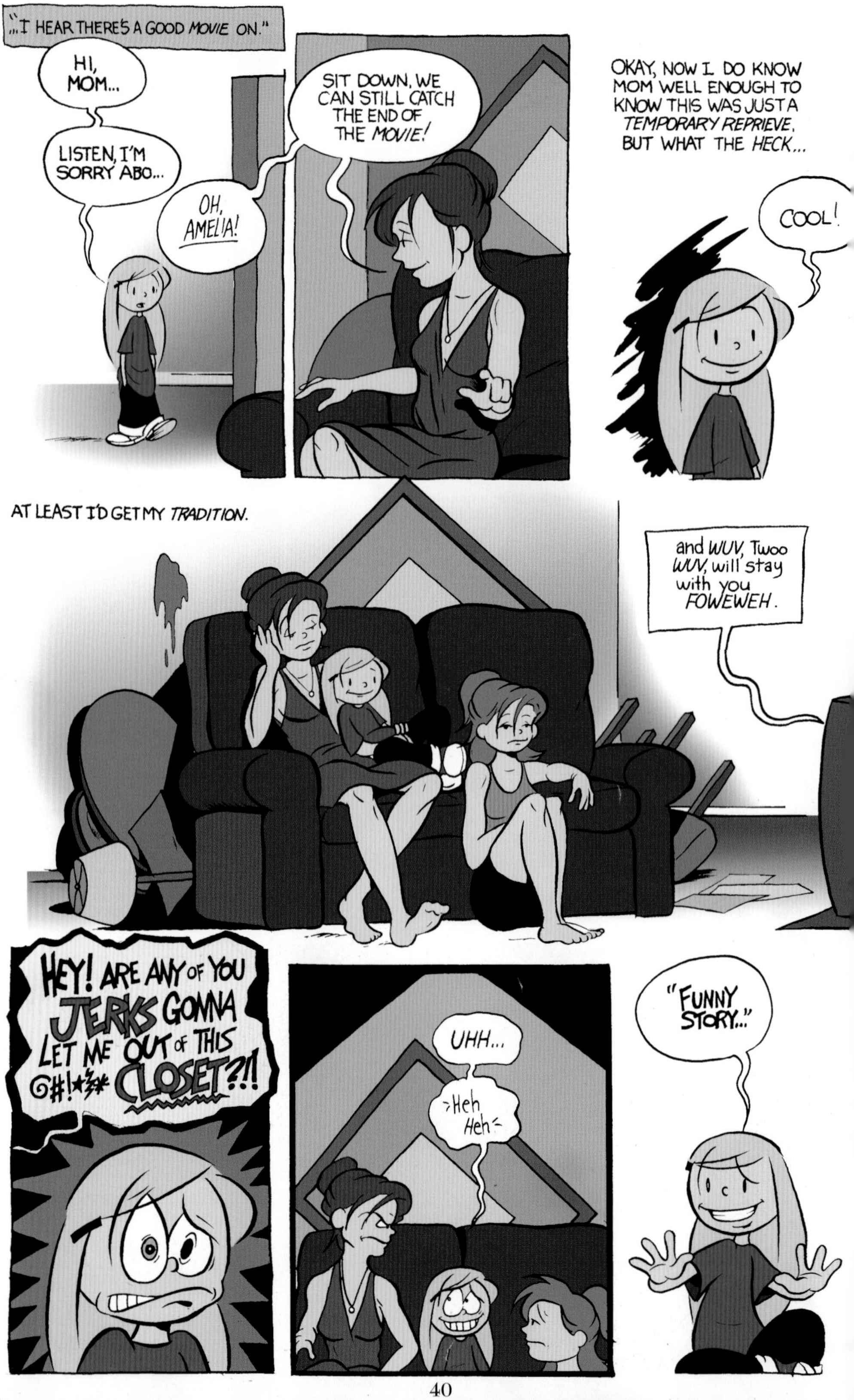
"...I HEAR THERE'S A GOOD MOVIE ON."
HI, MOM...
LISTEN, I'M SORRY ABO...
OH, AMELIA!
SIT DOWN, WE CAN STILL CATCH THE END OF THE MOVIE!
OKAY, NOW I DO KNOW MOM WELL ENOUGH TO KNOW THIS WAS JUST A TEMPORARY REPRIEVE, BUT WHAT THE HECK...
COOL!
AT LEAST I'D GET MY TRADITION.
and WUV, Twoo WUV, will stay with you FOWEWEH.
HEY! ARE ANY OF YOU JERKS GONNA LET ME OUT OF THIS @#!*%* CLOSET?!!
UHH...
Heh Heh
"FUNNY STORY..."

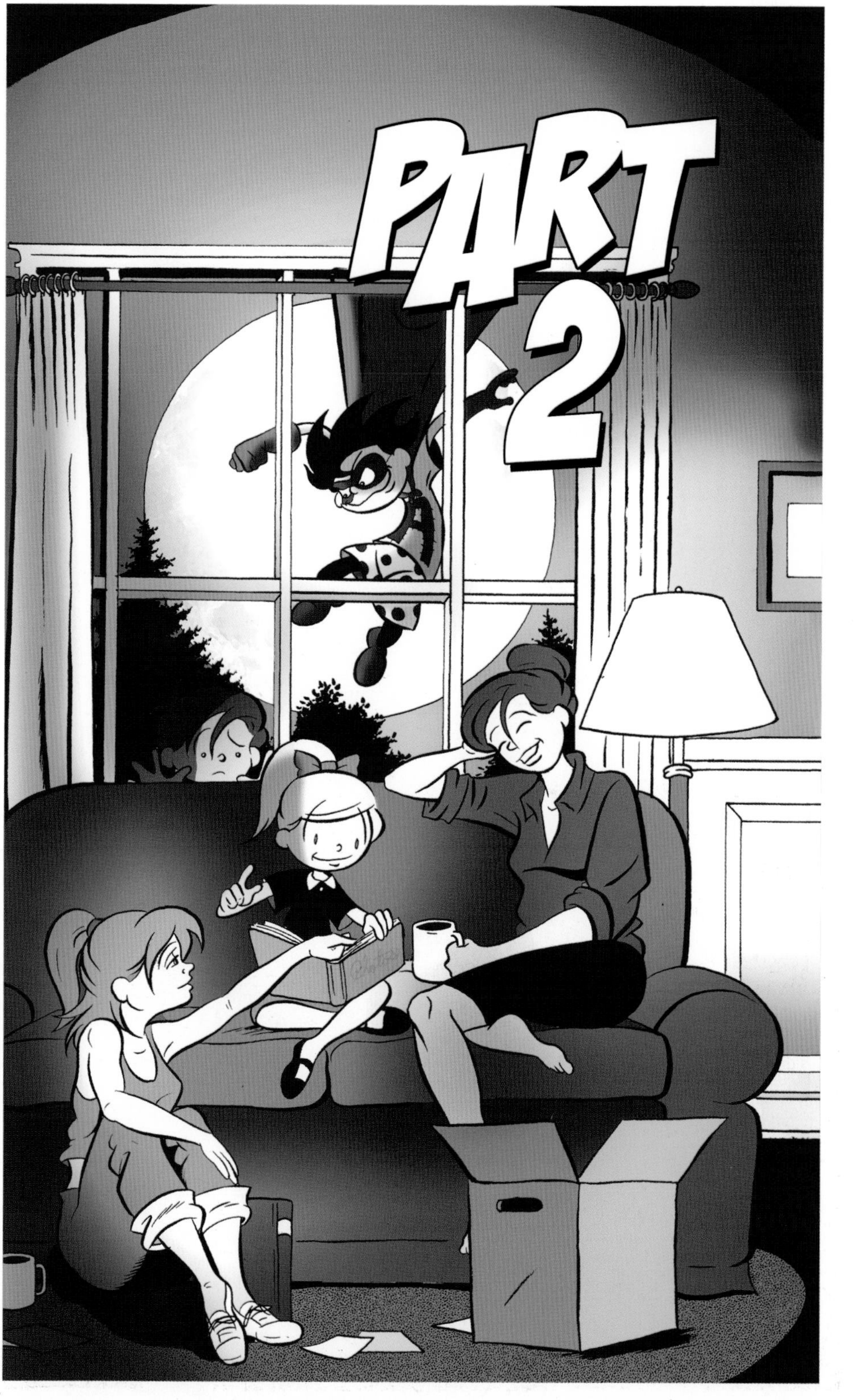
PART
2

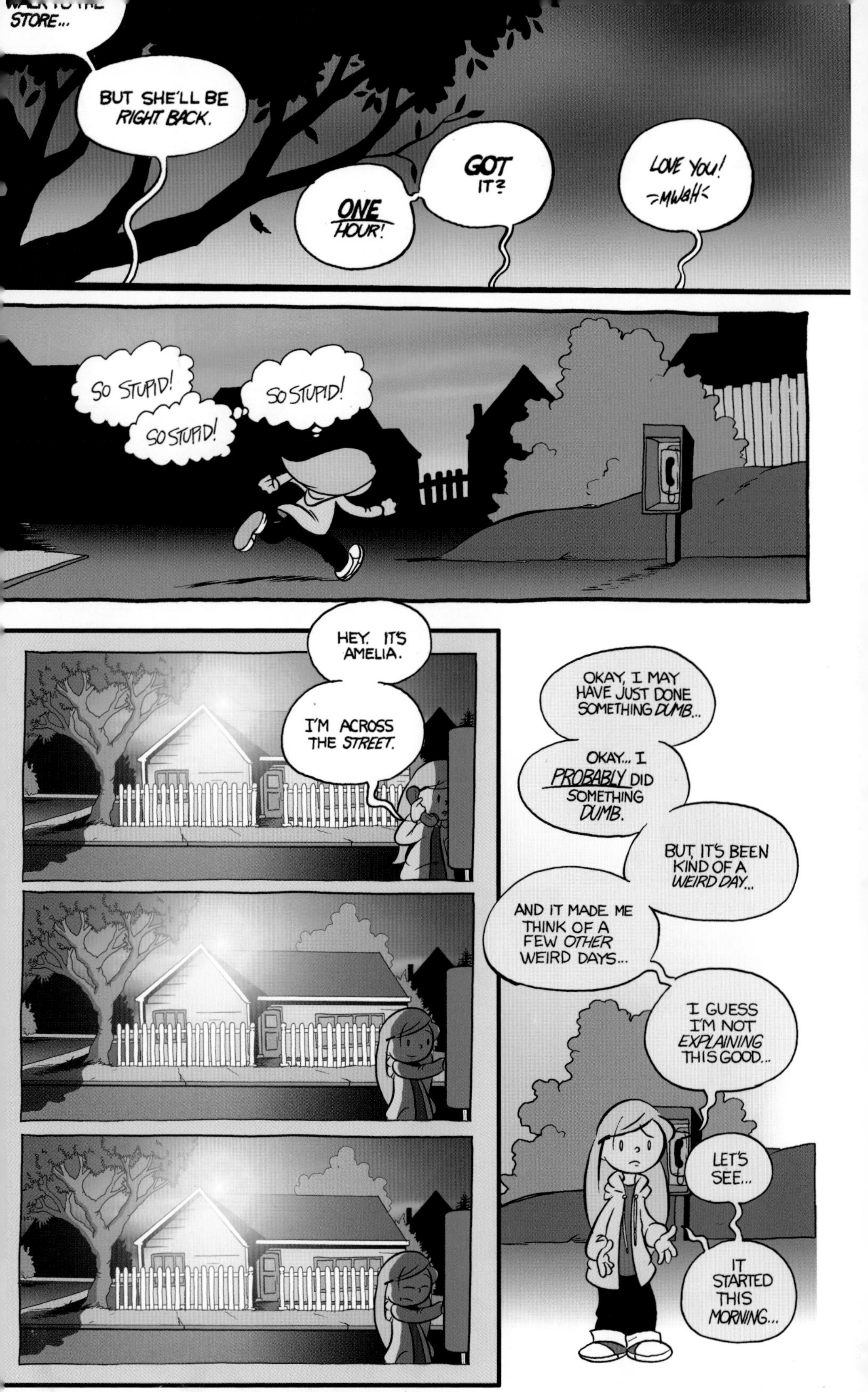
STORE...
BUT SHE'LL BE RIGHT BACK.
ONE HOUR!
GOT IT?
LOVE YOU! =MWAH<
SO STUPID!
SO STUPID!
SO STUPID!
HEY. IT'S AMELIA.
I'M ACROSS THE STREET.
OKAY, I MAY HAVE JUST DONE SOMETHING DUMB...
OKAY... I PROBABLY DID SOMETHING DUMB.
BUT, IT'S BEEN KIND OF A WEIRD DAY...
AND IT MADE ME THINK OF A FEW OTHER WEIRD DAYS...
I GUESS I'M NOT EXPLAINING THIS GOOD...
LET'S SEE...
IT STARTED THIS MORNING...

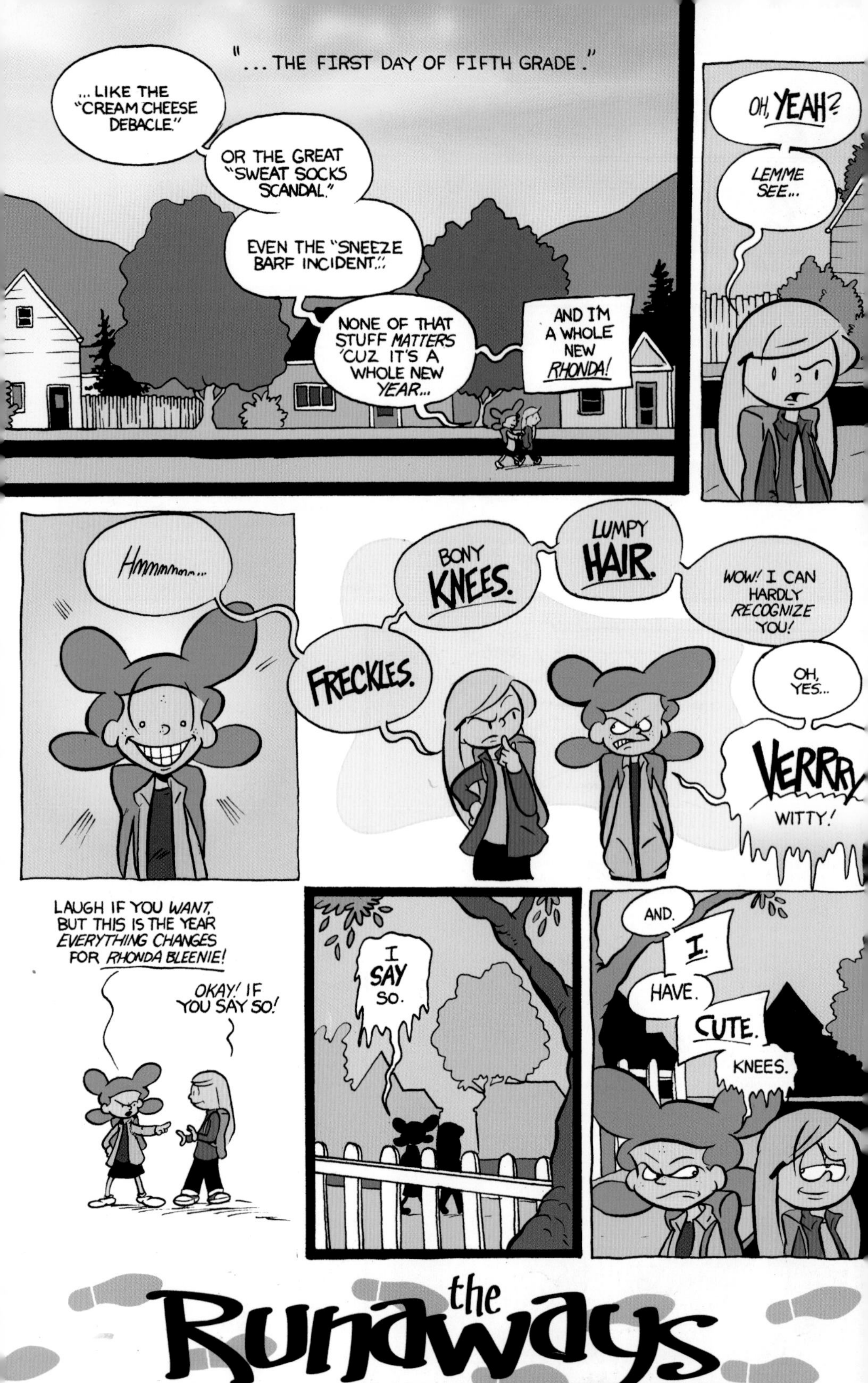
"... THE FIRST DAY OF FIFTH GRADE."
...LIKE THE "CREAM CHEESE DEBACLE."
OR THE GREAT "SWEAT SOCKS SCANDAL."
EVEN THE "SNEEZE BARF INCIDENT."
NONE OF THAT STUFF MATTERS 'CUZ IT'S A WHOLE NEW YEAR...
AND I'M A WHOLE NEW RHONDA!
OH, YEAH?
LEMME SEE...
Hmmmmm...
FRECKLES.
BONY KNEES.
LUMPY HAIR.
WOW! I CAN HARDLY RECOGNIZE YOU!
OH, YES...
VERRRY WITTY!
LAUGH IF YOU WANT, BUT THIS IS THE YEAR EVERYTHING CHANGES FOR RHONDA BLEENIE!
OKAY! IF YOU SAY SO!
I SAY SO.
AND.
I.
HAVE.
CUTE.
KNEES.
the Runaways

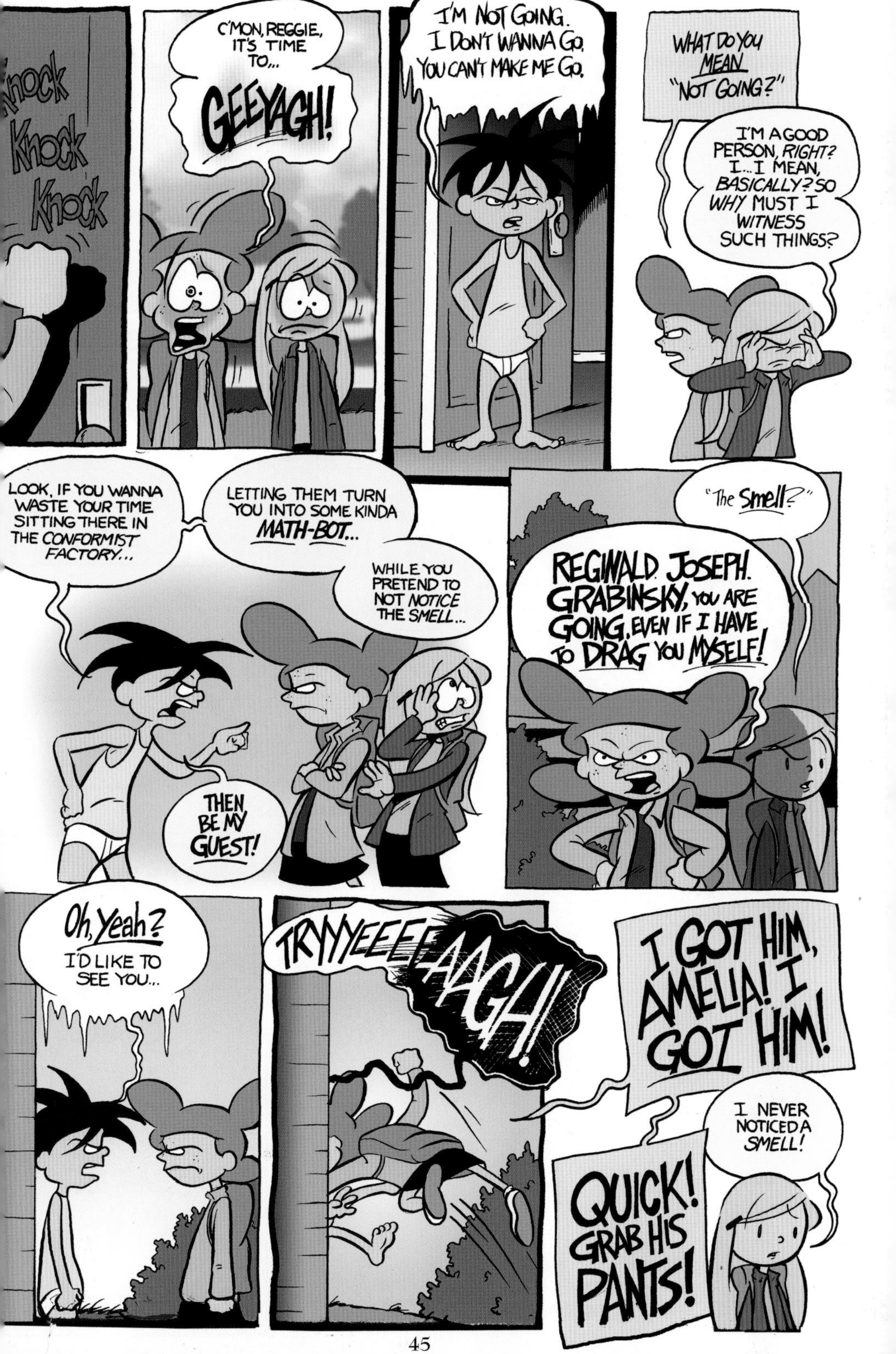
Knock
Knock
Knock
C'MON, REGGIE, IT'S TIME TO...
GEEYAGH!
I'M NOT GOING. I DON'T WANNA GO. YOU CAN'T MAKE ME GO.
WHAT DO YOU MEAN "NOT GOING?"
I'M A GOOD PERSON, RIGHT? I...I MEAN, BASICALLY? SO WHY MUST I WITNESS SUCH THINGS?
LOOK, IF YOU WANNA WASTE YOUR TIME SITTING THERE IN THE CONFORMIST FACTORY...
LETTING THEM TURN YOU INTO SOME KINDA MATH-BOT...
WHILE YOU PRETEND TO NOT NOTICE THE SMELL...
THEN BE MY GUEST!
"The Smell?"
REGINALD. JOSEPH. GRABINSKY, YOU ARE GOING, EVEN IF I HAVE TO DRAG YOU MYSELF!
Oh, Yeah? I'D LIKE TO SEE YOU...
TRYYYEEEEAAAGH!
I GOT HIM, AMELIA! I GOT HIM!
QUICK! GRAB HIS PANTS!
I NEVER NOTICED A SMELL!

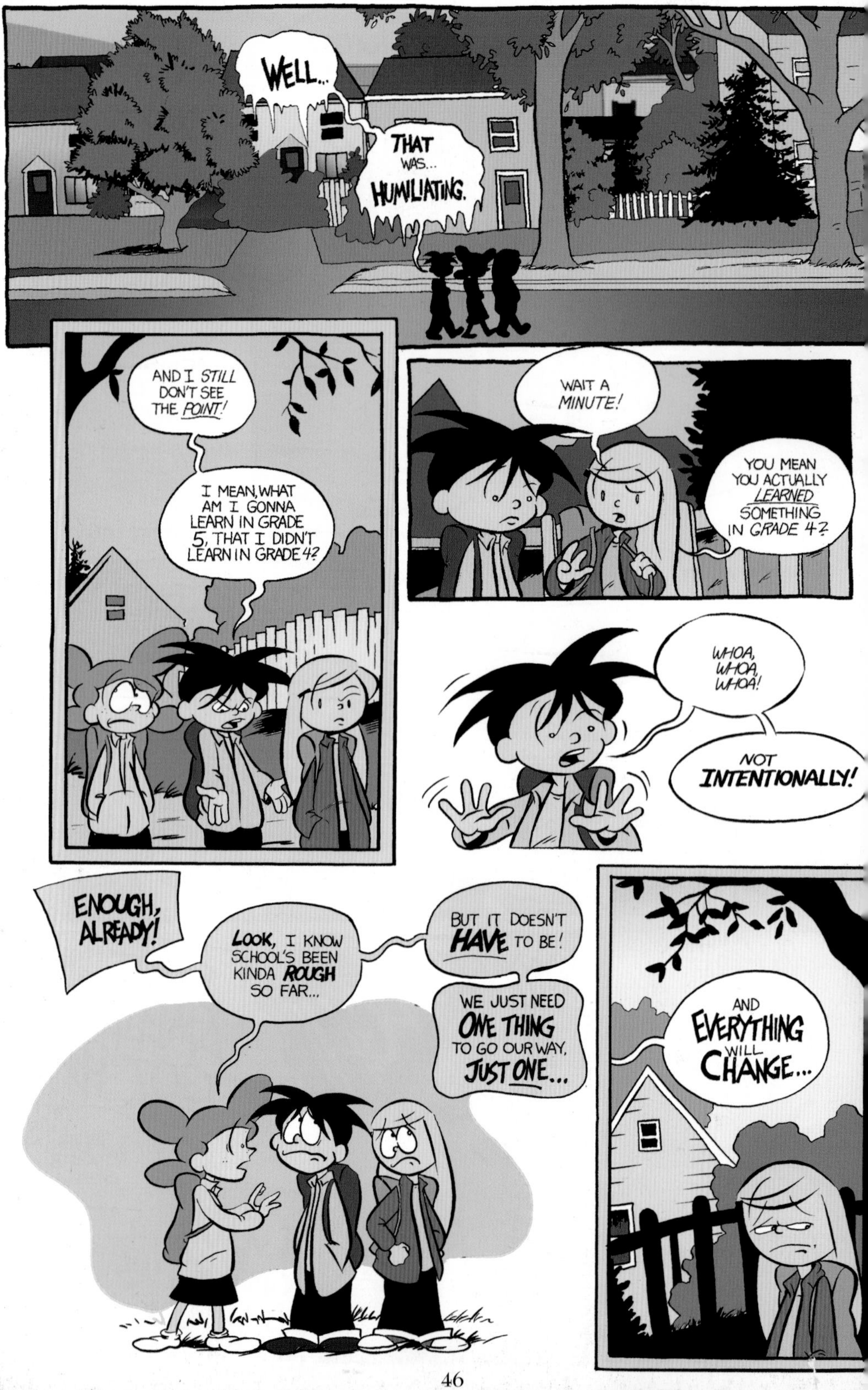
WELL...
THAT WAS... HUMILIATING.
AND I STILL DON'T SEE THE POINT!
I MEAN, WHAT AM I GONNA LEARN IN GRADE 5, THAT I DIDN'T LEARN IN GRADE 4?
WAIT A MINUTE!
YOU MEAN YOU ACTUALLY LEARNED SOMETHING IN GRADE 4?
WHOA, WHOA, WHOA!
NOT INTENTIONALLY!
ENOUGH, ALREADY!
LOOK, I KNOW SCHOOL'S BEEN KINDA ROUGH SO FAR...
BUT IT DOESN'T HAVE TO BE!
WE JUST NEED ONE THING TO GO OUR WAY, JUST ONE...
AND EVERYTHING WILL CHANGE...

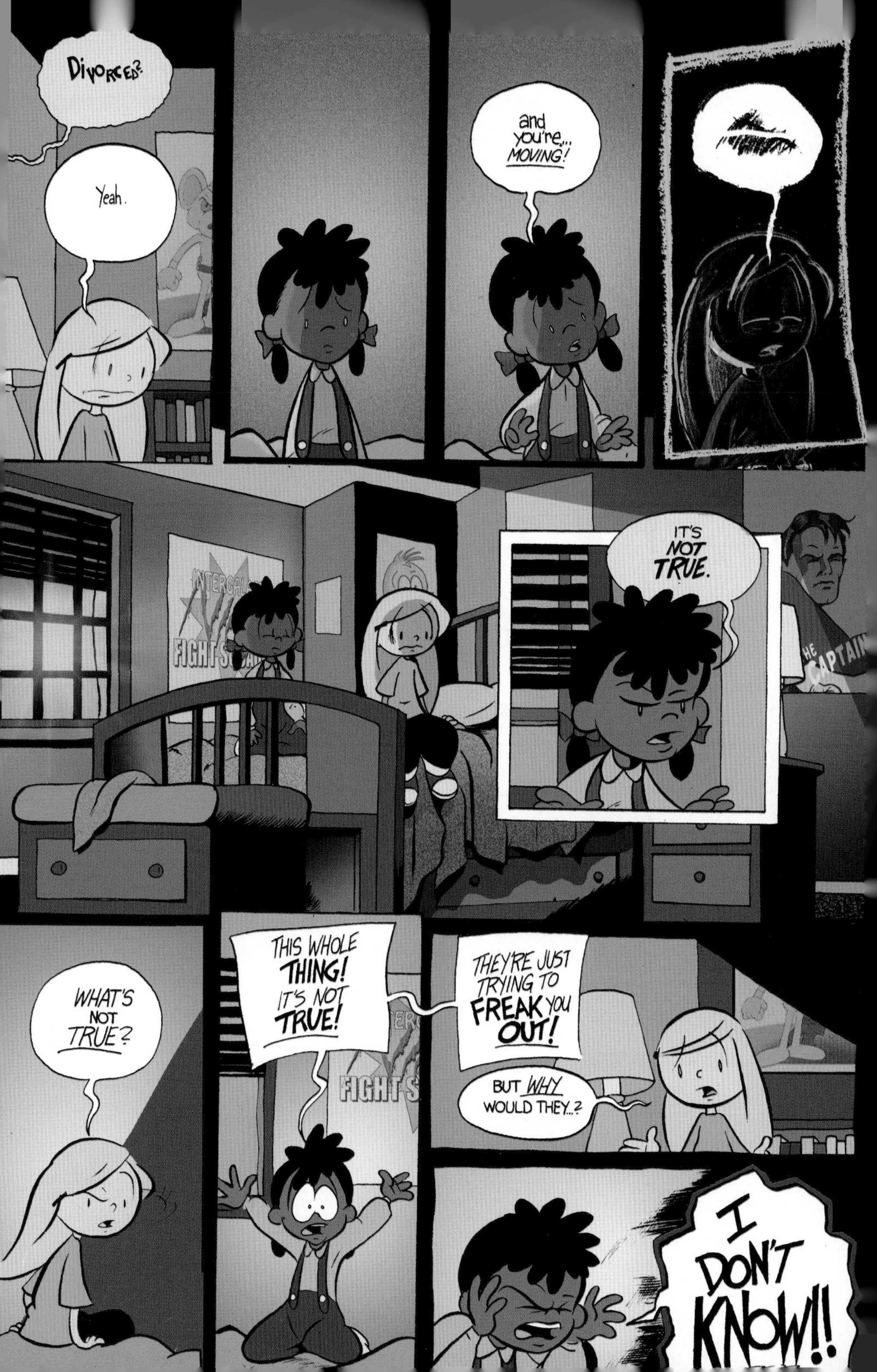

DIVORCED?
Yeah.
and you're... MOVING!
IT'S NOT TRUE.
WHAT'S NOT TRUE?
THIS WHOLE THING! IT'S NOT TRUE!
THEY'RE JUST TRYING TO FREAK YOU OUT!
BUT WHY WOULD THEY...?
I DON'T KNOW!!

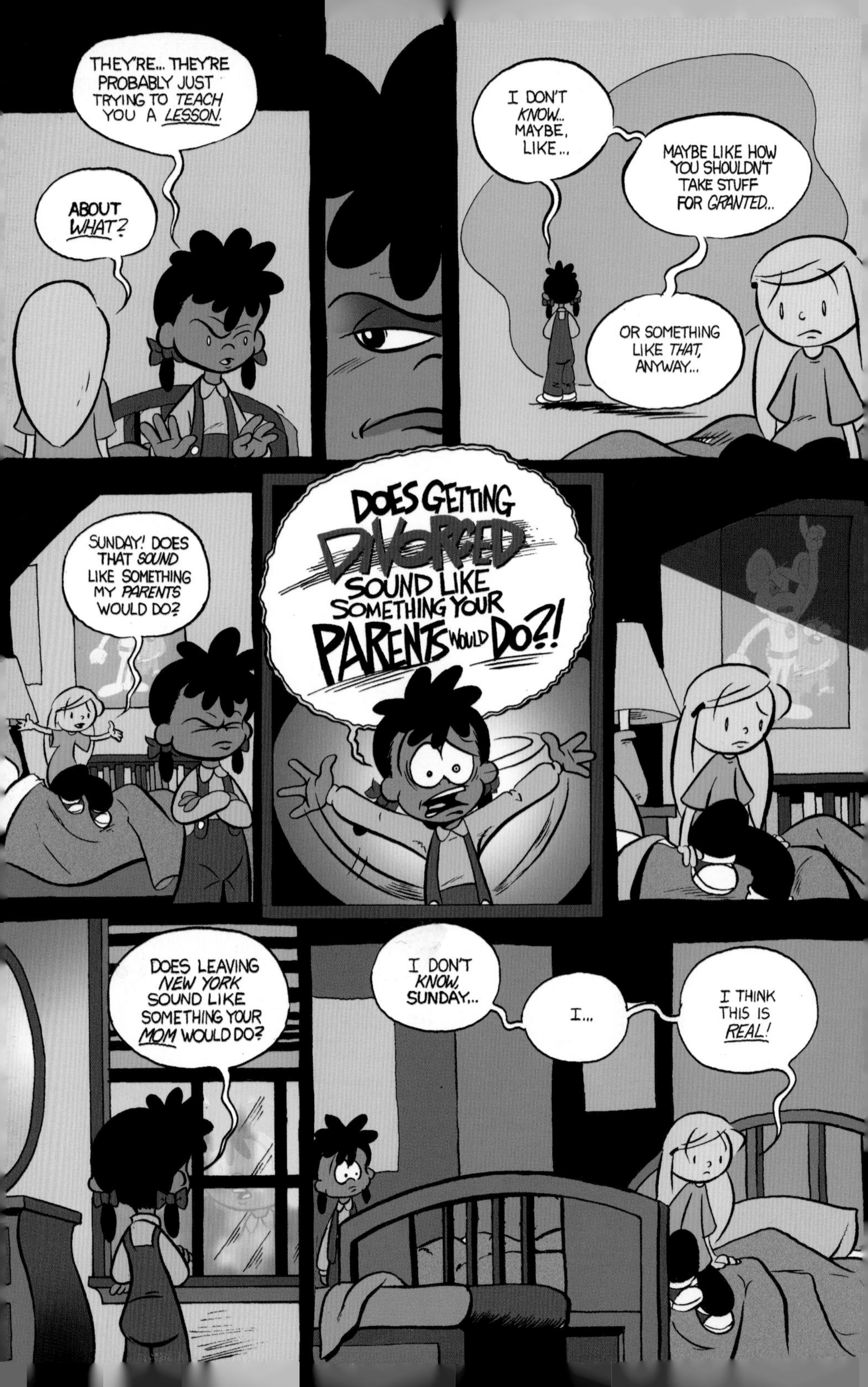

ABOUT WHAT?
THEY'RE... THEY'RE PROBABLY JUST TRYING TO TEACH YOU A LESSON.
I DON'T KNOW... MAYBE, LIKE...
MAYBE LIKE HOW YOU SHOULDN'T TAKE STUFF FOR GRANTED...
OR SOMETHING LIKE THAT, ANYWAY...
SUNDAY! DOES THAT SOUND LIKE SOMETHING MY PARENTS WOULD DO?
DOES GETTING DIVORCED SOUND LIKE SOMETHING YOUR PARENTS WOULD DO?!
DOES LEAVING NEW YORK SOUND LIKE SOMETHING YOUR MOM WOULD DO?
I DON'T KNOW, SUNDAY...
I...
I THINK THIS IS REAL!

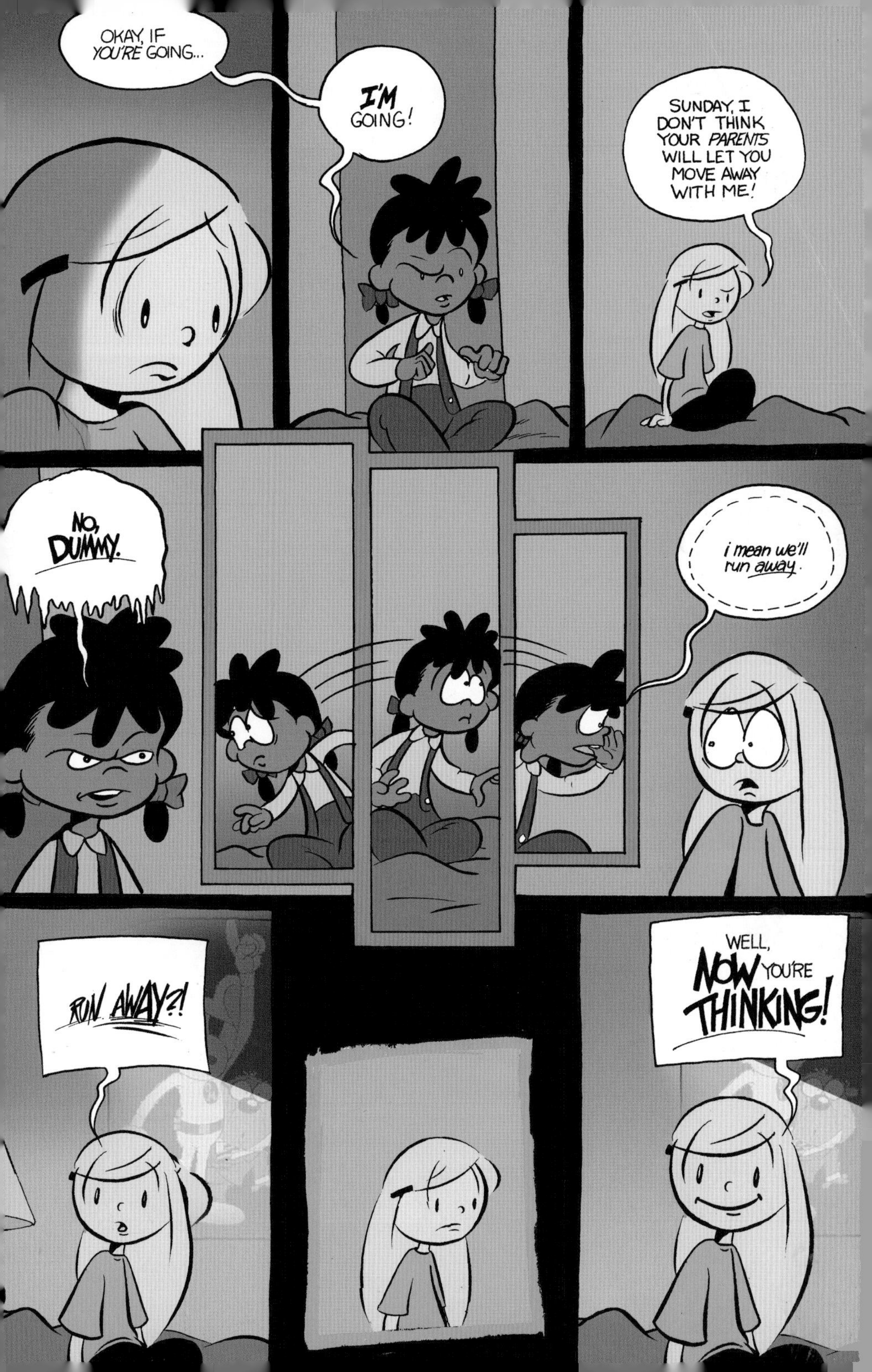
OKAY, IF YOU'RE GOING...
I'M GOING!
SUNDAY, I DON'T THINK YOUR PARENTS WILL LET YOU MOVE AWAY WITH ME!
NO, DUMMY.
i mean we'll run away.
RUN AWAY?!
WELL, NOW YOU'RE THINKING!

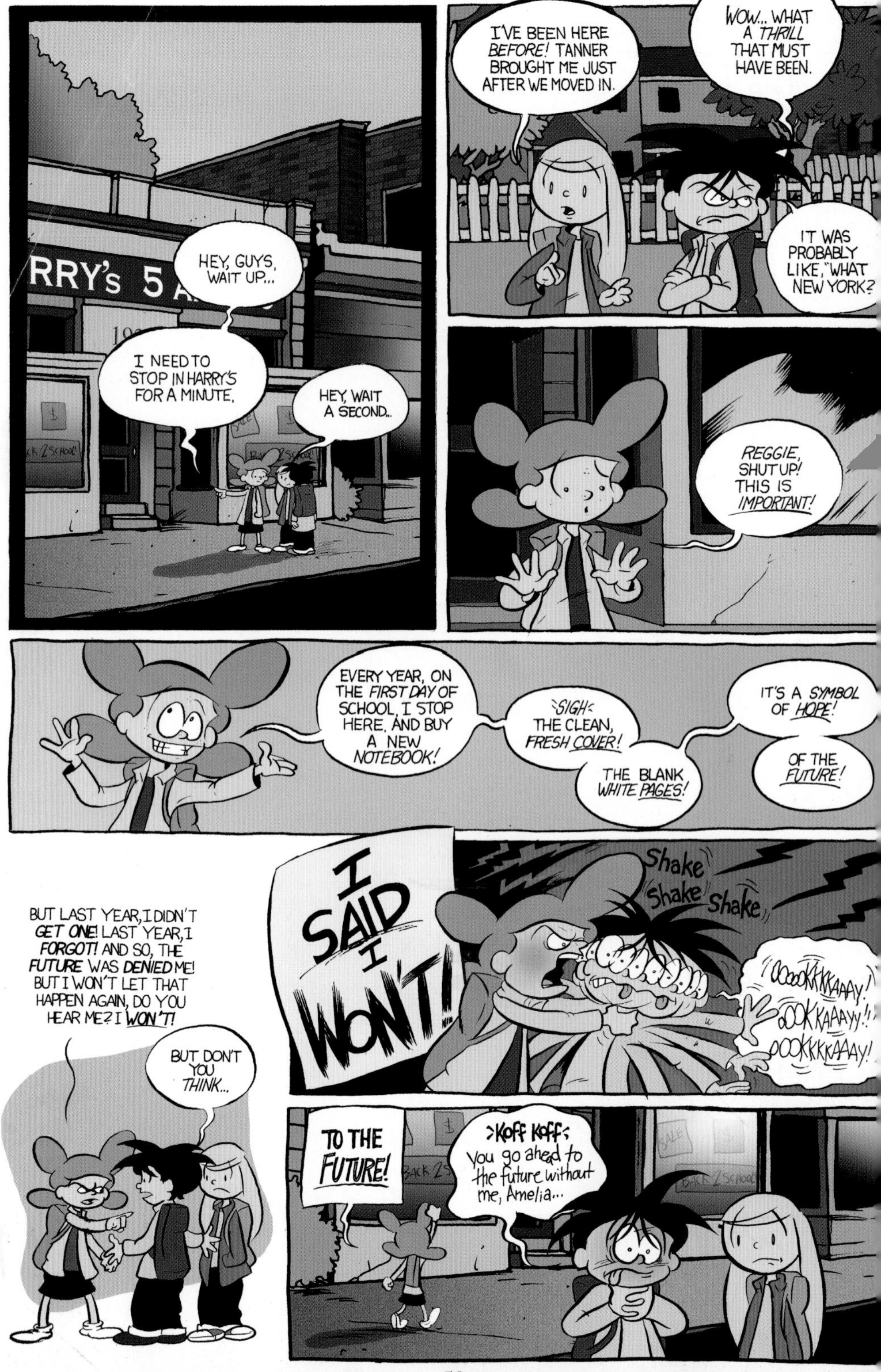
RRY's 5 A
HEY, GUYS, WAIT UP...
I NEED TO STOP IN HARRY'S FOR A MINUTE.
HEY, WAIT A SECOND..
I'VE BEEN HERE BEFORE! TANNER BROUGHT ME JUST AFTER WE MOVED IN.
WOW... WHAT A THRILL THAT MUST HAVE BEEN.
IT WAS PROBABLY LIKE, "WHAT NEW YORK?
REGGIE, SHUT UP! THIS IS IMPORTANT!
EVERY YEAR, ON THE FIRST DAY OF SCHOOL, I STOP HERE, AND BUY A NEW NOTEBOOK!
SIGH THE CLEAN, FRESH COVER!
THE BLANK WHITE PAGES!
IT'S A SYMBOL OF HOPE!
OF THE FUTURE!
BUT LAST YEAR, I DIDN'T GET ONE! LAST YEAR, I FORGOT! AND SO, THE FUTURE WAS DENIED ME! BUT I WON'T LET THAT HAPPEN AGAIN, DO YOU HEAR ME? I WON'T!
BUT DON'T YOU THINK...
I SAID I WON'T!
Shake Shake Shake
OOOOKKKKAAAY! OOOKKAAAYY! OOOKKKKAAAY!
TO THE FUTURE!
Koff Koff You go ahead to the future without me, Amelia...

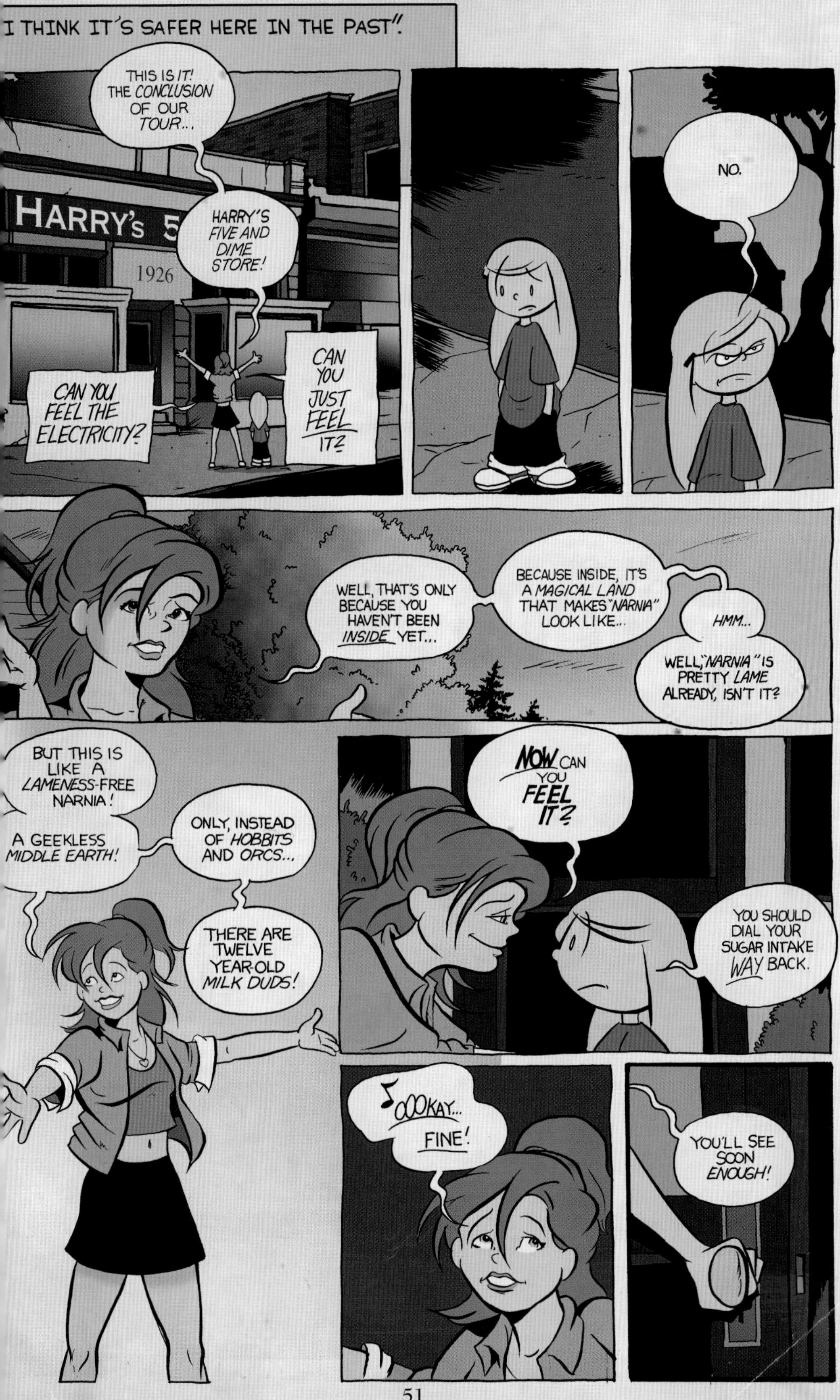

I THINK IT'S SAFER HERE IN THE PAST".
THIS IS IT! THE CONCLUSION OF OUR TOUR...
HARRY's 5
1926
HARRY'S FIVE AND DIME STORE!
CAN YOU FEEL THE ELECTRICITY?
CAN YOU JUST FEEL IT?
NO.
WELL, THAT'S ONLY BECAUSE YOU HAVEN'T BEEN INSIDE YET...
BECAUSE INSIDE, IT'S A MAGICAL LAND THAT MAKES "NARNIA" LOOK LIKE...
HMM...
WELL, "NARNIA" IS PRETTY LAME ALREADY, ISN'T IT?
BUT THIS IS LIKE A LAMENESS-FREE NARNIA!
A GEEKLESS MIDDLE EARTH!
ONLY, INSTEAD OF HOBBITS AND ORCS...
THERE ARE TWELVE YEAR-OLD MILK DUDS!
NOW CAN YOU FEEL IT?
YOU SHOULD DIAL YOUR SUGAR INTAKE WAY BACK.
OOOKAY... FINE!
YOU'LL SEE SOON ENOUGH!

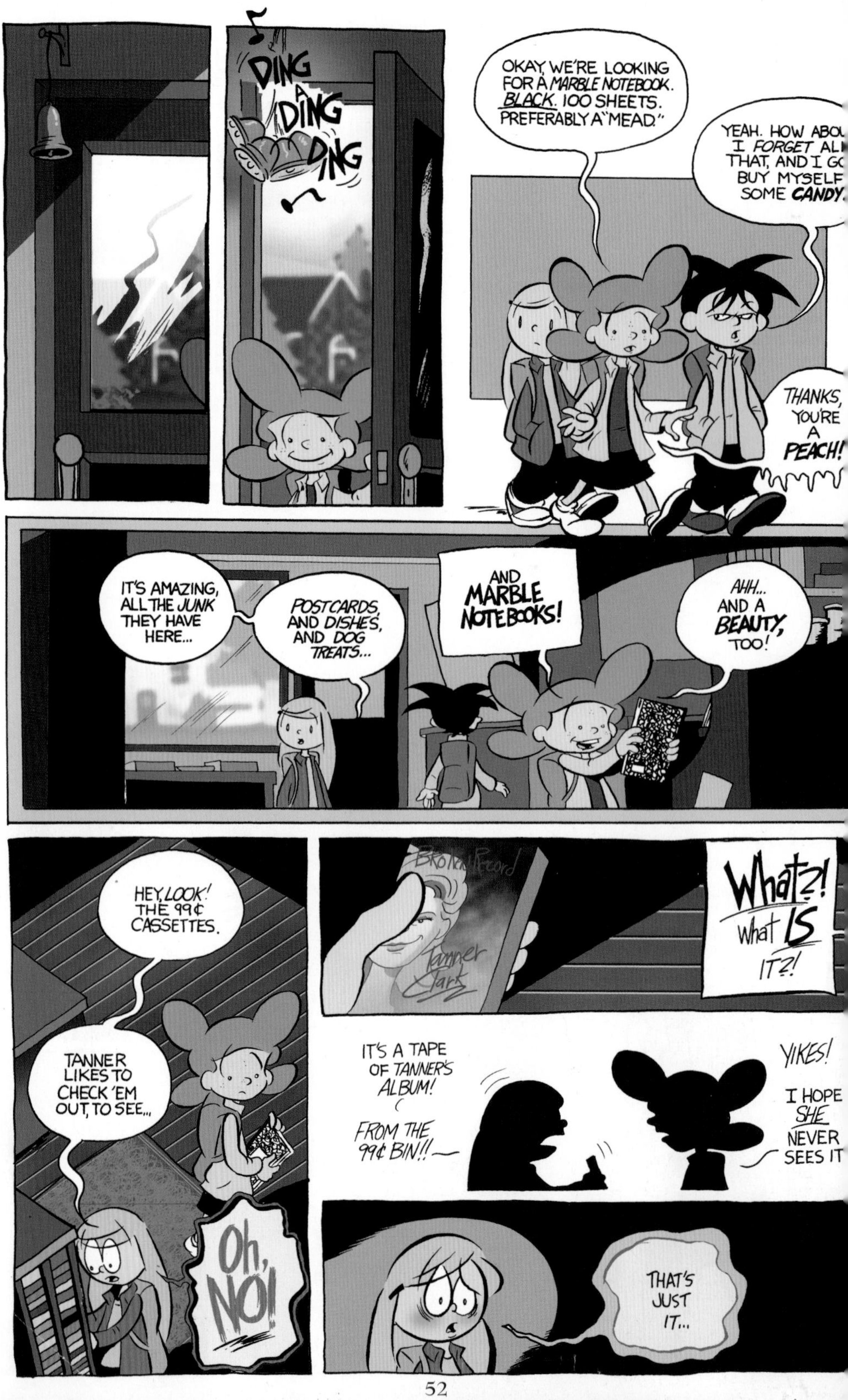
DING A DING DING
OKAY, WE'RE LOOKING FOR A MARBLE NOTEBOOK. BLACK. 100 SHEETS. PREFERABLY A "MEAD."
YEAH. HOW ABOU I FORGET AL THAT, AND I GO BUY MYSELF SOME CANDY.
THANKS, YOU'RE A PEACH!
IT'S AMAZING, ALL THE JUNK THEY HAVE HERE...
POSTCARDS, AND DISHES, AND DOG TREATS...
AND MARBLE NOTEBOOKS!
AHH... AND A BEAUTY, TOO!
HEY, LOOK! THE 99¢ CASSETTES.
TANNER LIKES TO CHECK 'EM OUT, TO SEE...
Oh, NO!
Tanner Clark
What?! What IS IT?!
IT'S A TAPE OF TANNER'S ALBUM!
FROM THE 99¢ BIN!!
YIKES!
I HOPE SHE NEVER SEES IT
THAT'S JUST IT...

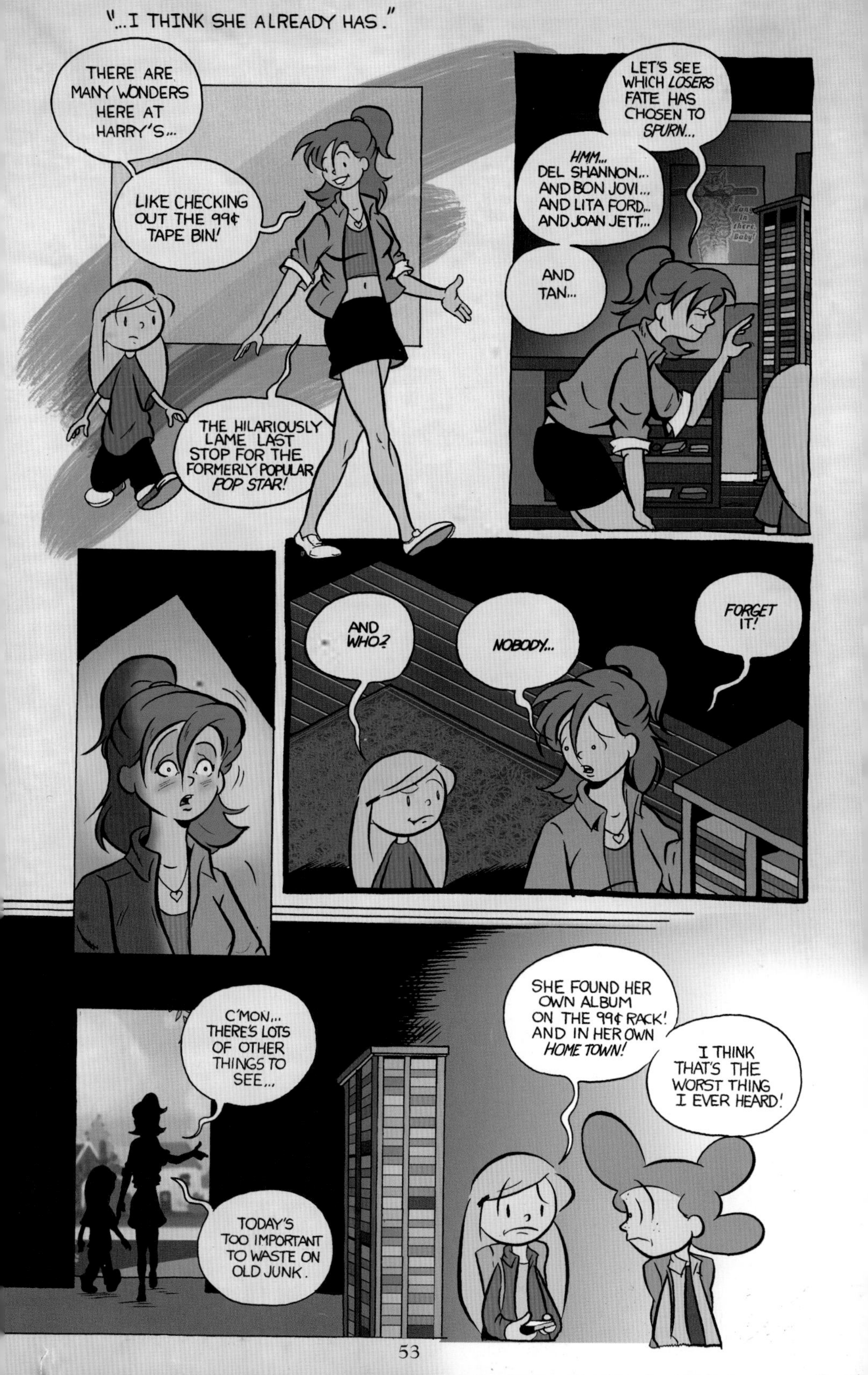
"...I THINK SHE ALREADY HAS."
THERE ARE MANY WONDERS HERE AT HARRY'S...
LIKE CHECKING OUT THE 99¢ TAPE BIN!
THE HILARIOUSLY LAME LAST STOP FOR THE FORMERLY POPULAR *POP STAR!*
LET'S SEE WHICH *LOSERS* FATE HAS CHOSEN TO *SPURN*...
HMM... DEL SHANNON... AND BON JOVI... AND LITA FORD... AND JOAN JETT...
AND TAN...
AND *WHO?*
NOBODY...
FORGET IT!
C'MON... THERE'S LOTS OF OTHER THINGS TO SEE...
TODAY'S TOO IMPORTANT TO WASTE ON OLD JUNK.
SHE FOUND HER OWN ALBUM ON THE 99¢ RACK! AND IN HER OWN *HOME TOWN!*
I THINK THAT'S THE WORST THING I EVER HEARD!

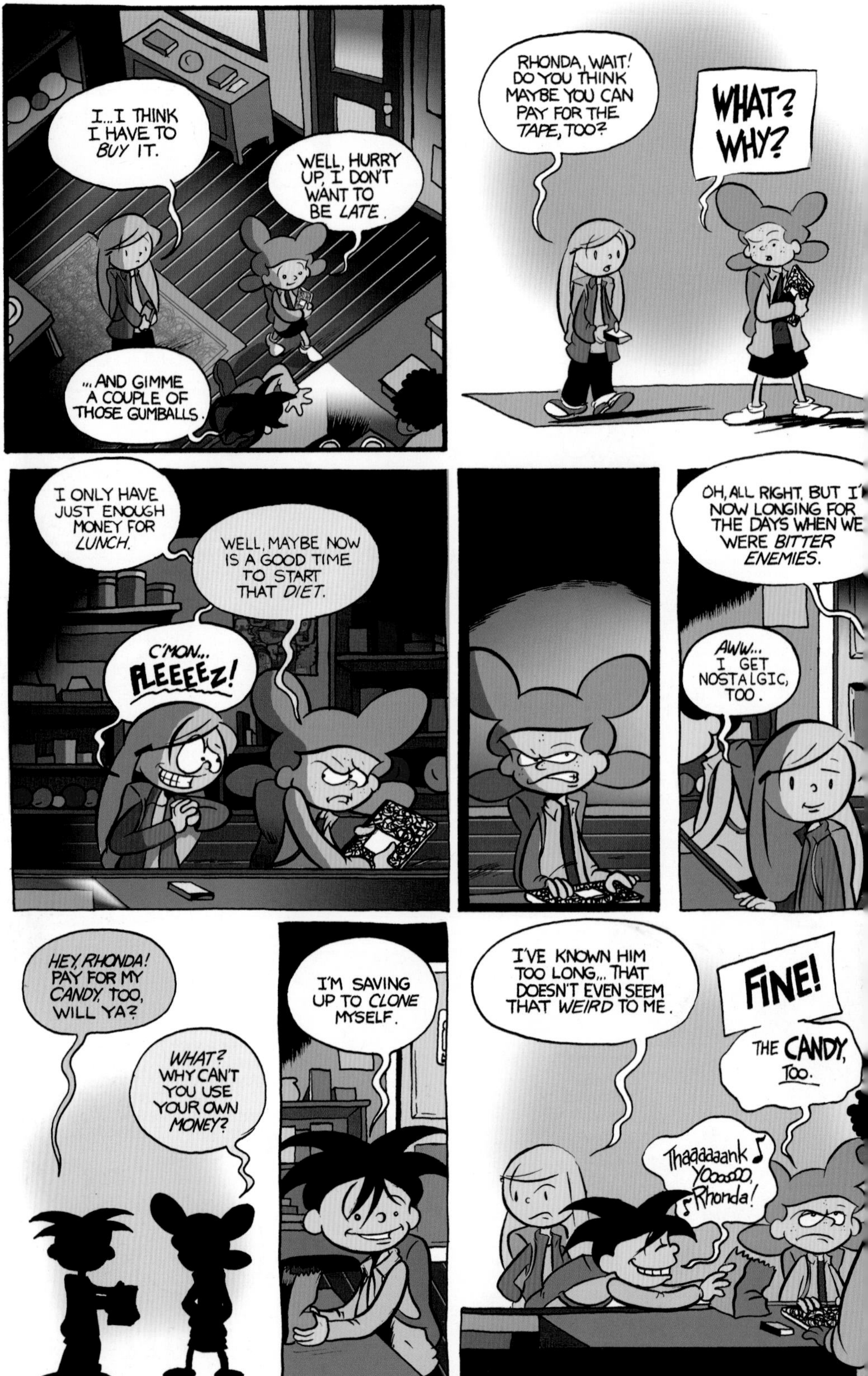
I...I THINK I HAVE TO *BUY* IT.
WELL, HURRY UP, I DON'T WANT TO BE *LATE*.
...AND GIMME A COUPLE OF THOSE GUMBALLS.
RHONDA, WAIT! DO YOU THINK MAYBE YOU CAN PAY FOR THE *TAPE*, TOO?
WHAT? WHY?
I ONLY HAVE JUST ENOUGH MONEY FOR *LUNCH*.
WELL, MAYBE NOW IS A GOOD TIME TO START THAT *DIET*.
C'MON... PLEEEEZ!
OH, ALL RIGHT, BUT I'M NOW LONGING FOR THE DAYS WHEN WE WERE *BITTER ENEMIES*.
AWW... I GET NOSTALGIC, TOO.
HEY, RHONDA! PAY FOR MY *CANDY*, TOO, WILL YA?
WHAT? WHY CAN'T YOU USE YOUR OWN *MONEY*?
I'M SAVING UP TO *CLONE* MYSELF.
I'VE KNOWN HIM TOO LONG... THAT DOESN'T EVEN SEEM THAT *WEIRD* TO ME.
FINE!
THE CANDY, TOO.
Thaaaaaank Yooooooo, Rhonda!

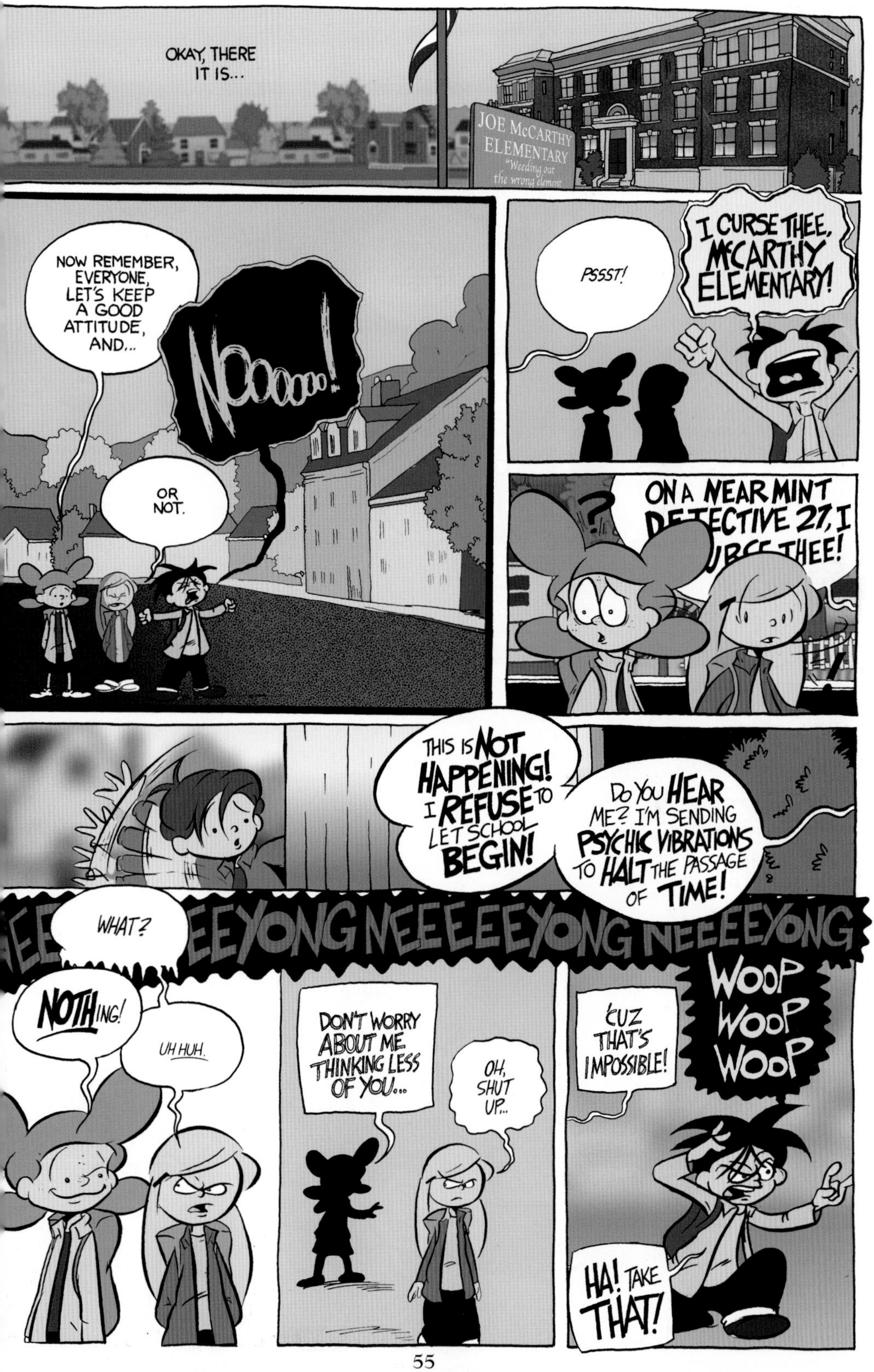
OKAY, THERE IT IS...
JOE McCARTHY ELEMENTARY
"Weeding out the wrong element"
NOW REMEMBER, EVERYONE, LET'S KEEP A GOOD ATTITUDE, AND...
NOOOOOO!
OR NOT.
PSSST!
I CURSE THEE, McCARTHY ELEMENTARY!
ON A NEAR MINT DETECTIVE 27, I CURSE THEE!
THIS IS NOT HAPPENING! I REFUSE TO LET SCHOOL BEGIN!
DO YOU HEAR ME? I'M SENDING PSYCHIC VIBRATIONS TO HALT THE PASSAGE OF TIME!
WHAT?
EEYONG NEEEEEEYONG NEEEEEYONG
NOTHING!
UH HUH.
DON'T WORRY ABOUT ME THINKING LESS OF YOU...
OH, SHUT UP...
'CUZ THAT'S IMPOSSIBLE!
WOOP WOOP WOOP
HA! TAKE THAT!

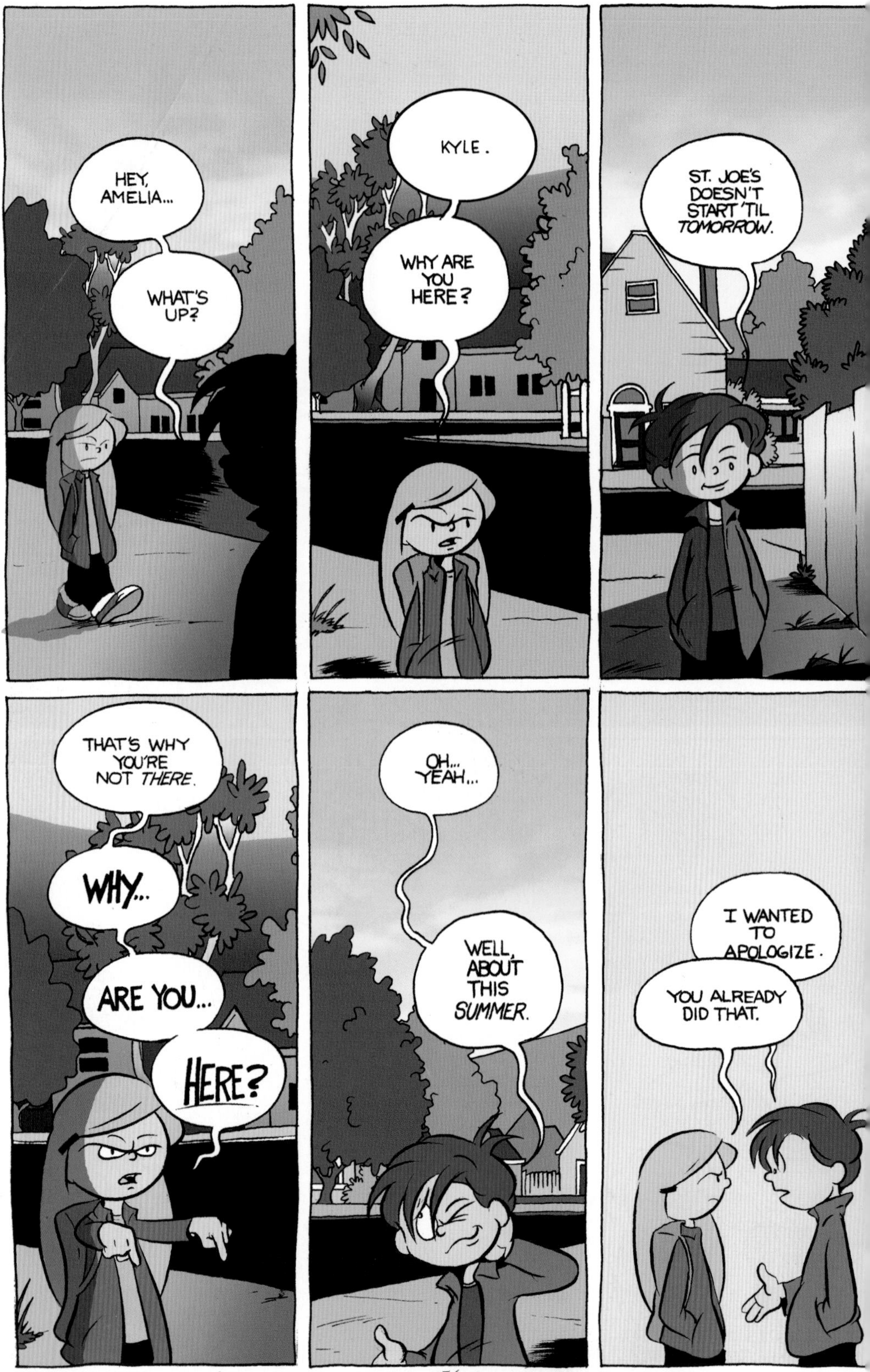
HEY, AMELIA...
WHAT'S UP?
KYLE.
WHY ARE YOU HERE?
ST. JOE'S DOESN'T START 'TIL TOMORROW.
THAT'S WHY YOU'RE NOT THERE.
WHY...
ARE YOU...
HERE?
OH... YEAH...
WELL, ABOUT THIS SUMMER.
I WANTED TO APOLOGIZE.
YOU ALREADY DID THAT.

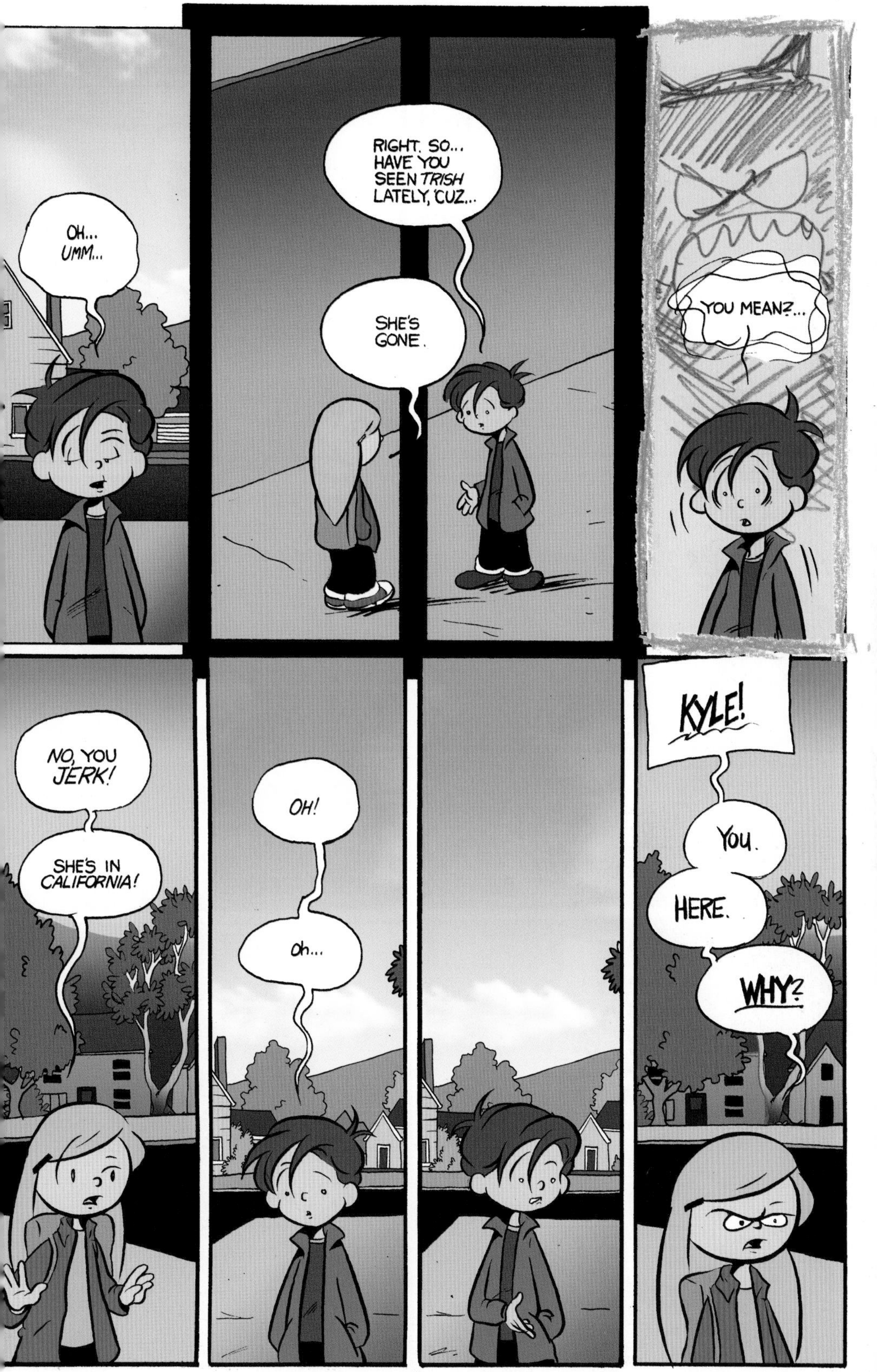
OH... UMM...
RIGHT. SO... HAVE YOU SEEN TRISH LATELY, 'CUZ...
SHE'S GONE.
YOU MEANZ...
NO, YOU JERK!
SHE'S IN CALIFORNIA!
OH!
Oh...
KYLE!
You.
HERE.
WHY?

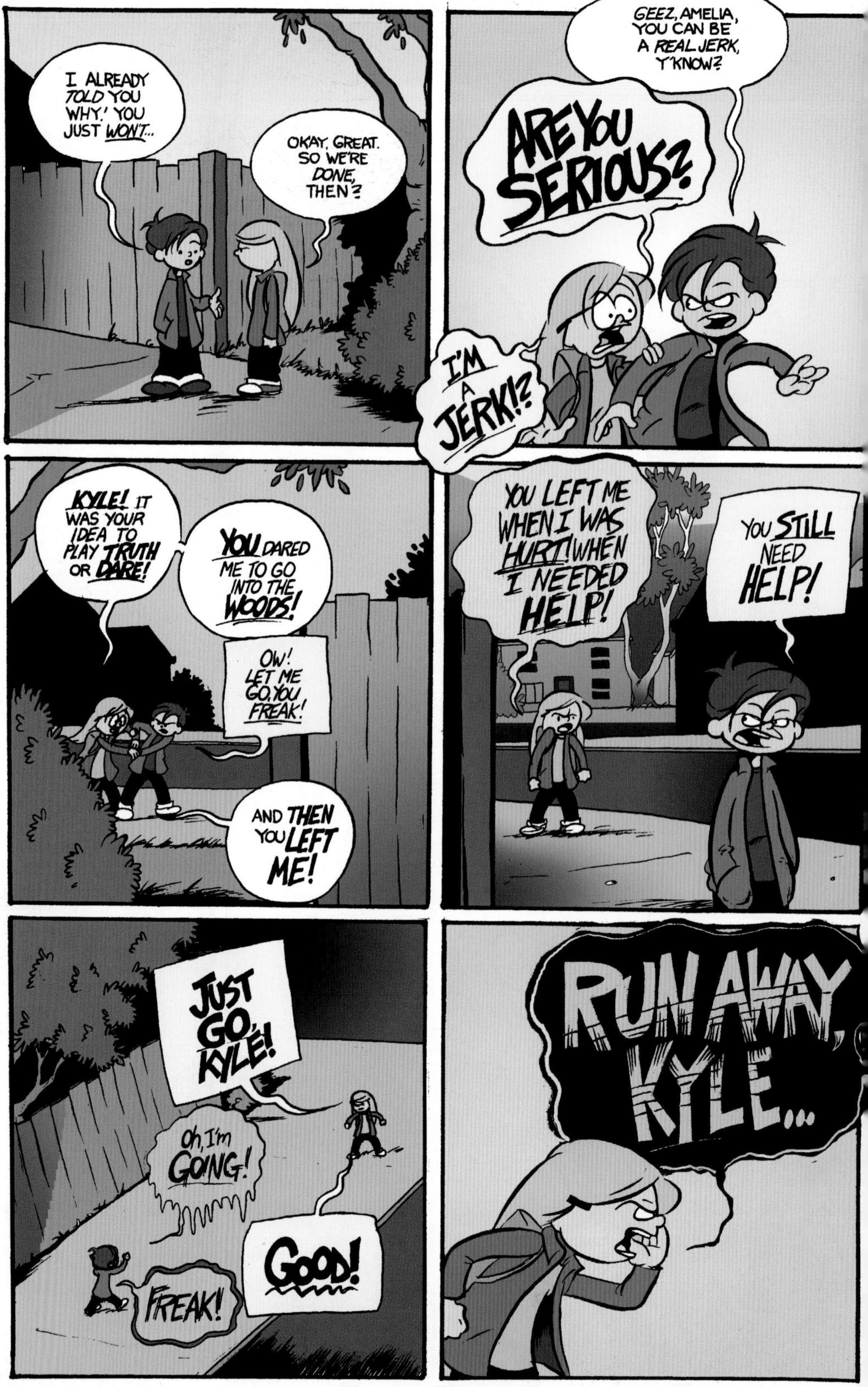
I ALREADY TOLD YOU WHY.' YOU JUST WON'T...
OKAY, GREAT. SO WE'RE DONE, THEN?
GEEZ, AMELIA, YOU CAN BE A REAL JERK, Y'KNOW?
ARE YOU SERIOUS?
I'M A JERK!?
KYLE! IT WAS YOUR IDEA TO PLAY TRUTH OR DARE!
YOU DARED ME TO GO INTO THE WOODS!
OW! LET ME GO, YOU FREAK!
AND THEN YOU LEFT ME!
YOU LEFT ME WHEN I WAS HURT! WHEN I NEEDED HELP!
YOU STILL NEED HELP!
JUST GO, KYLE!
Oh, I'm GOING!
GOOD!
FREAK!
RUN AWAY, KYLE...

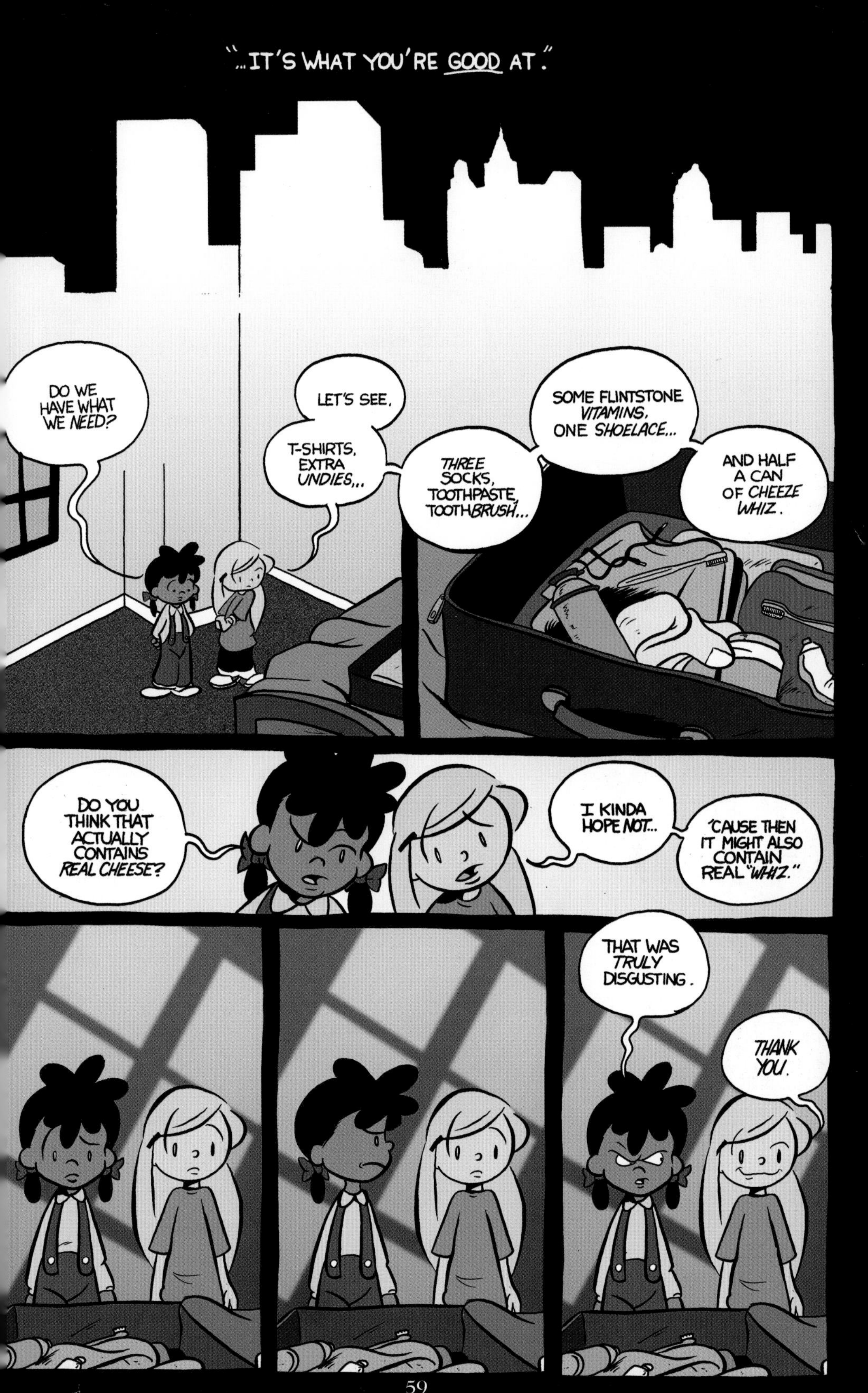
"...IT'S WHAT YOU'RE GOOD AT."
DO WE HAVE WHAT WE NEED?
LET'S SEE.
T-SHIRTS, EXTRA UNDIES,..
THREE SOCKS, TOOTHPASTE, TOOTHBRUSH...
SOME FLINTSTONE VITAMINS, ONE SHOELACE...
AND HALF A CAN OF CHEEZE WHIZ.
DO YOU THINK THAT ACTUALLY CONTAINS REAL CHEESE?
I KINDA HOPE NOT...
'CAUSE THEN IT MIGHT ALSO CONTAIN REAL "WHIZ."
THAT WAS TRULY DISGUSTING.
THANK YOU.

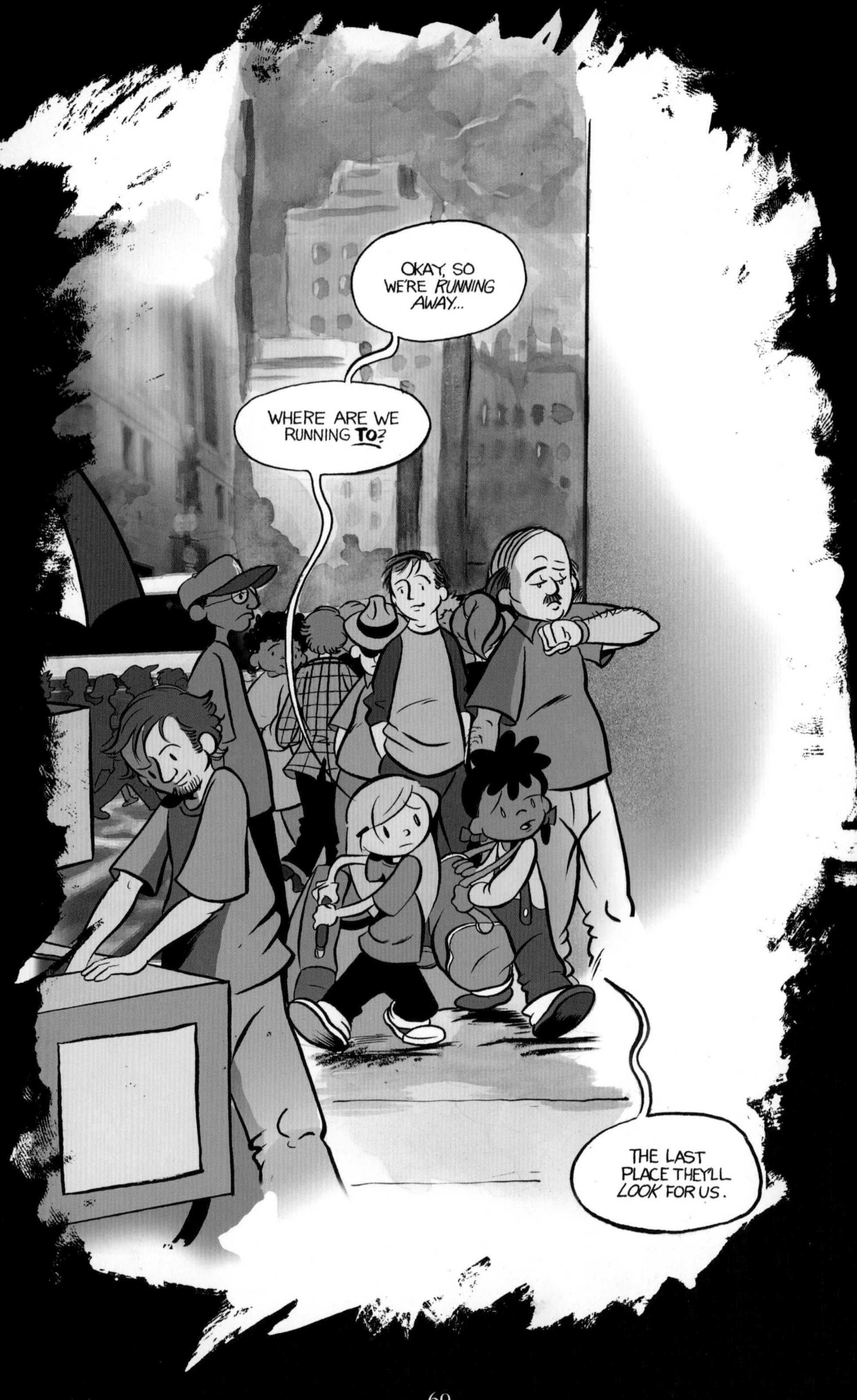
OKAY, SO WE'RE RUNNING AWAY...
WHERE ARE WE RUNNING TO?
THE LAST PLACE THEY'LL LOOK FOR US.

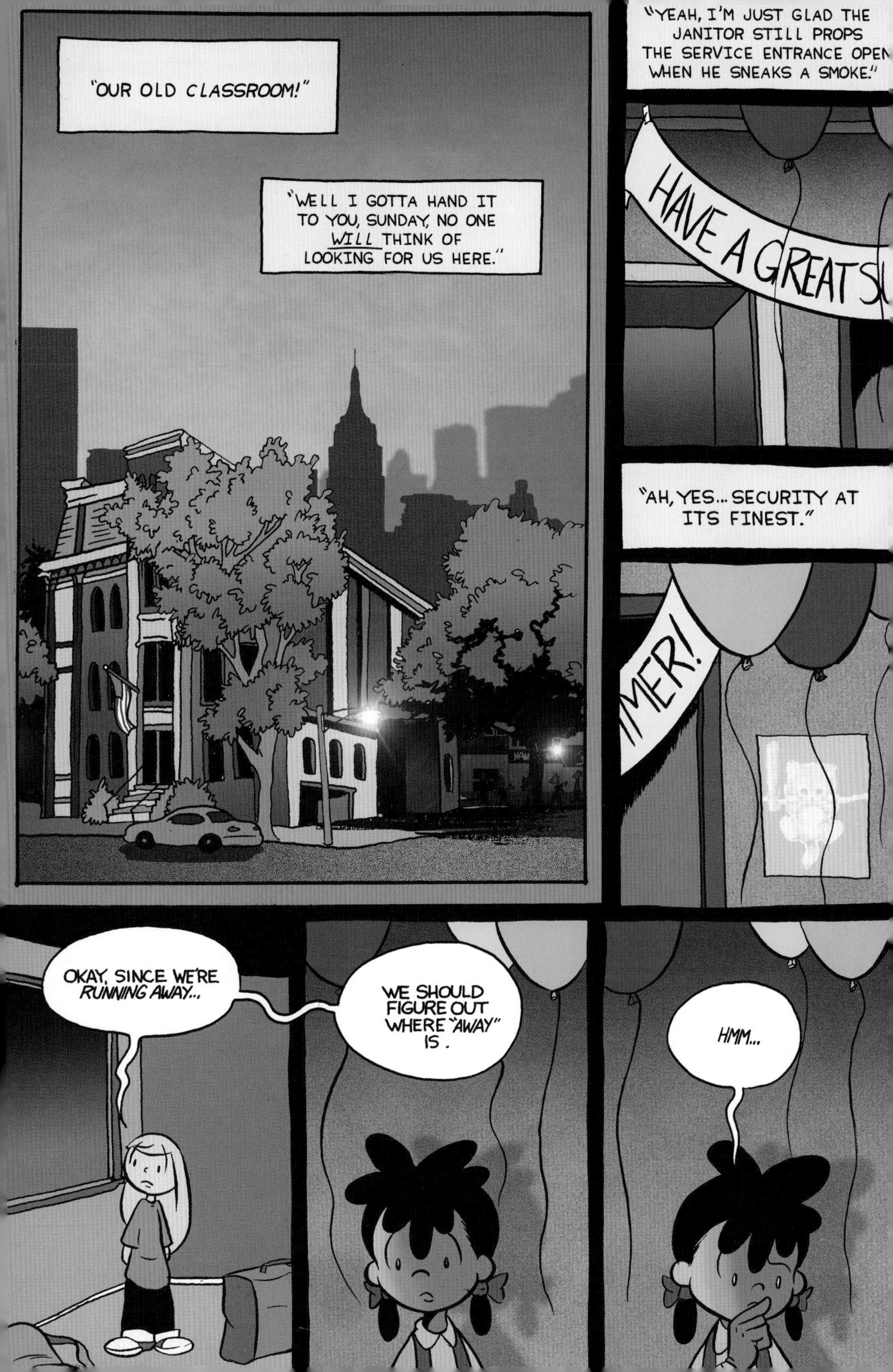
"OUR OLD CLASSROOM!"
"WELL I GOTTA HAND IT TO YOU, SUNDAY, NO ONE WILL THINK OF LOOKING FOR US HERE."
"YEAH, I'M JUST GLAD THE JANITOR STILL PROPS THE SERVICE ENTRANCE OPEN WHEN HE SNEAKS A SMOKE."
HAVE A GREAT SU
"AH, YES... SECURITY AT ITS FINEST."
MMER!
OKAY, SINCE WE'RE RUNNING AWAY...
WE SHOULD FIGURE OUT WHERE "AWAY" IS.
HMM...

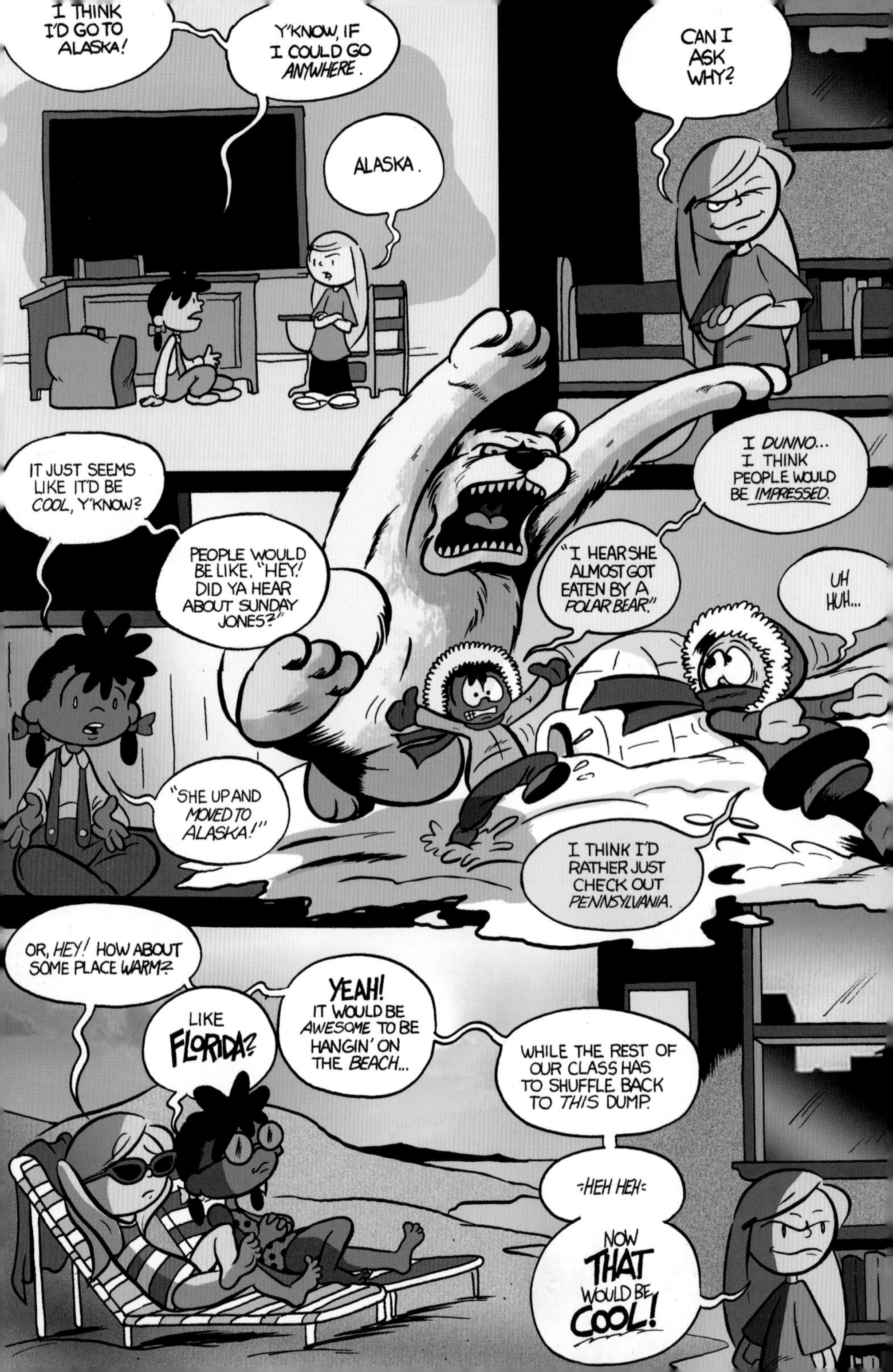
I THINK I'D GO TO ALASKA!
Y'KNOW, IF I COULD GO *ANYWHERE*.
ALASKA.
CAN I ASK WHY?
IT JUST SEEMS LIKE IT'D BE *COOL*, Y'KNOW?
PEOPLE WOULD BE LIKE, "HEY! DID YA HEAR ABOUT SUNDAY JONES?"
"SHE UP AND *MOVED TO ALASKA!*"
"I HEAR SHE ALMOST GOT EATEN BY A *POLAR BEAR*."
I *DUNNO*... I THINK PEOPLE WOULD BE *IMPRESSED*.
UH HUH...
I THINK I'D RATHER JUST CHECK OUT *PENNSYLVANIA*.
OR, *HEY!* HOW ABOUT SOME PLACE *WARM*?
LIKE FLORIDA?
YEAH! IT WOULD BE *AWESOME* TO BE HANGIN' ON THE *BEACH*...
WHILE THE REST OF OUR CLASS HAS TO SHUFFLE BACK TO *THIS* DUMP.
HEH HEH
NOW THAT WOULD BE COOL!

"WE'D NEVER HAVE TO SEE THOSE *JERKS* AGAIN."

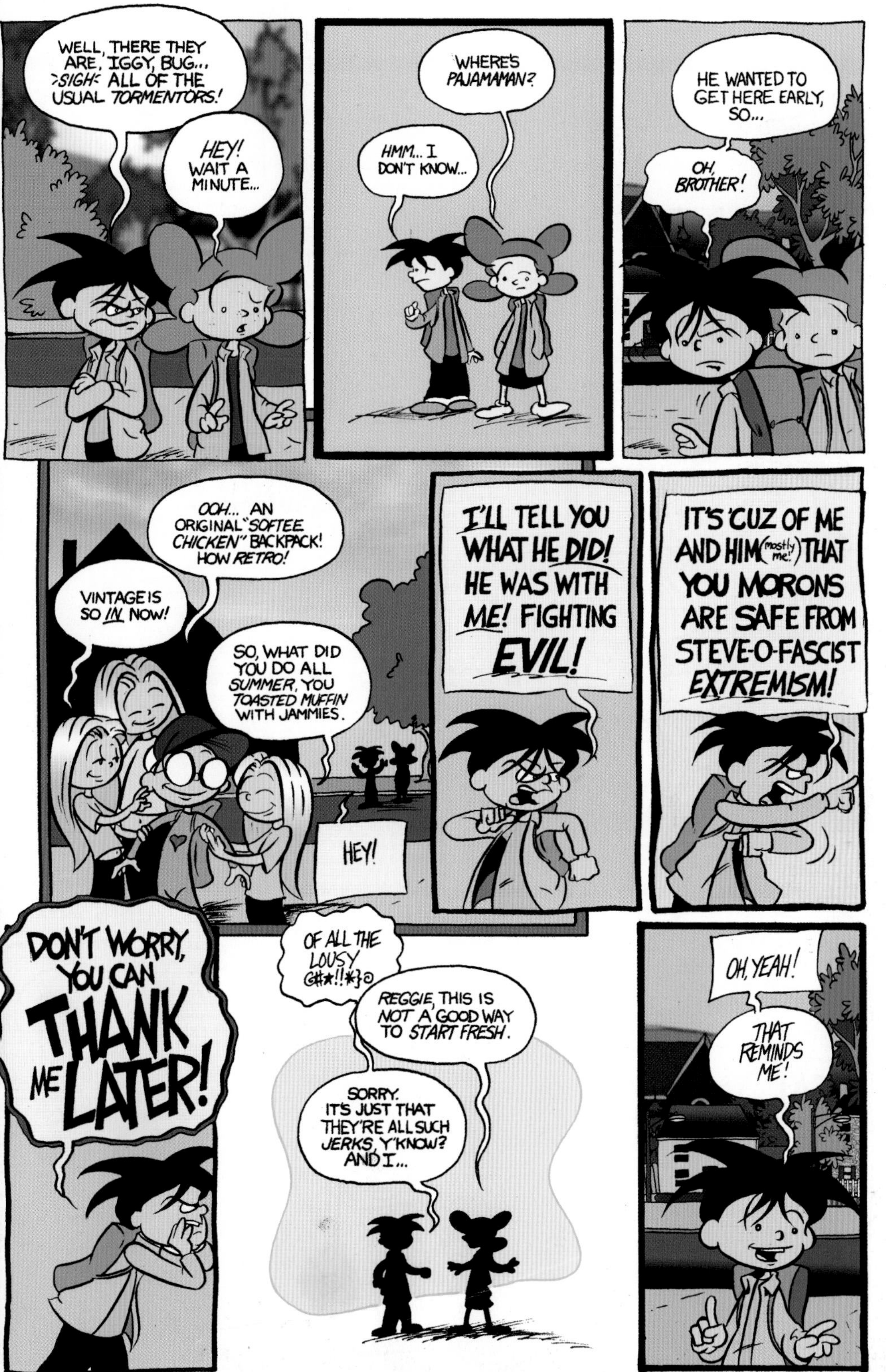
WELL, THERE THEY ARE, IGGY, BUG... >SIGH< ALL OF THE USUAL TORMENTORS!
HEY! WAIT A MINUTE...
WHERE'S PAJAMAMAN?
HMM... I DON'T KNOW...
HE WANTED TO GET HERE EARLY, SO...
OH, BROTHER!
OOH... AN ORIGINAL "SOFTEE CHICKEN" BACKPACK! HOW RETRO!
VINTAGE IS SO IN NOW!
SO, WHAT DID YOU DO ALL SUMMER, YOU TOASTED MUFFIN WITH JAMMIES.
HEY!
I'LL TELL YOU WHAT HE DID! HE WAS WITH ME! FIGHTING EVIL!
IT'S 'CUZ OF ME AND HIM (mostly me!) THAT YOU MORONS ARE SAFE FROM STEVE-O-FASCIST EXTREMISM!
DON'T WORRY, YOU CAN THANK ME LATER!
OF ALL THE LOUSY G#*!!*}@
REGGIE, THIS IS NOT A GOOD WAY TO START FRESH.
SORRY. IT'S JUST THAT THEY'RE ALL SUCH JERKS, Y'KNOW? AND I...
OH, YEAH!
THAT REMINDS ME!

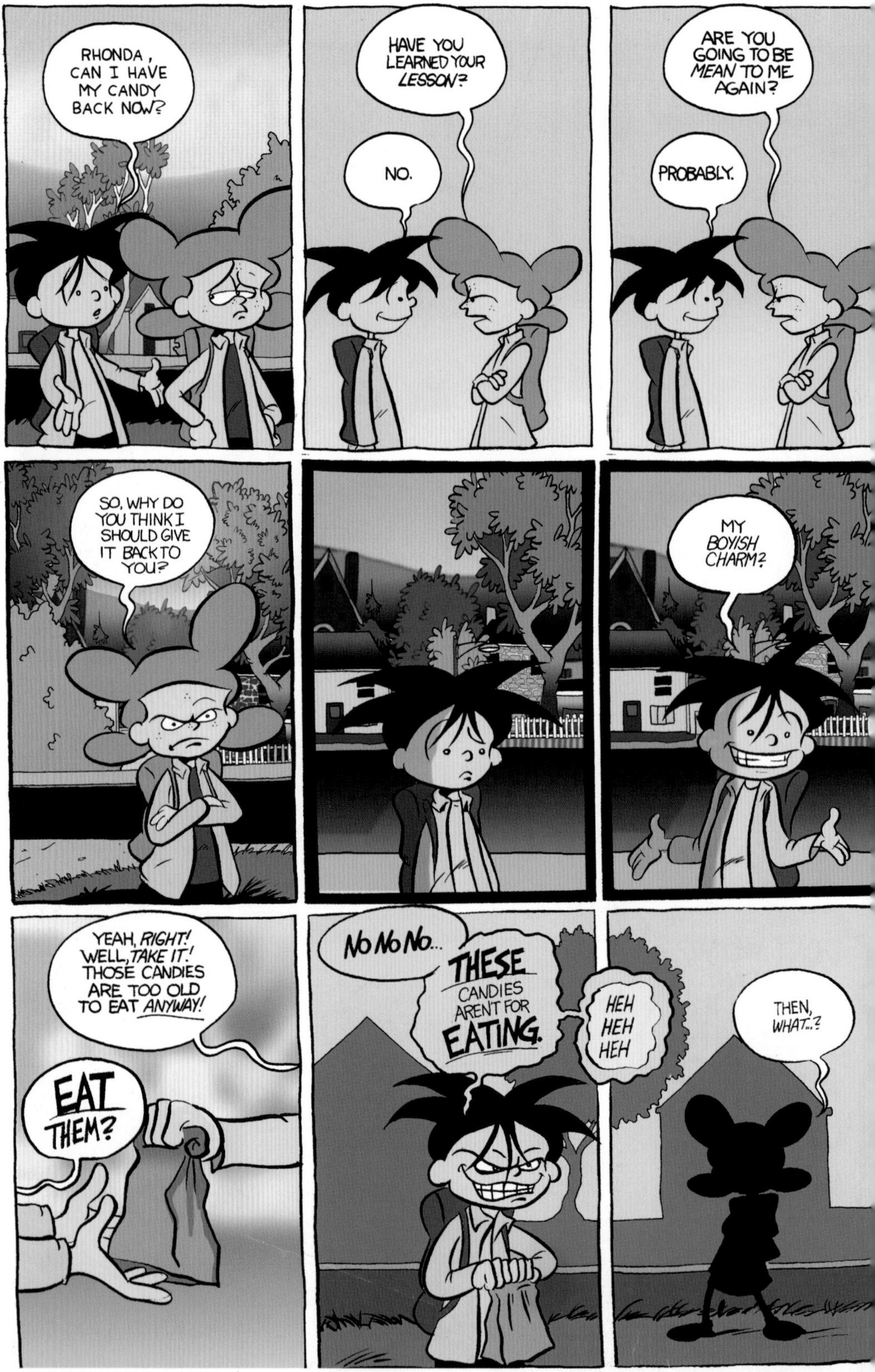
RHONDA, CAN I HAVE MY CANDY BACK NOW?
HAVE YOU LEARNED YOUR LESSON?
NO.
ARE YOU GOING TO BE MEAN TO ME AGAIN?
PROBABLY.
SO, WHY DO YOU THINK I SHOULD GIVE IT BACK TO YOU?
MY BOYISH CHARM?
YEAH, RIGHT! WELL, TAKE IT! THOSE CANDIES ARE TOO OLD TO EAT ANYWAY!
EAT THEM?
No No No...
THESE CANDIES AREN'T FOR EATING.
HEH HEH HEH
THEN, WHAT...?

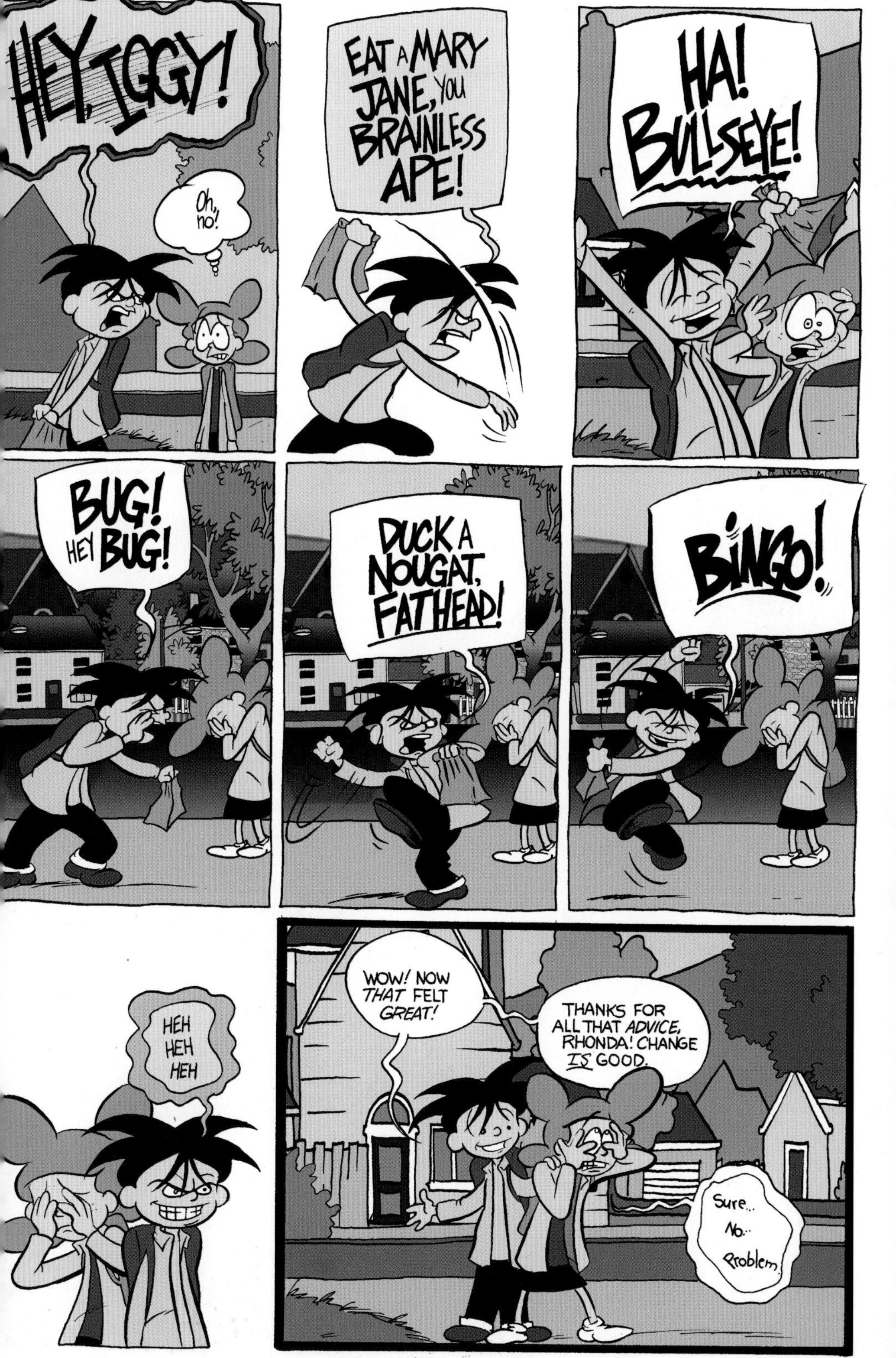
HEY, IGGY!
Oh, no!
EAT A MARY JANE, YOU BRAINLESS APE!
HA! BULLSEYE!
BUG! HEY BUG!
DUCK A NOUGAT, FATHEAD!
BINGO!
HEH HEH HEH
WOW! NOW THAT FELT GREAT!
THANKS FOR ALL THAT ADVICE, RHONDA! CHANGE IS GOOD.
Sure... No... Problem.

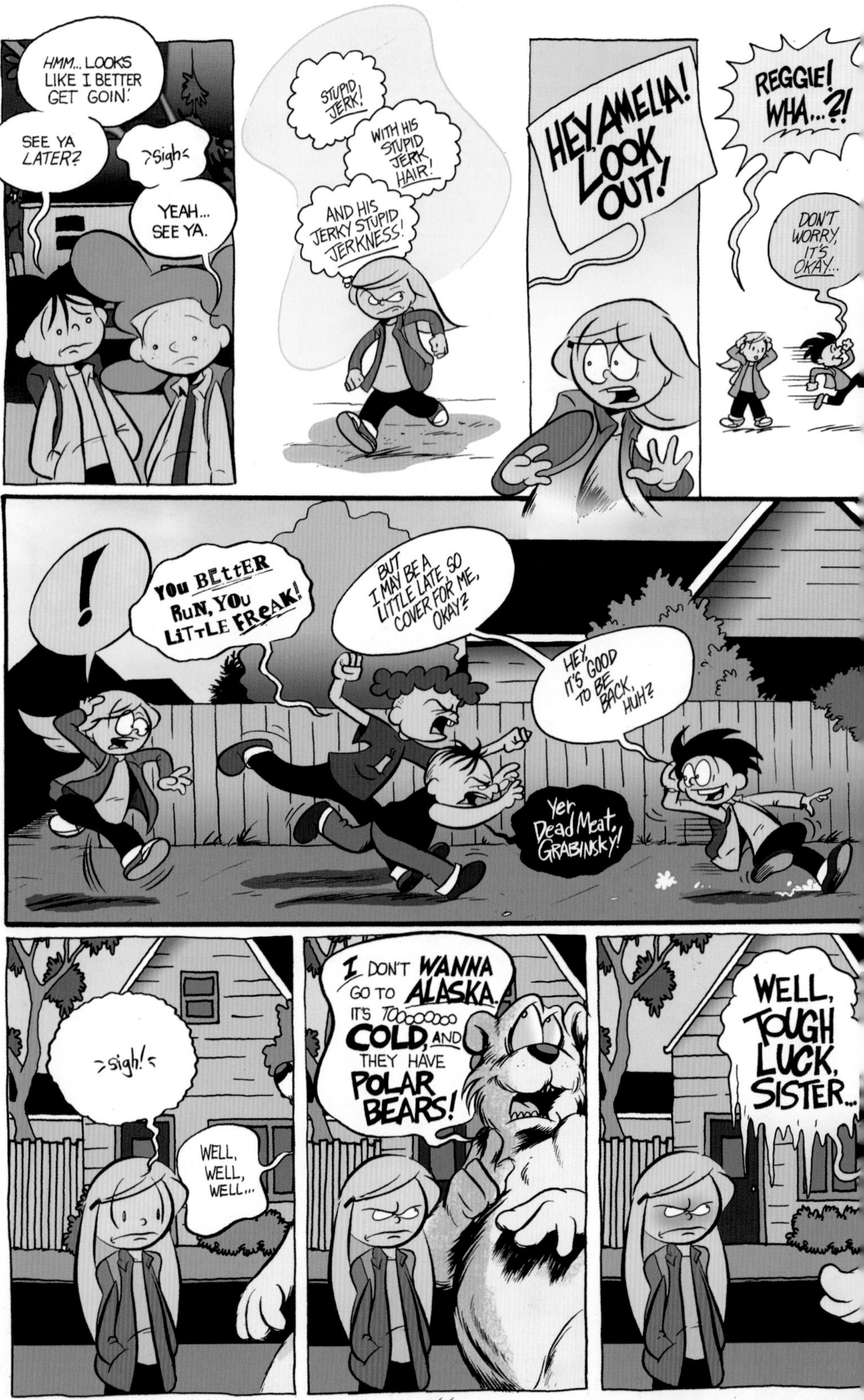

HMM... LOOKS LIKE I BETTER GET GOIN'.
SEE YA LATER?
>sigh<
YEAH... SEE YA.
STUPID JERK!
WITH HIS STUPID JERK HAIR!
AND HIS JERKY STUPID JERKNESS!
HEY, AMELIA! LOOK OUT!
REGGIE! WHA...?!
DON'T WORRY, IT'S OKAY...
!
YOU BETTER RUN, YOU LITTLE FREAK!
BUT I MAY BE A LITTLE LATE, SO COVER FOR ME, OKAY?
HEY, IT'S GOOD TO BE BACK, HUH?
Yer Dead Meat, GRABINSKY!
>sigh!<
WELL, WELL, WELL...
I DON'T WANNA GO TO ALASKA. IT'S TOOOOOOOO COLD, AND THEY HAVE POLAR BEARS!
WELL, TOUGH LUCK, SISTER...

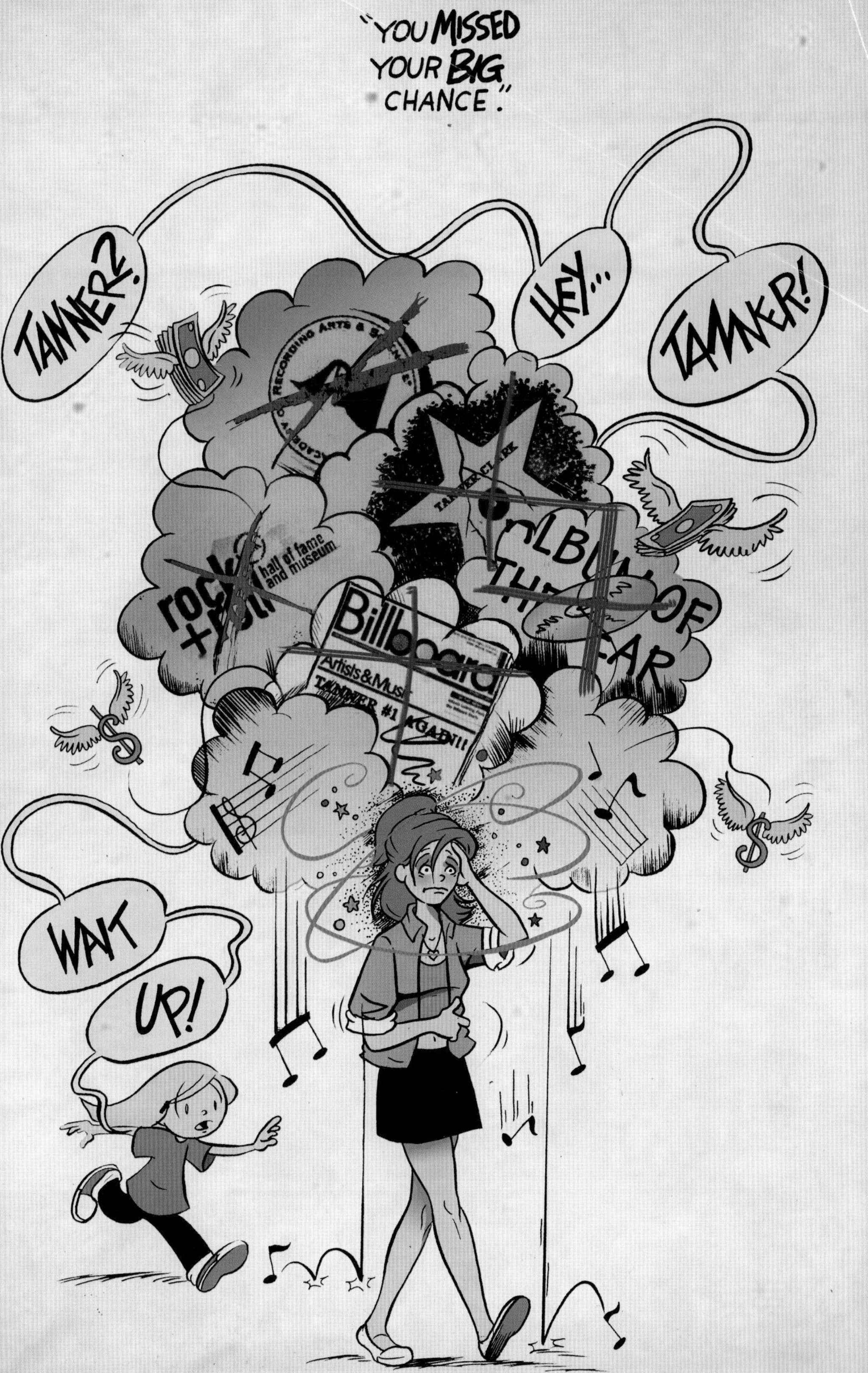
"YOU MISSED YOUR BIG CHANCE."
TANNER?
HEY...
TANNER!
hall of fame and museum
Billboard
Artists & Music
WAIT UP!

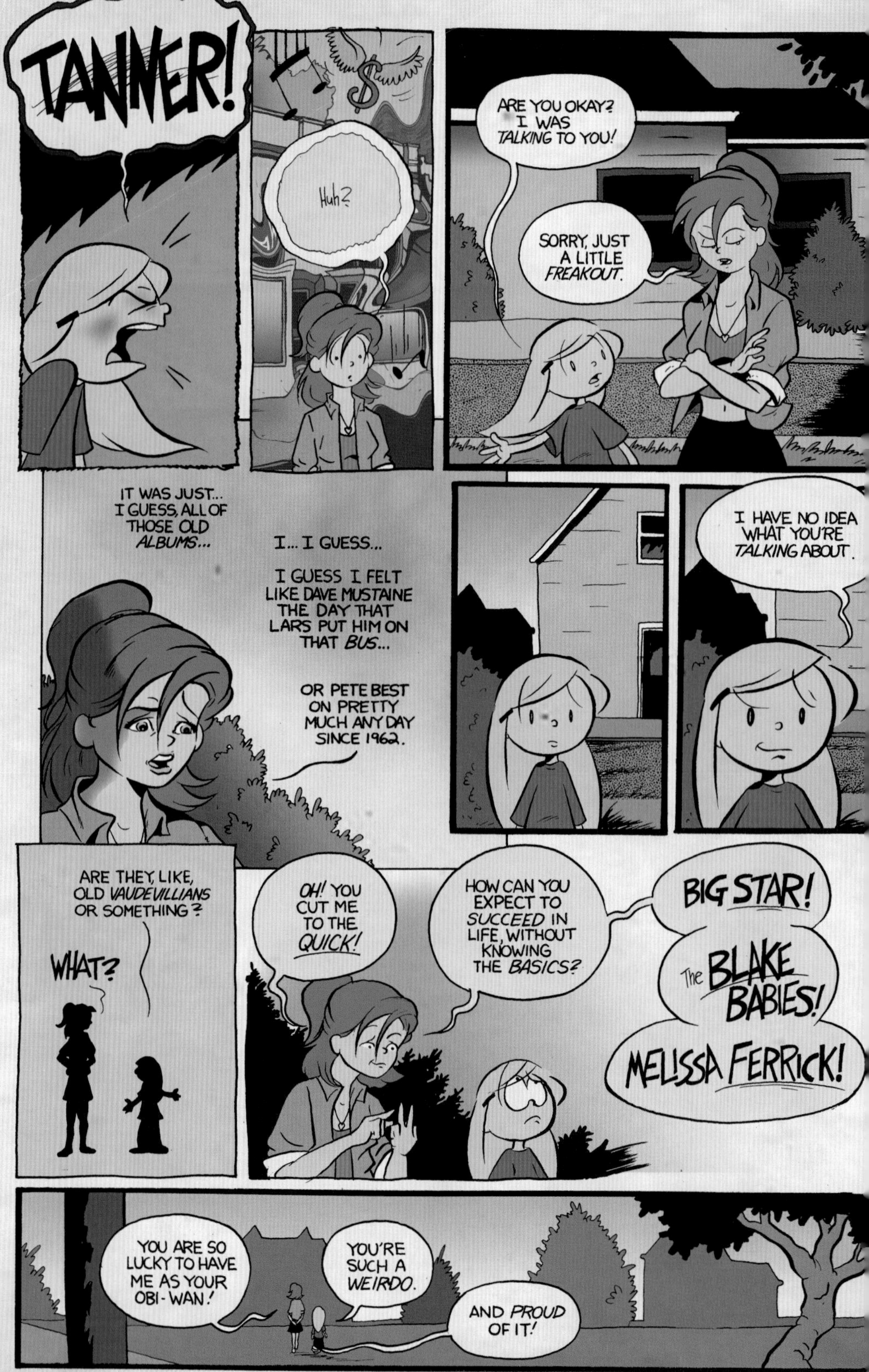
TANNER!
Huh?
ARE YOU OKAY? I WAS TALKING TO YOU!
SORRY, JUST A LITTLE FREAKOUT.
IT WAS JUST... I GUESS, ALL OF THOSE OLD ALBUMS...
I... I GUESS...
I GUESS I FELT LIKE DAVE MUSTAINE THE DAY THAT LARS PUT HIM ON THAT BUS...
OR PETE BEST ON PRETTY MUCH ANY DAY SINCE 1962.
I HAVE NO IDEA WHAT YOU'RE TALKING ABOUT.
ARE THEY, LIKE, OLD VAUDEVILLIANS OR SOMETHING?
WHAT?
OH! YOU CUT ME TO THE QUICK!
HOW CAN YOU EXPECT TO SUCCEED IN LIFE, WITHOUT KNOWING THE BASICS?
BIG STAR!
The BLAKE BABIES!
MELISSA FERRICK!
YOU ARE SO LUCKY TO HAVE ME AS YOUR OBI-WAN!
YOU'RE SUCH A WEIRDO.
AND PROUD OF IT!

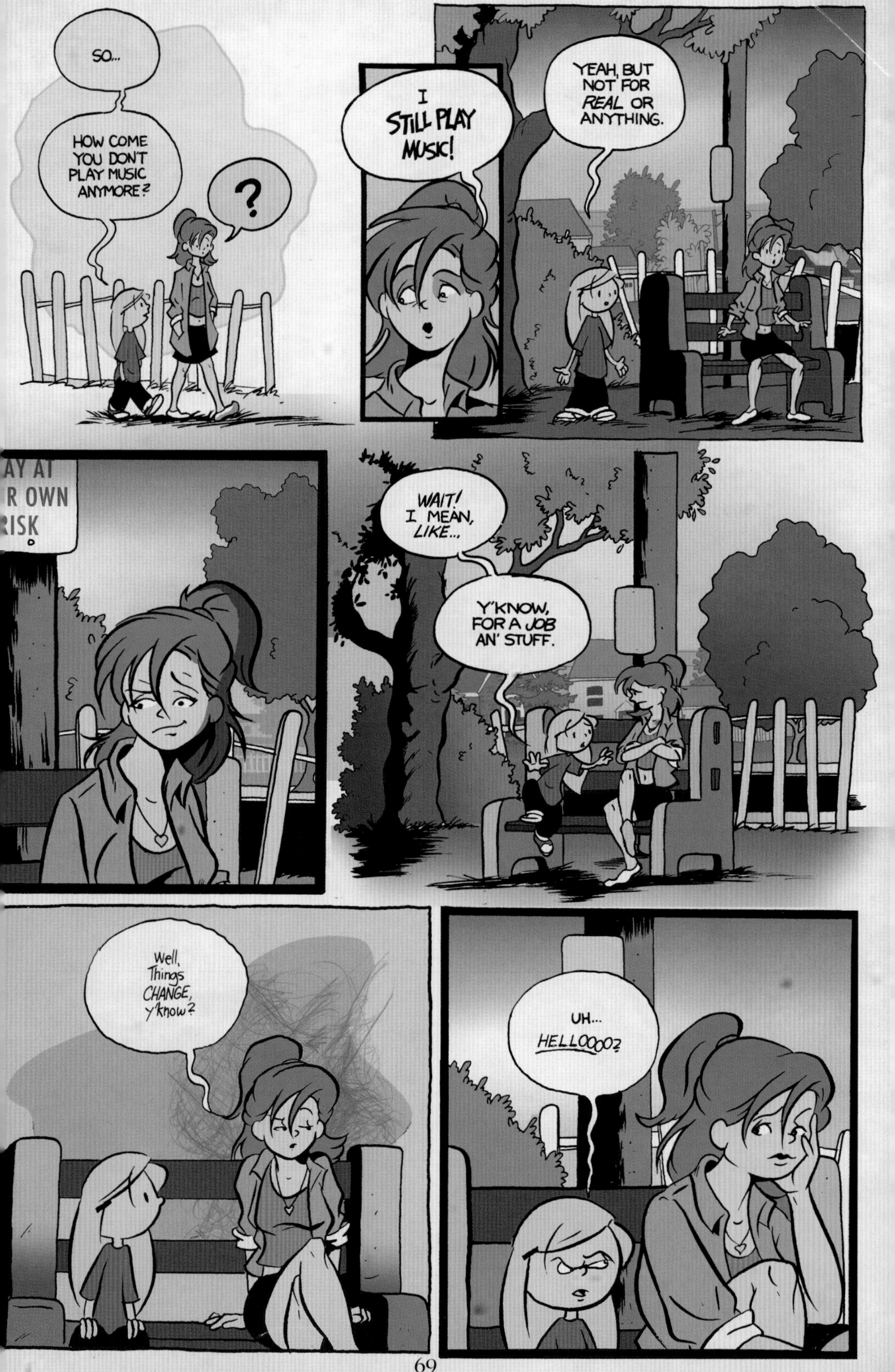
SO...
HOW COME YOU DON'T PLAY MUSIC ANYMORE?
?
I STILL PLAY MUSIC!
YEAH, BUT NOT FOR REAL OR ANYTHING.
AY AT R OWN ISK
WAIT! I MEAN, LIKE...
Y'KNOW, FOR A JOB AN' STUFF.
Well, Things CHANGE, y'know?
UH... HELLOOOO?

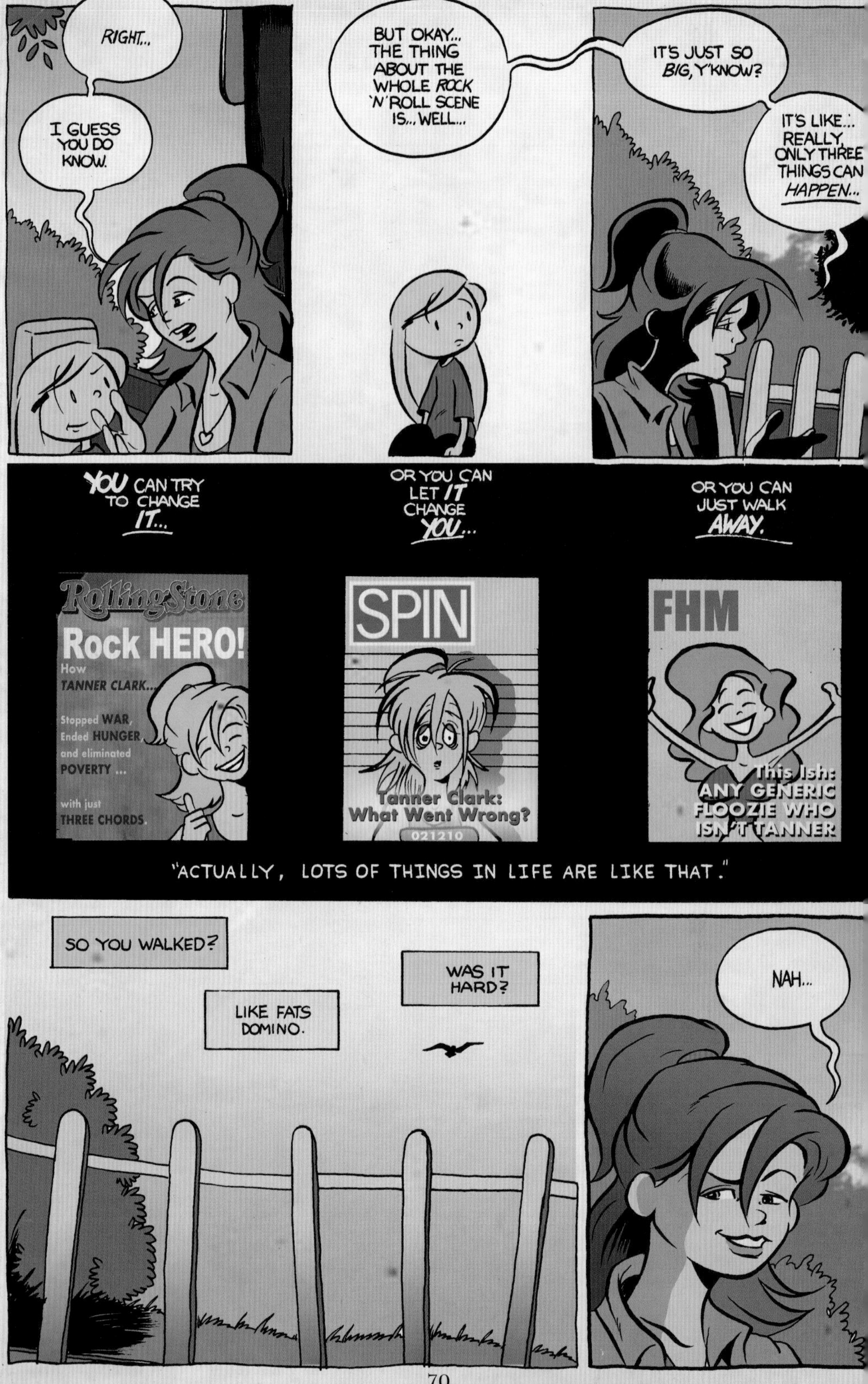
RIGHT...
I GUESS YOU DO KNOW.
BUT OKAY... THE THING ABOUT THE WHOLE ROCK 'N' ROLL SCENE IS... WELL...
IT'S JUST SO BIG, Y'KNOW?
IT'S LIKE... REALLY, ONLY THREE THINGS CAN HAPPEN...
YOU CAN TRY TO CHANGE IT...
OR YOU CAN LET IT CHANGE YOU...
OR YOU CAN JUST WALK AWAY.
Rolling Stone
Rock HERO!
How TANNER CLARK... Stopped WAR, Ended HUNGER, and eliminated POVERTY ... with just THREE CHORDS.
SPIN
Tanner Clark: What Went Wrong?
021210
FHM
This Ish: ANY GENERIC FLOOZIE WHO ISN'T TANNER
"ACTUALLY, LOTS OF THINGS IN LIFE ARE LIKE THAT."
SO YOU WALKED?
LIKE FATS DOMINO.
WAS IT HARD?
NAH...

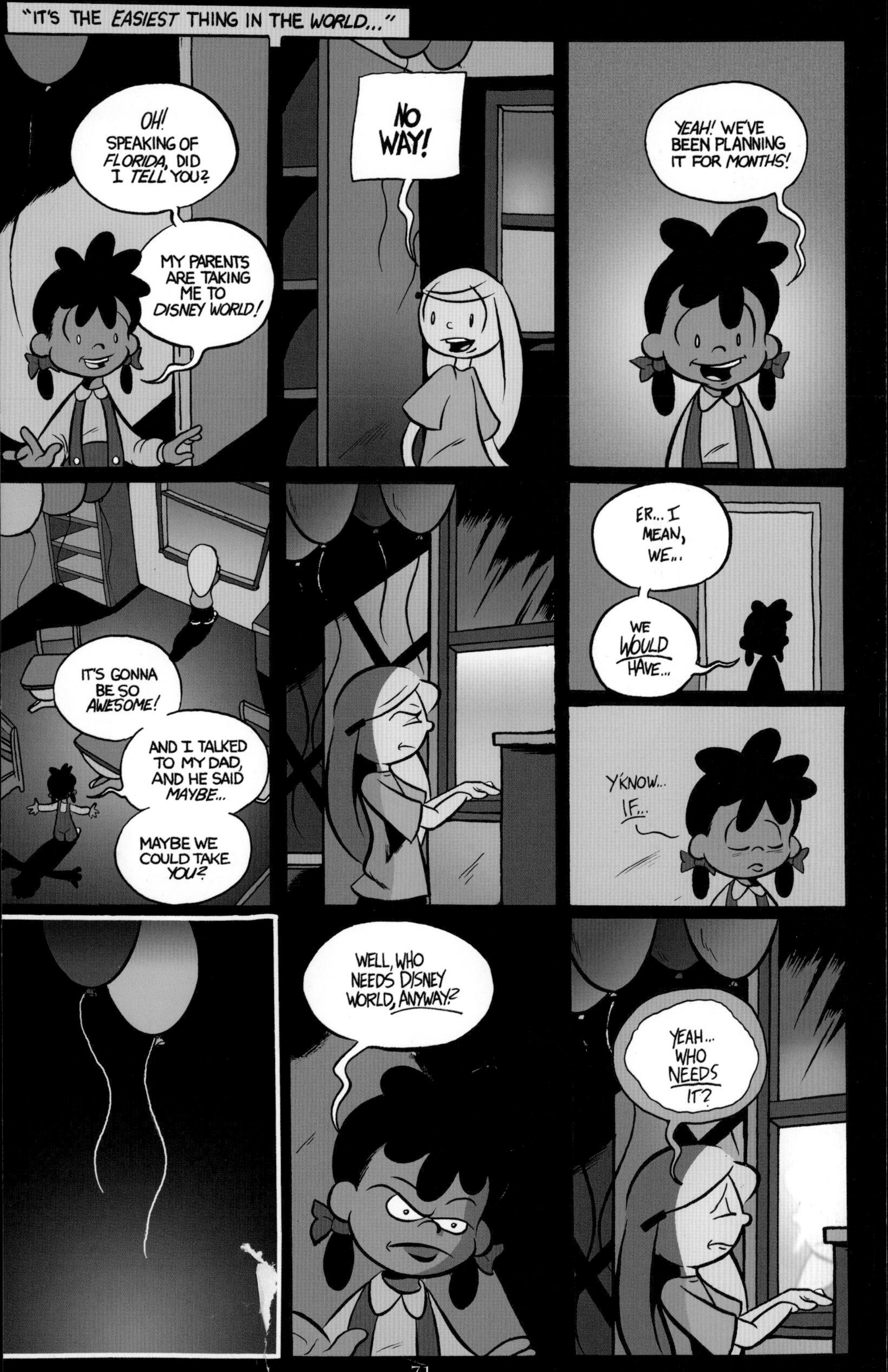
"IT'S THE EASIEST THING IN THE WORLD..."
OH! SPEAKING OF FLORIDA, DID I TELL YOU?
MY PARENTS ARE TAKING ME TO DISNEY WORLD!
NO WAY!
YEAH! WE'VE BEEN PLANNING IT FOR MONTHS!
IT'S GONNA BE SO AWESOME!
AND I TALKED TO MY DAD, AND HE SAID MAYBE...
MAYBE WE COULD TAKE YOU?
ER... I MEAN, WE...
WE WOULD HAVE...
Y'KNOW... IF...
WELL, WHO NEEDS DISNEY WORLD, ANYWAY?
YEAH... WHO NEEDS IT?

"SUNDAY?"

"LET'S GO HOME."

OKAY, SO WE STINK AT *RUNNING AWAY!*

HEY! I THINK THIS IS A SUCCESS.

HOW?

FREE BALLOON, FOR ONE THING.

PLUS, AT LEAST YOU GOT FARTHER THAN THE LAST TIME YOU TRIED.

I THOUGHT WE WERE NEVER GONNA *MENTION* THAT AGAIN.

ARE YOU *KIDDING?* I...

OH, NO!

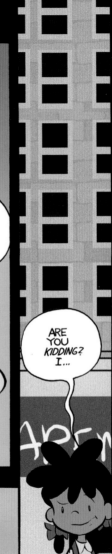

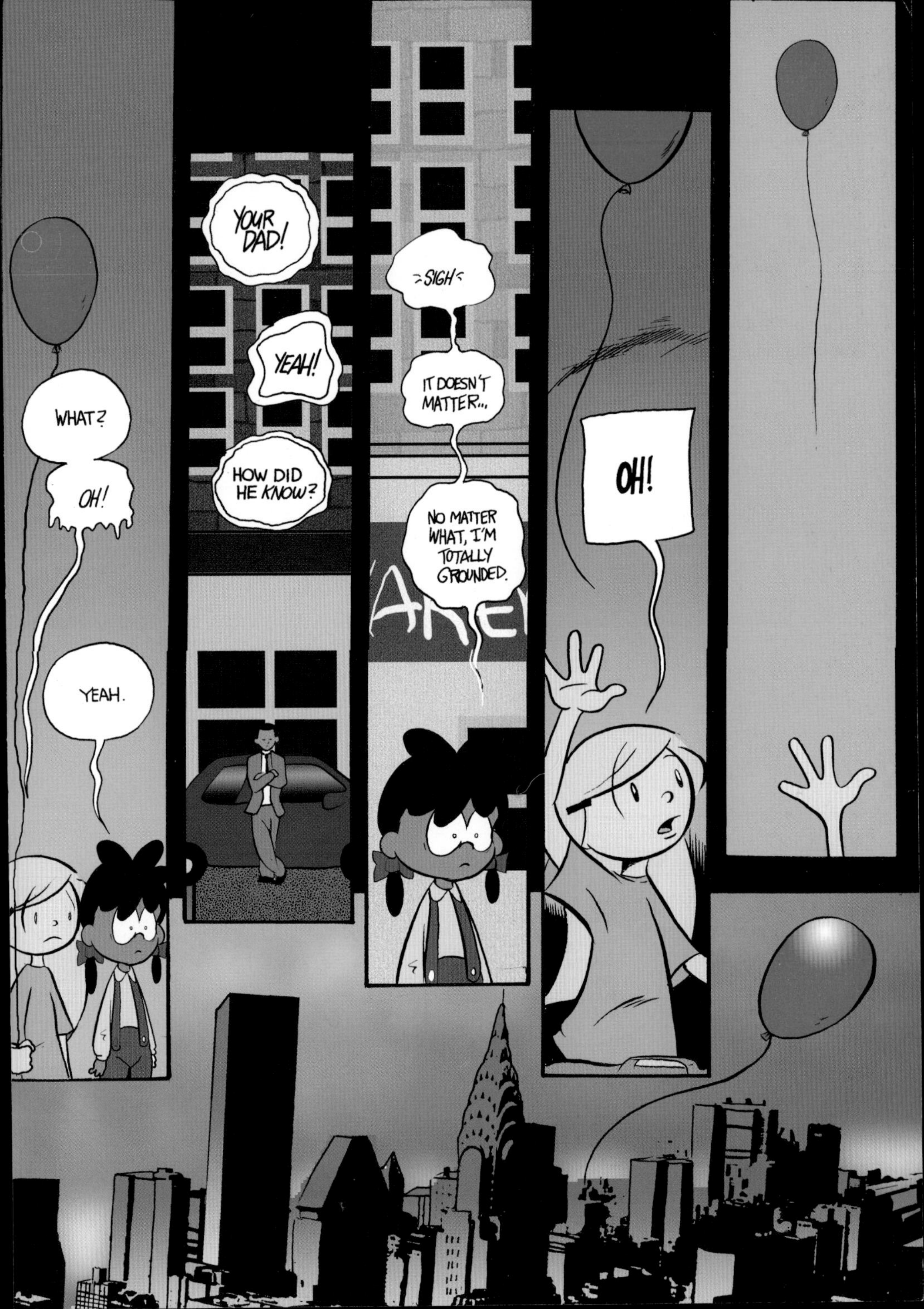
WHAT?
OH!
YEAH.
YOUR DAD!
YEAH!
HOW DID HE KNOW?
SIGH
IT DOESN'T MATTER...
NO MATTER WHAT, I'M TOTALLY GROUNDED.
OH!

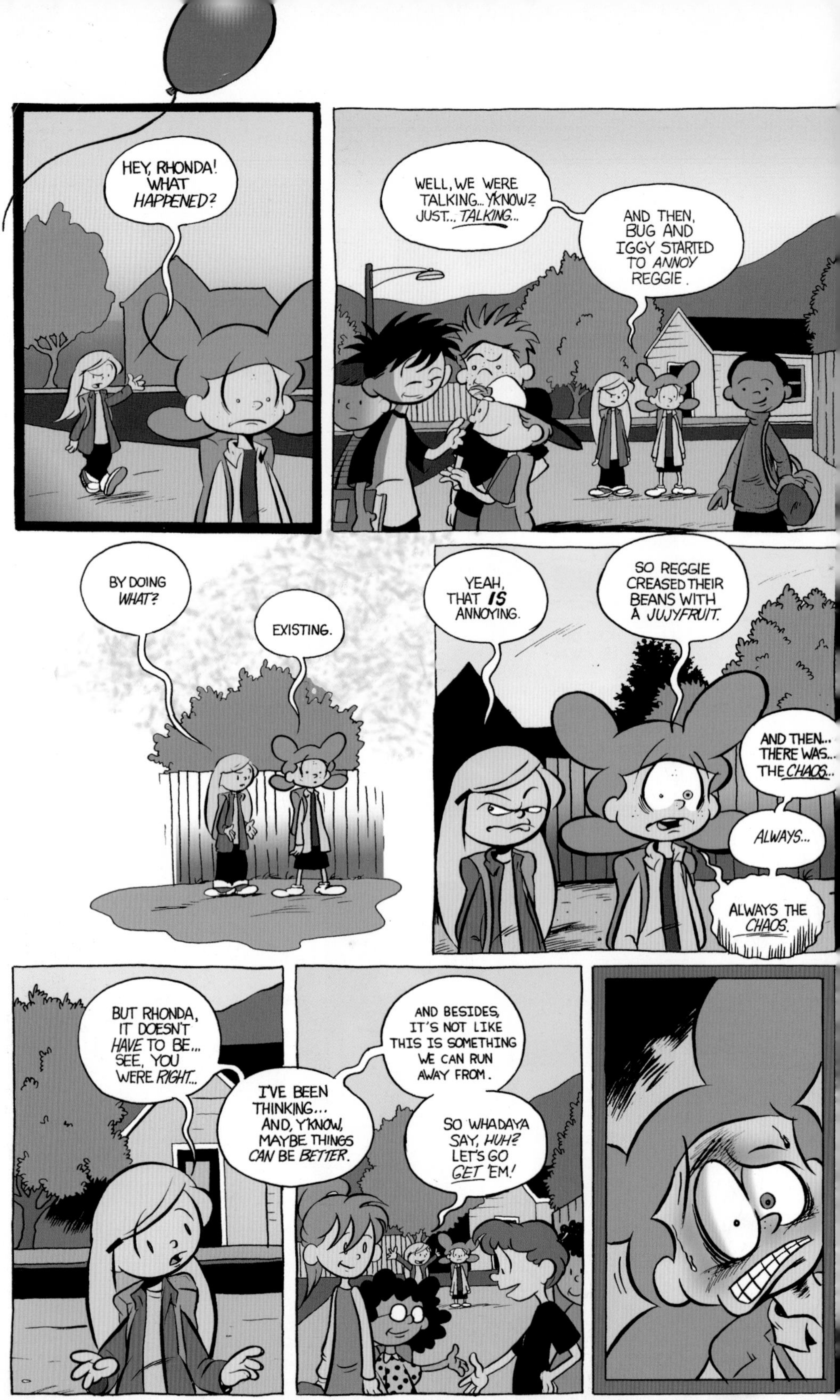
HEY, RHONDA! WHAT HAPPENED?
WELL, WE WERE TALKING... Y'KNOW? JUST... TALKING...
AND THEN, BUG AND IGGY STARTED TO ANNOY REGGIE.
BY DOING WHAT?
EXISTING.
YEAH, THAT IS ANNOYING.
SO REGGIE CREASED THEIR BEANS WITH A JUJYFRUIT.
AND THEN... THERE WAS... THE CHAOS...
ALWAYS...
ALWAYS THE CHAOS.
BUT RHONDA, IT DOESN'T HAVE TO BE... SEE, YOU WERE RIGHT...
I'VE BEEN THINKING... AND, Y'KNOW, MAYBE THINGS CAN BE BETTER.
AND BESIDES, IT'S NOT LIKE THIS IS SOMETHING WE CAN RUN AWAY FROM.
SO WHADAYA SAY, HUH? LET'S GO GET 'EM!

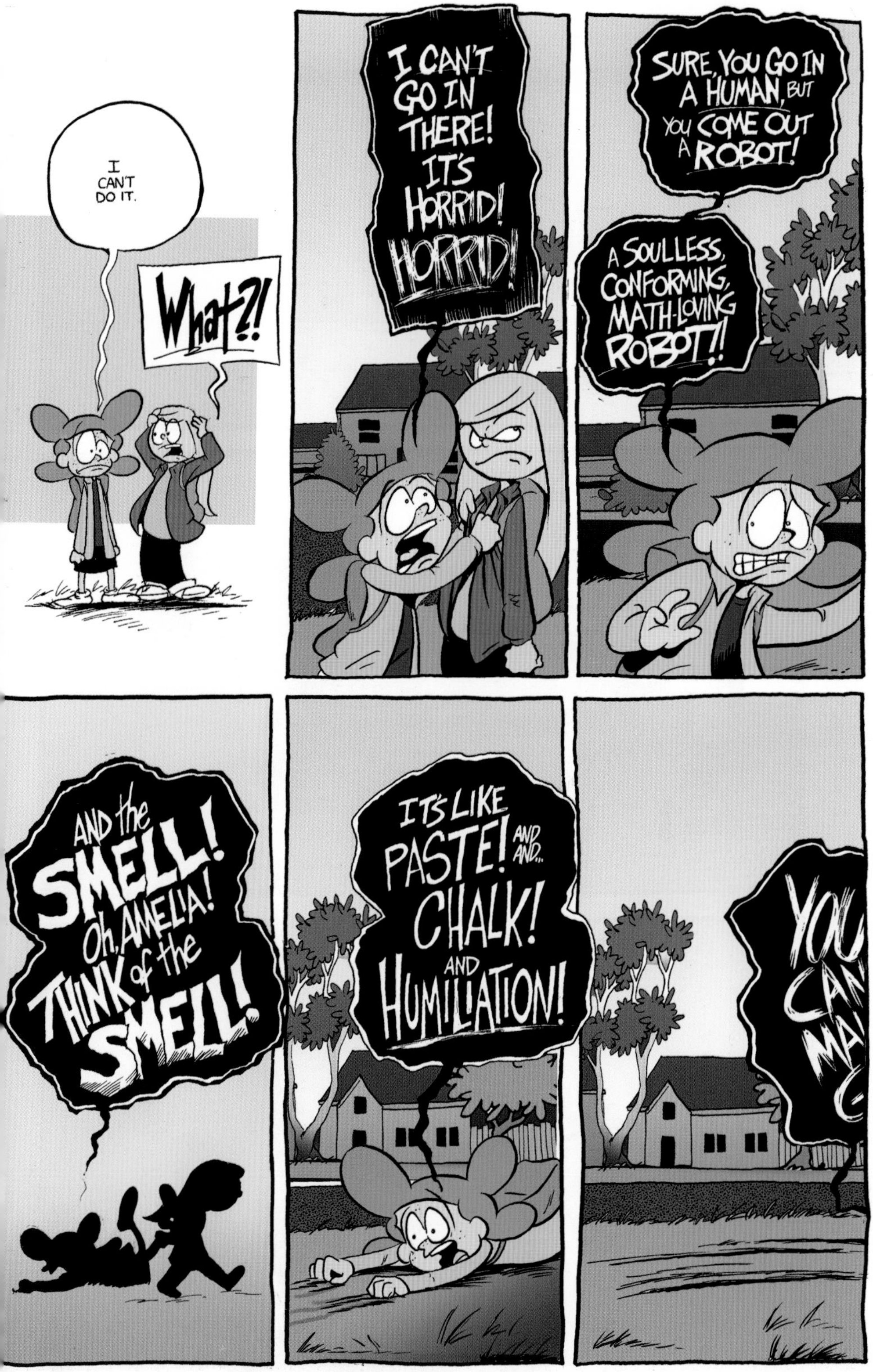

I CAN'T DO IT.
What?!
I CAN'T GO IN THERE! IT'S HORRID! HORRID!
SURE, YOU GO IN A HUMAN, BUT YOU COME OUT A ROBOT!
A SOULLESS, CONFORMING, MATH-LOVING ROBOT!!
AND the SMELL! Oh, AMELIA! THINK of the SMELL!
IT'S LIKE PASTE! AND AND... CHALK! AND HUMILIATION!

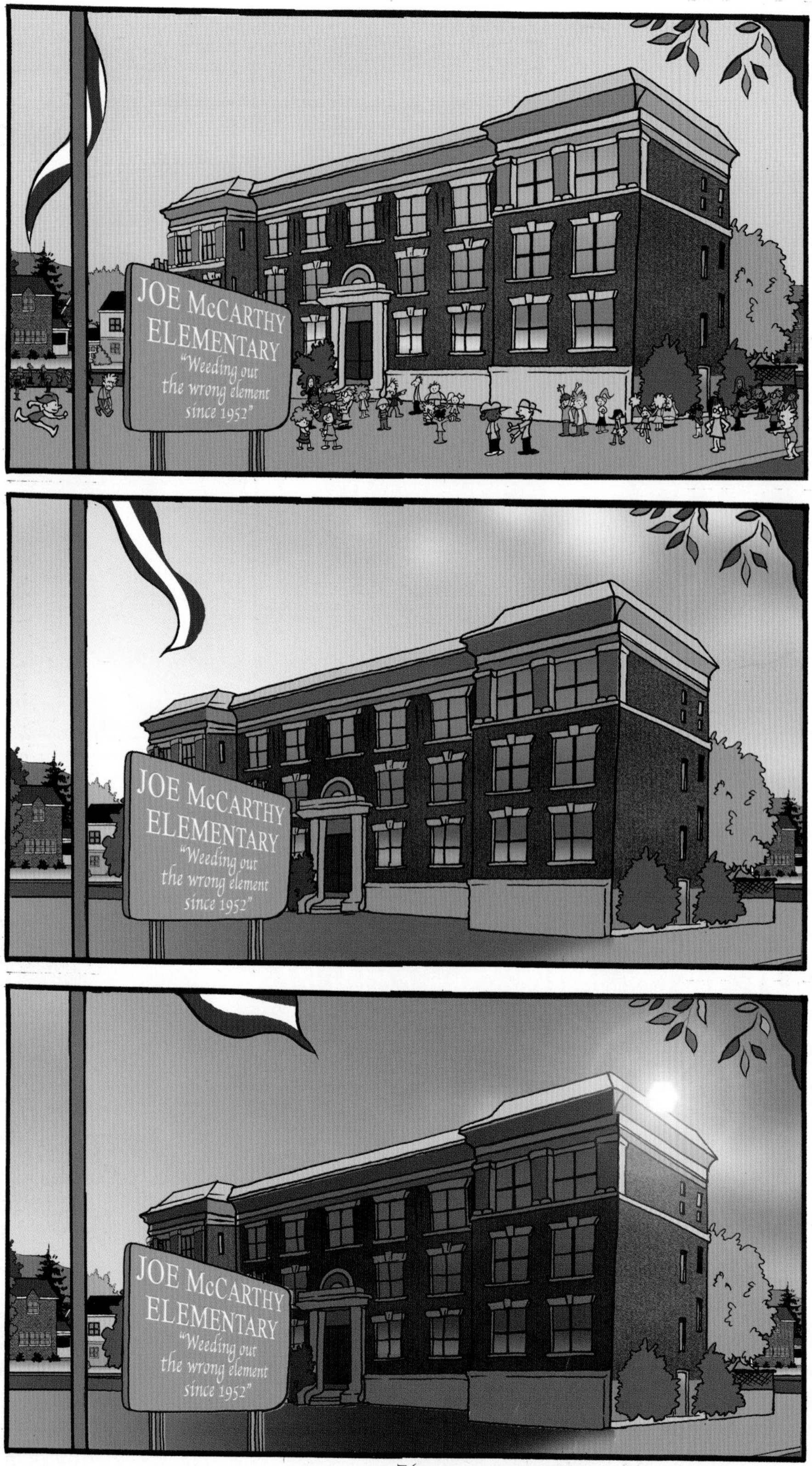
JOE McCARTHY
ELEMENTARY
"Weeding out
the wrong element
since 1952"
JOE McCARTHY
ELEMENTARY
"Weeding out
the wrong element
since 1952"
JOE McCARTHY
ELEMENTARY
"Weeding out
the wrong element
since 1952"

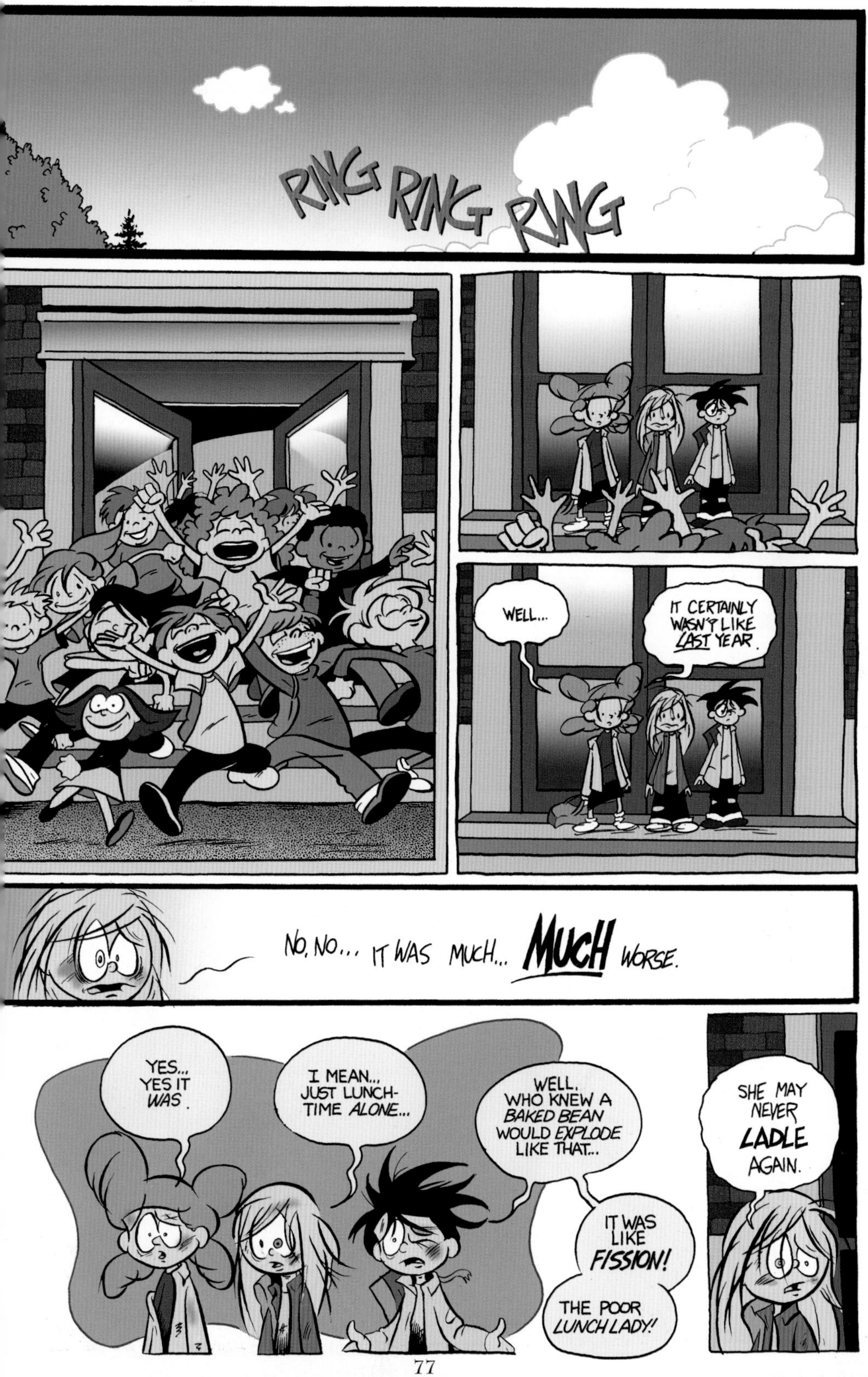
RING RING RING
WELL...
IT CERTAINLY WASN'T LIKE LAST YEAR.
NO, NO... IT WAS MUCH... MUCH WORSE.
YES... YES IT WAS.
I MEAN... JUST LUNCH-TIME ALONE...
WELL, WHO KNEW A BAKED BEAN WOULD EXPLODE LIKE THAT...
IT WAS LIKE FISSION!
THE POOR LUNCH LADY!
SHE MAY NEVER LADLE AGAIN.

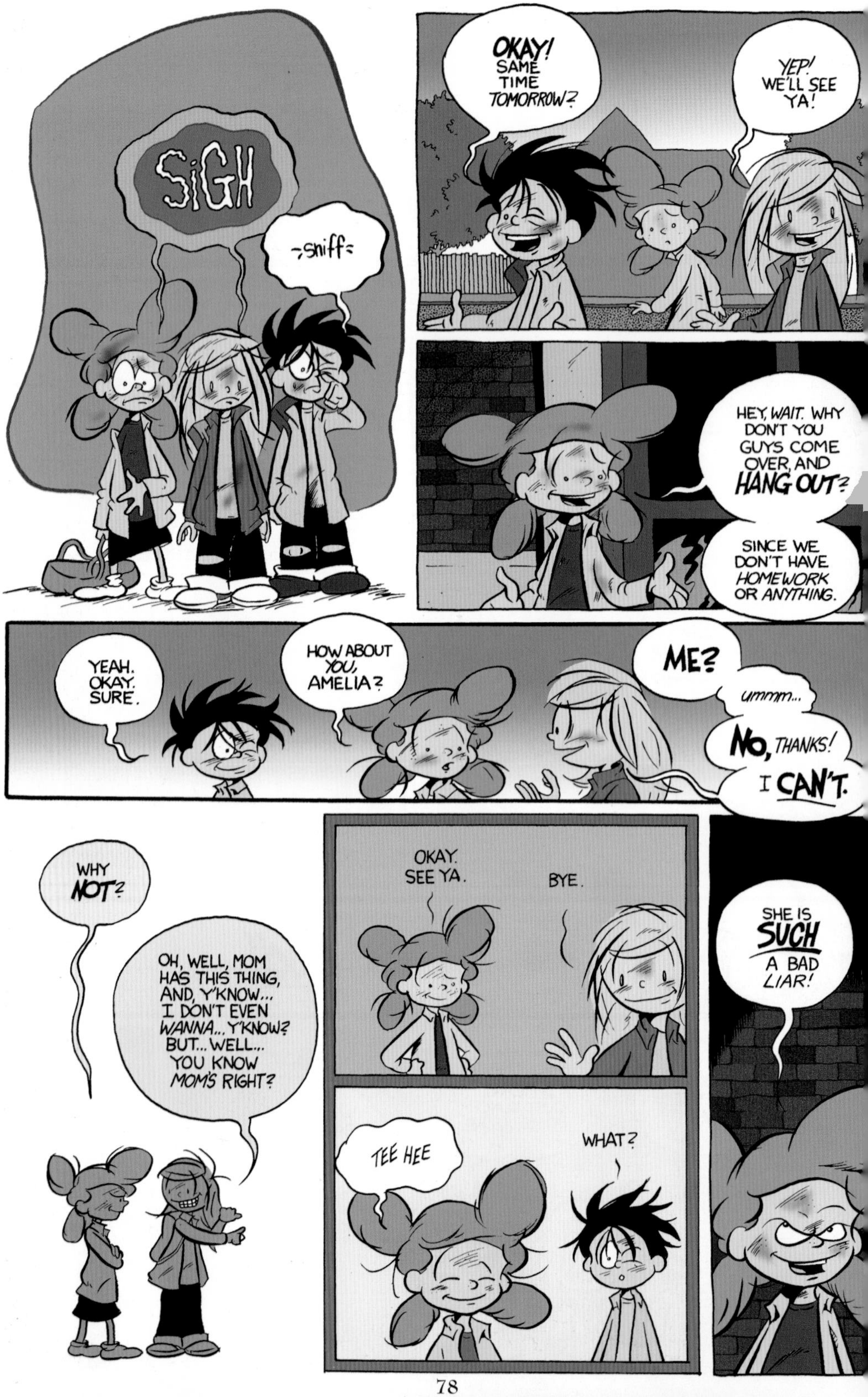
SiGH
-sniff-
OKAY! SAME TIME TOMORROW?
YEP! WE'LL SEE YA!
HEY, WAIT. WHY DON'T YOU GUYS COME OVER, AND HANG OUT?
SINCE WE DON'T HAVE HOMEWORK OR ANYTHING.
YEAH. OKAY. SURE.
HOW ABOUT YOU, AMELIA?
ME?
ummm...
NO, THANKS!
I CAN'T.
WHY NOT?
OH, WELL, MOM HAS THIS THING, AND, Y'KNOW... I DON'T EVEN WANNA... Y'KNOW? BUT... WELL... YOU KNOW MOM'S RIGHT?
OKAY. SEE YA.
BYE.
SHE IS SUCH A BAD LIAR!
TEE HEE
WHAT?

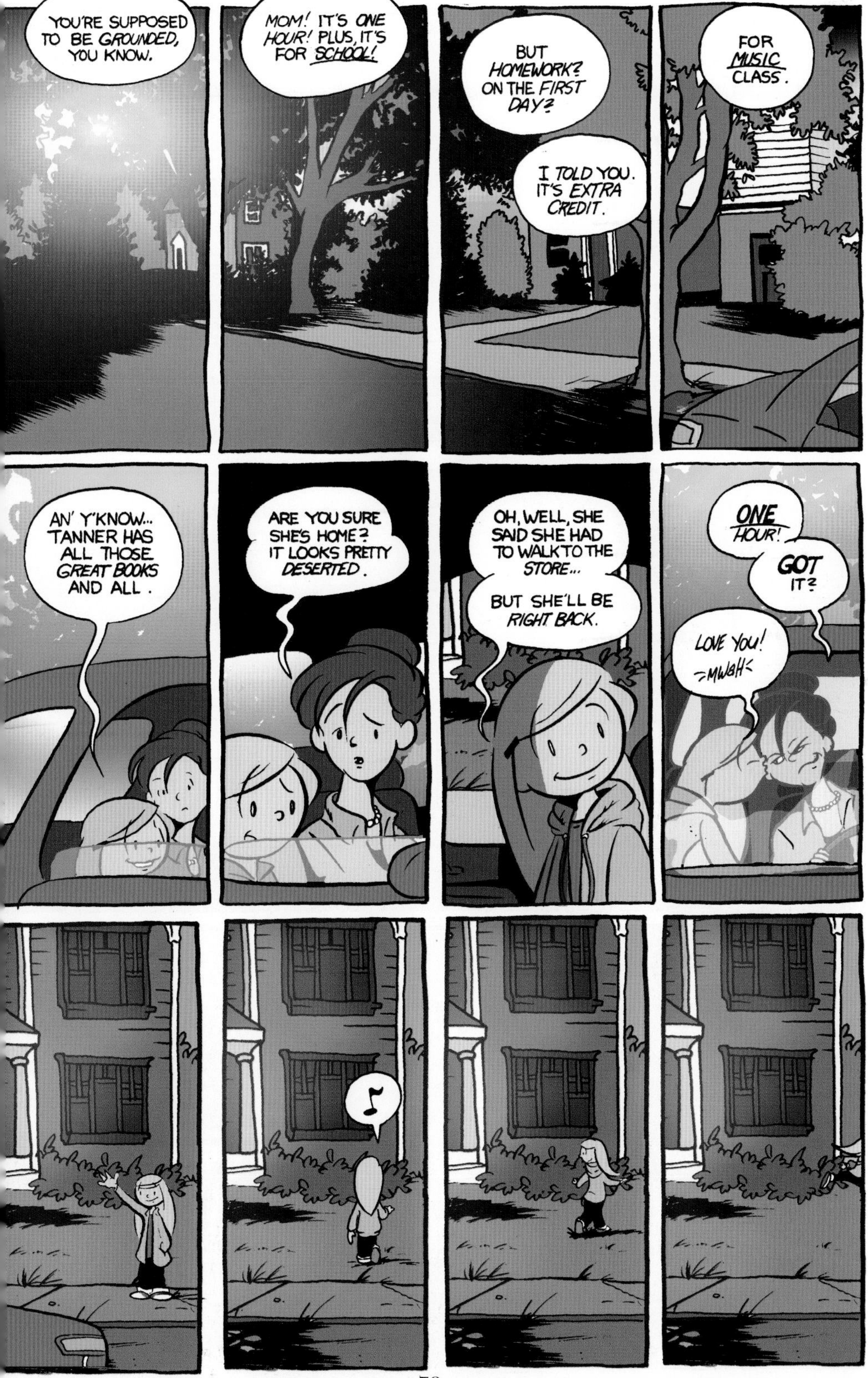
YOU'RE SUPPOSED TO BE GROUNDED, YOU KNOW.
MOM! IT'S ONE HOUR! PLUS, IT'S FOR SCHOOL!
BUT HOMEWORK? ON THE FIRST DAY?
I TOLD YOU. IT'S EXTRA CREDIT.
FOR MUSIC CLASS.
AN' Y'KNOW... TANNER HAS ALL THOSE GREAT BOOKS AND ALL.
ARE YOU SURE SHE'S HOME? IT LOOKS PRETTY DESERTED.
OH, WELL, SHE SAID SHE HAD TO WALK TO THE STORE...
BUT SHE'LL BE RIGHT BACK.
ONE HOUR!
GOT IT?
LOVE YOU!
MWAH

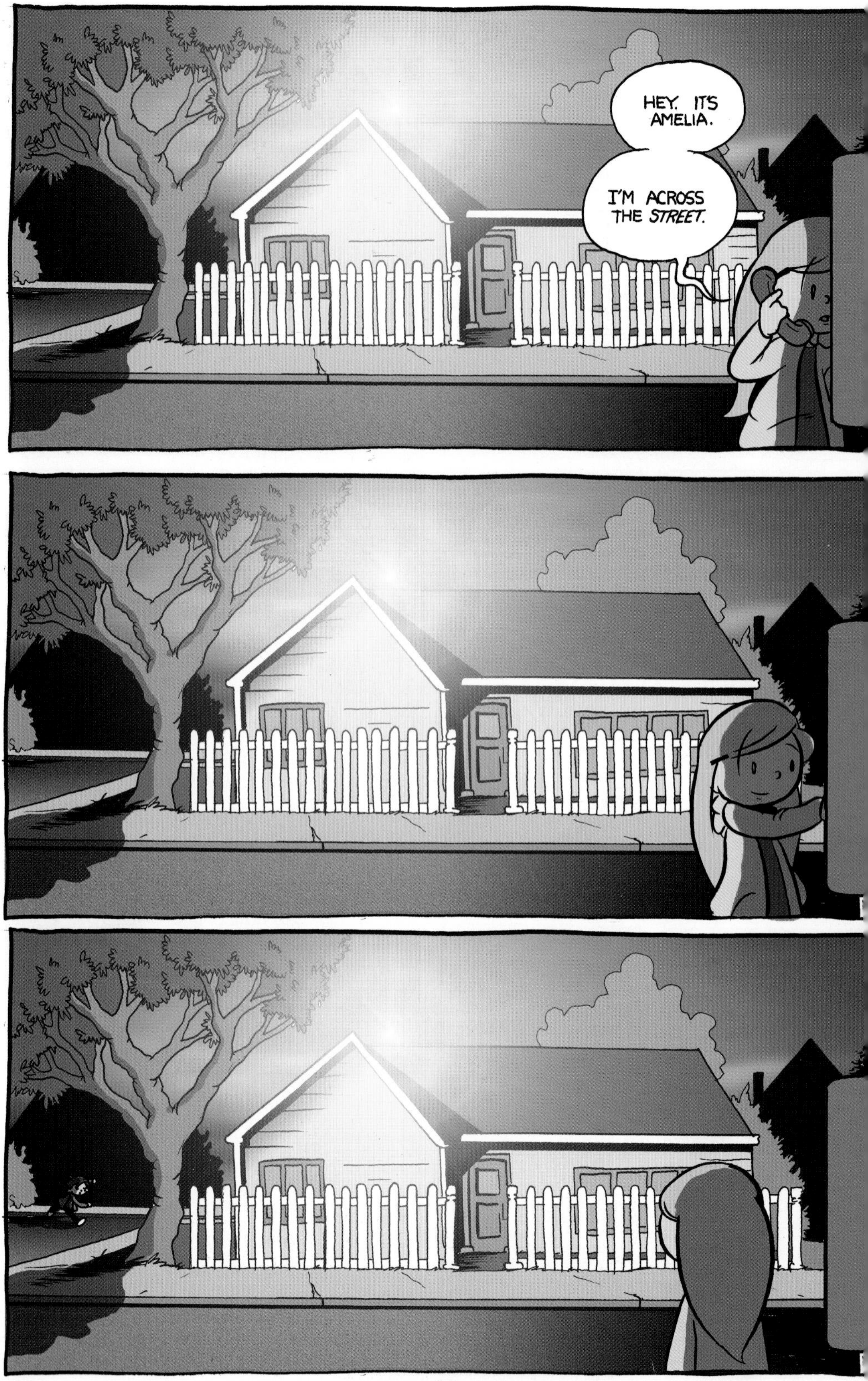
HEY. IT'S AMELIA.
I'M ACROSS THE *STREET*.

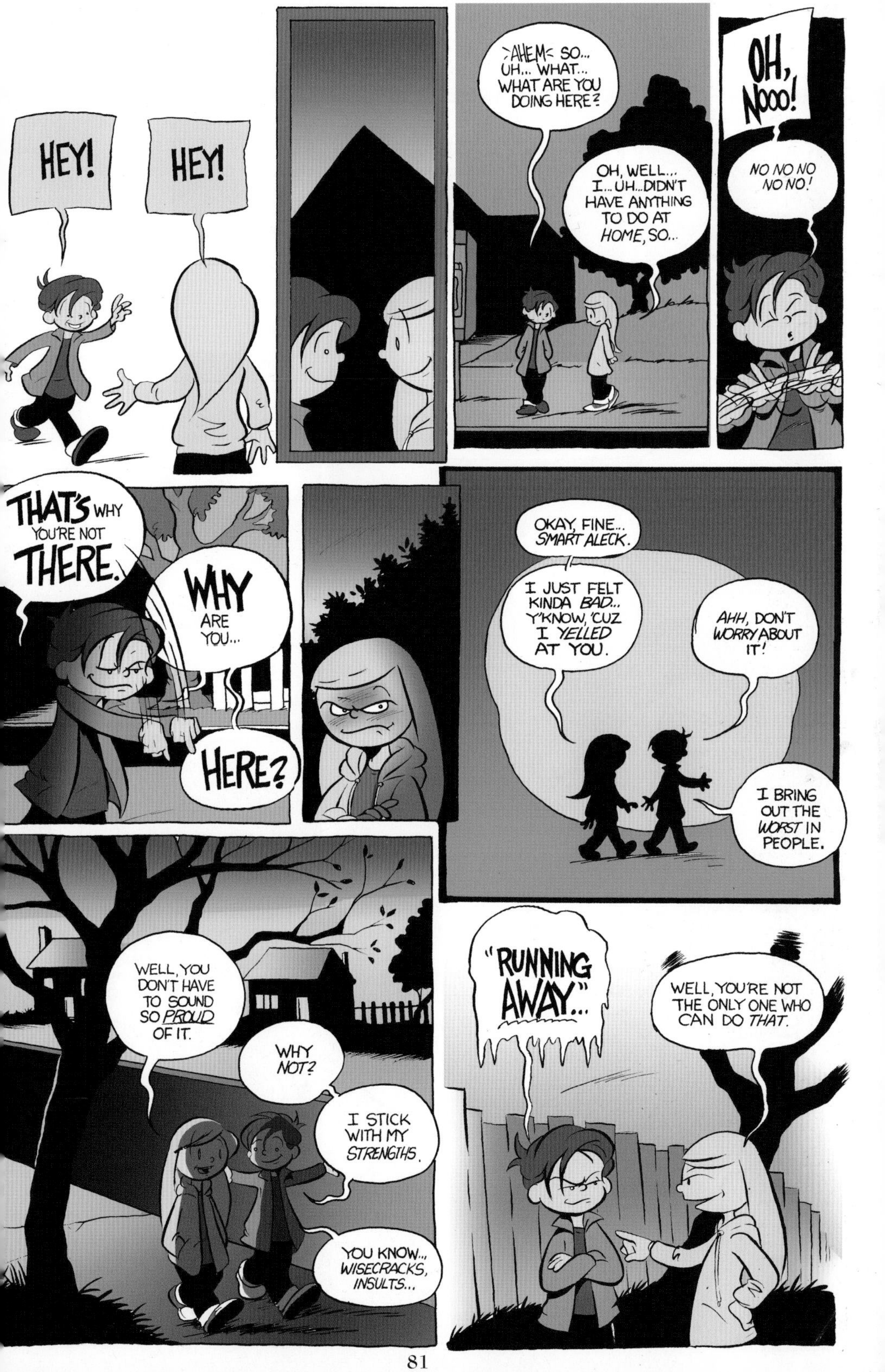
HEY!
HEY!
>AHEM< SO... UH... WHAT... WHAT ARE YOU DOING HERE?
OH, WELL... I... UH... DIDN'T HAVE ANYTHING TO DO AT HOME, SO...
OH, Nooo!
NO NO NO NO NO!
THAT'S WHY YOU'RE NOT THERE.
WHY ARE YOU...
HERE?
OKAY, FINE... SMART ALECK.
I JUST FELT KINDA BAD... Y'KNOW, 'CUZ I YELLED AT YOU.
AHH, DON'T WORRY ABOUT IT!
I BRING OUT THE WORST IN PEOPLE.
WELL, YOU DON'T HAVE TO SOUND SO PROUD OF IT.
WHY NOT?
I STICK WITH MY STRENGTHS.
YOU KNOW... WISECRACKS, INSULTS...
"RUNNING AWAY"...
WELL, YOU'RE NOT THE ONLY ONE WHO CAN DO THAT.

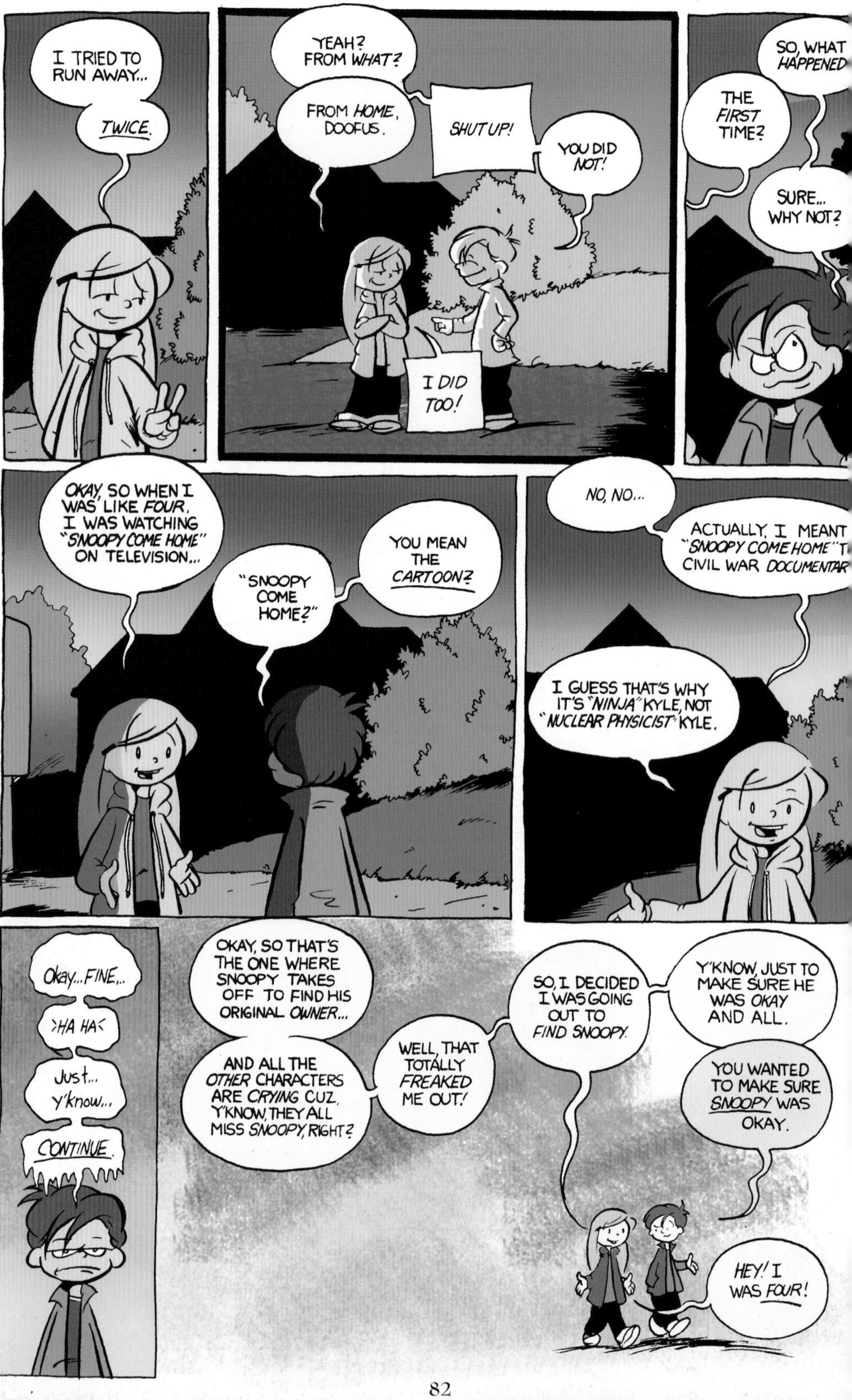
I TRIED TO RUN AWAY...
TWICE.
YEAH? FROM WHAT?
FROM HOME, DOOFUS.
SHUT UP!
YOU DID NOT!
I DID TOO!
THE FIRST TIME?
SO, WHAT HAPPENED
SURE... WHY NOT?
OKAY, SO WHEN I WAS LIKE FOUR, I WAS WATCHING "SNOOPY COME HOME" ON TELEVISION...
"SNOOPY COME HOME?"
YOU MEAN THE CARTOON?
NO, NO...
ACTUALLY, I MEANT "SNOOPY COME HOME" T CIVIL WAR DOCUMENTAR
I GUESS THAT'S WHY IT'S "NINJA" KYLE, NOT "NUCLEAR PHYSICIST" KYLE.
Okay...FINE...
>HA HA<
Just... y'know...
CONTINUE.
OKAY, SO THAT'S THE ONE WHERE SNOOPY TAKES OFF TO FIND HIS ORIGINAL OWNER...
AND ALL THE OTHER CHARACTERS ARE CRYING CUZ, Y'KNOW, THEY ALL MISS SNOOPY, RIGHT?
WELL, THAT TOTALLY FREAKED ME OUT!
SO, I DECIDED I WAS GOING OUT TO FIND SNOOPY.
Y'KNOW, JUST TO MAKE SURE HE WAS OKAY AND ALL.
YOU WANTED TO MAKE SURE SNOOPY WAS OKAY.
HEY! I WAS FOUR!

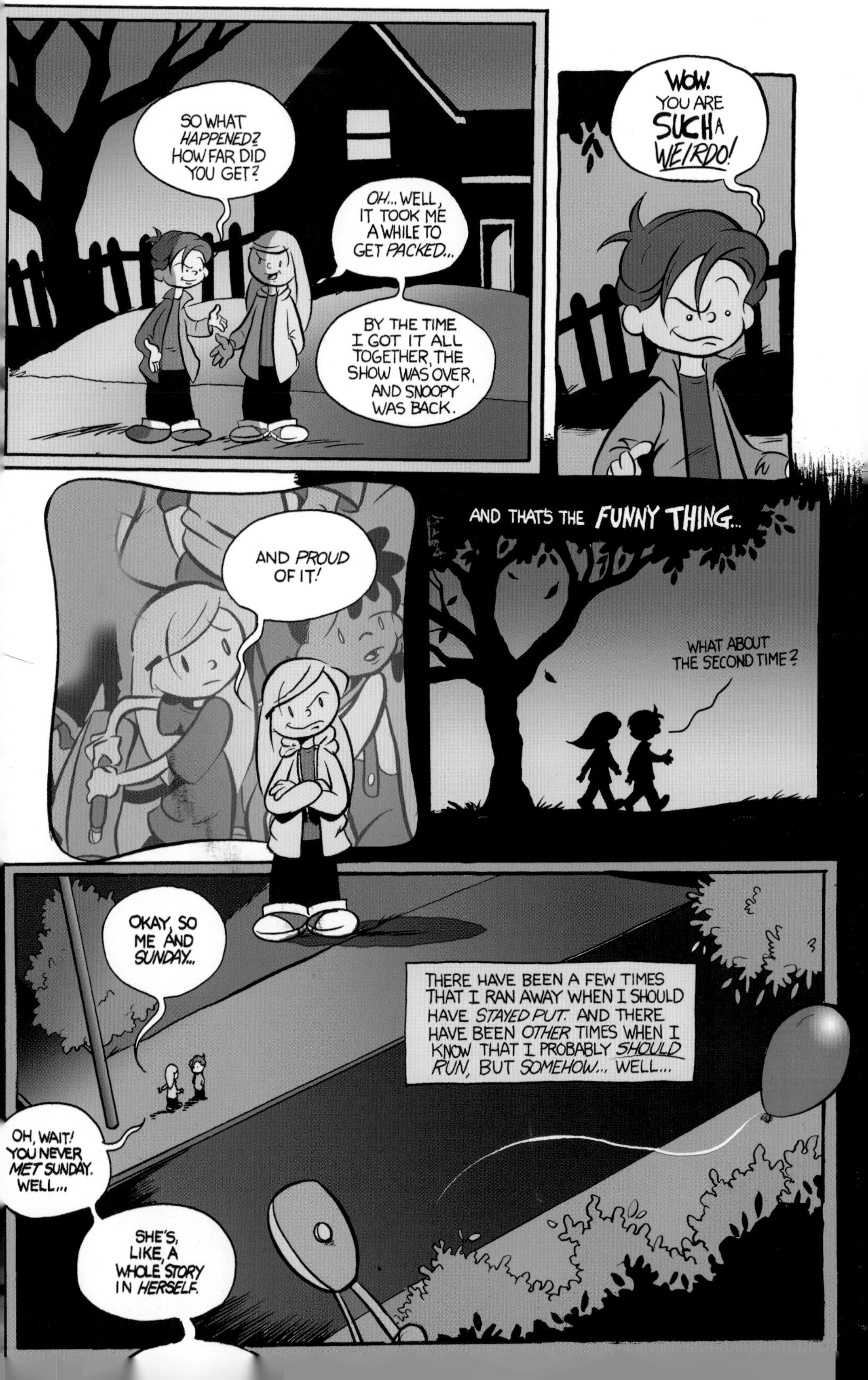
SO WHAT HAPPENED? HOW FAR DID YOU GET?
OH... WELL, IT TOOK ME A WHILE TO GET PACKED...
BY THE TIME I GOT IT ALL TOGETHER, THE SHOW WAS OVER, AND SNOOPY WAS BACK.
WOW. YOU ARE SUCH A WEIRDO!
AND PROUD OF IT!
AND THAT'S THE FUNNY THING...
WHAT ABOUT THE SECOND TIME?
OKAY, SO ME AND SUNDAY...
OH, WAIT! YOU NEVER MET SUNDAY. WELL...
SHE'S, LIKE, A WHOLE STORY IN HERSELF.
THERE HAVE BEEN A FEW TIMES THAT I RAN AWAY WHEN I SHOULD HAVE STAYED PUT. AND THERE HAVE BEEN OTHER TIMES WHEN I KNOW THAT I PROBABLY SHOULD RUN, BUT SOMEHOW... WELL...

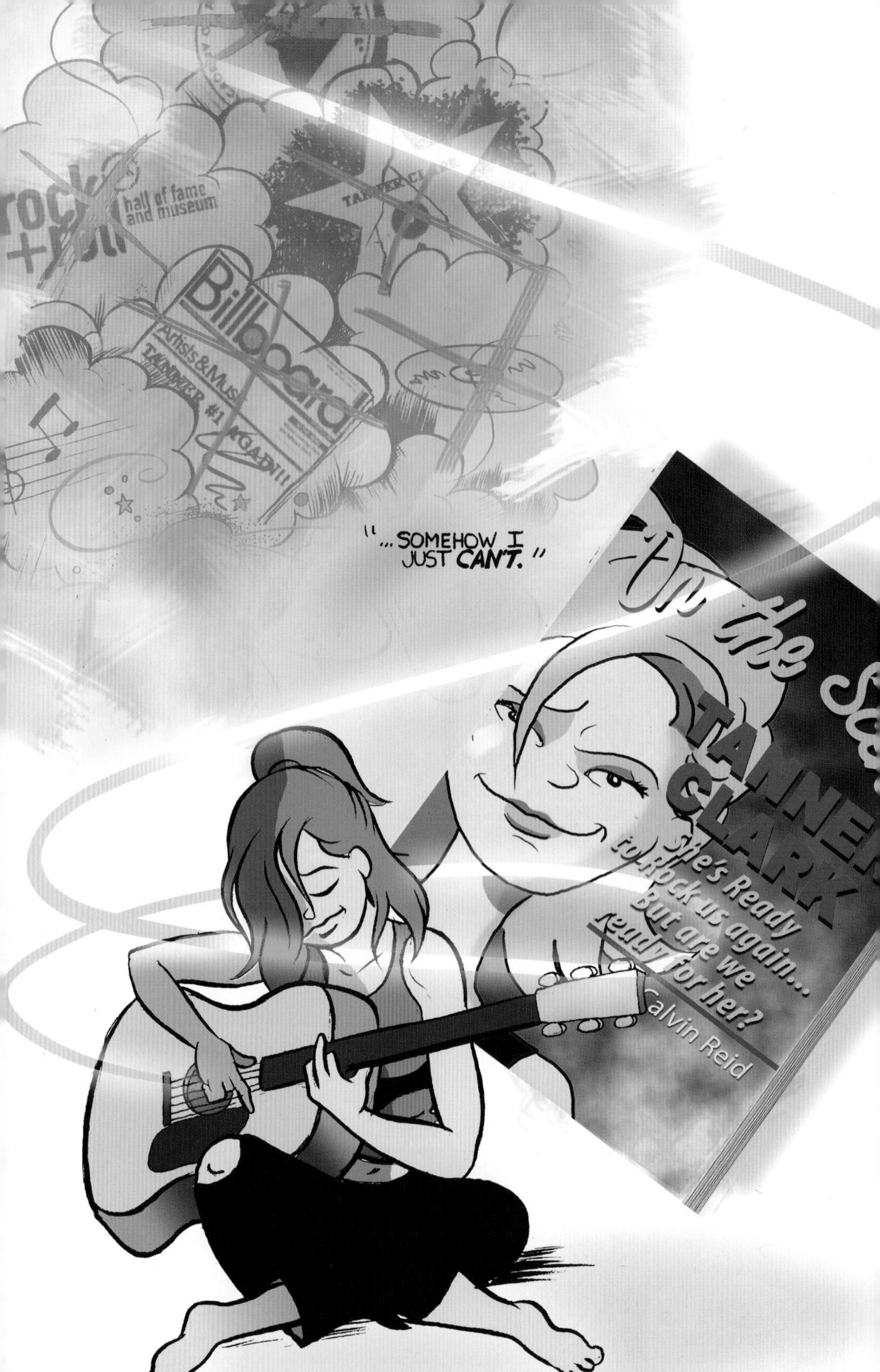
hall of fame
and museum
Billboard
"...SOMEHOW I JUST CAN'T."
CLARK
She's Ready
to Rock us again...
But are we
ready for her?
Calvin Reid

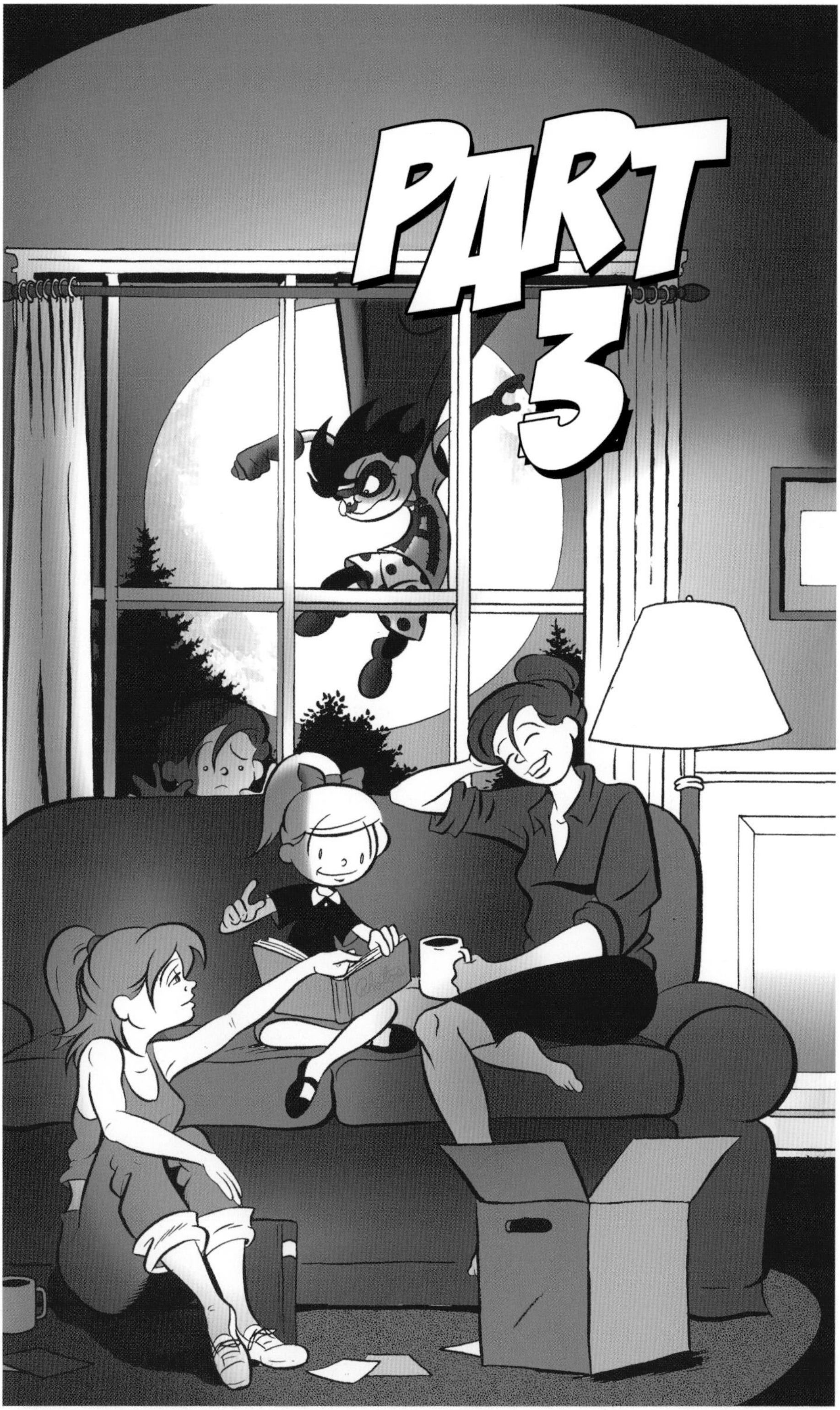
PART 3

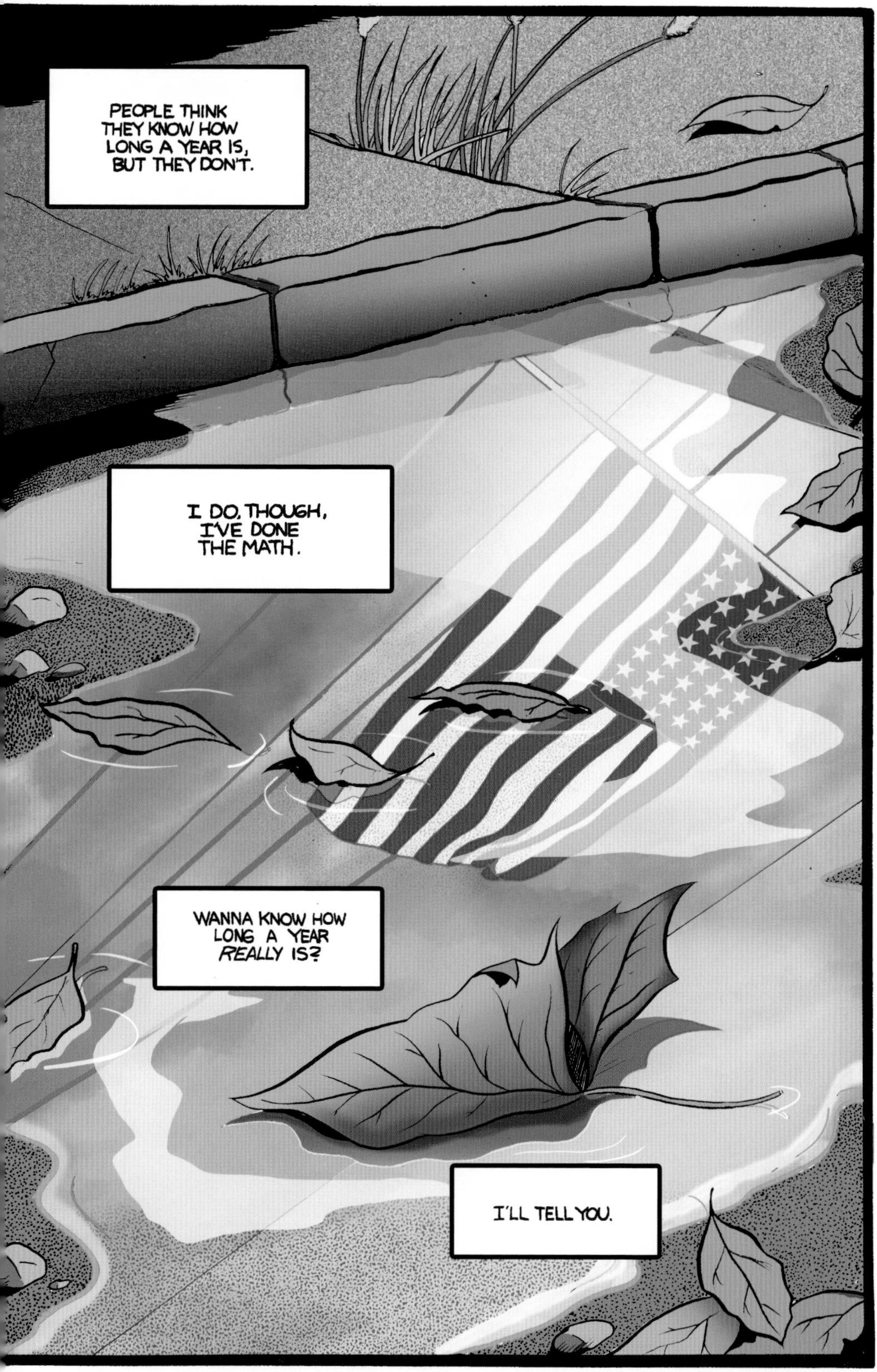
PEOPLE THINK THEY KNOW HOW LONG A YEAR IS, BUT THEY DON'T.
I DO, THOUGH. I'VE DONE THE MATH.
WANNA KNOW HOW LONG A YEAR *REALLY* IS?
I'LL TELL YOU.

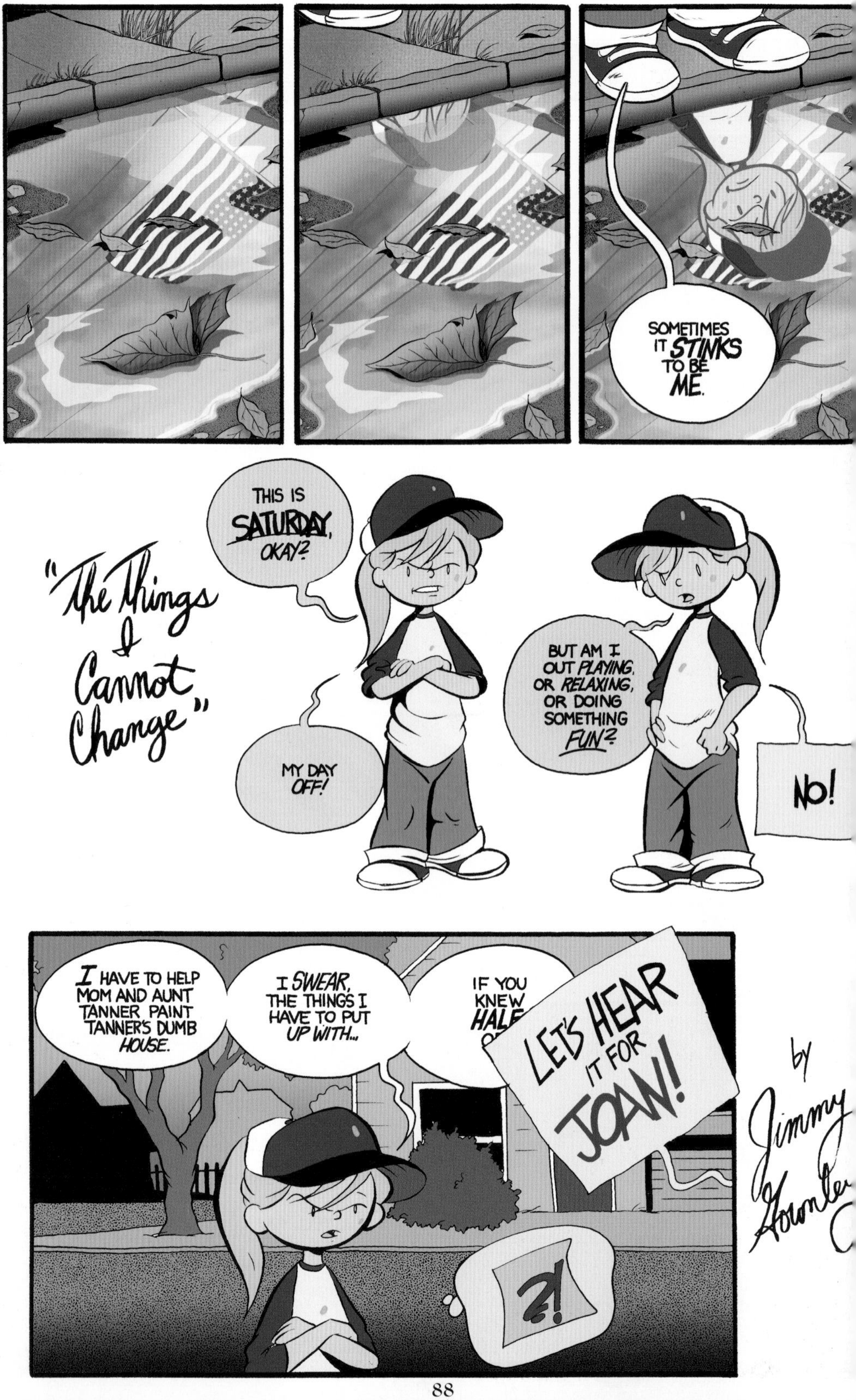
SOMETIMES IT STINKS TO BE ME.
"The Things I Cannot Change"
THIS IS SATURDAY, OKAY?
MY DAY OFF!
BUT AM I OUT PLAYING, OR RELAXING, OR DOING SOMETHING FUN?
NO!
I HAVE TO HELP MOM AND AUNT TANNER PAINT TANNER'S DUMB HOUSE.
I SWEAR, THE THINGS I HAVE TO PUT UP WITH...
IF YOU KNEW
LET'S HEAR IT FOR JOAN!
?!
by
Jimmy

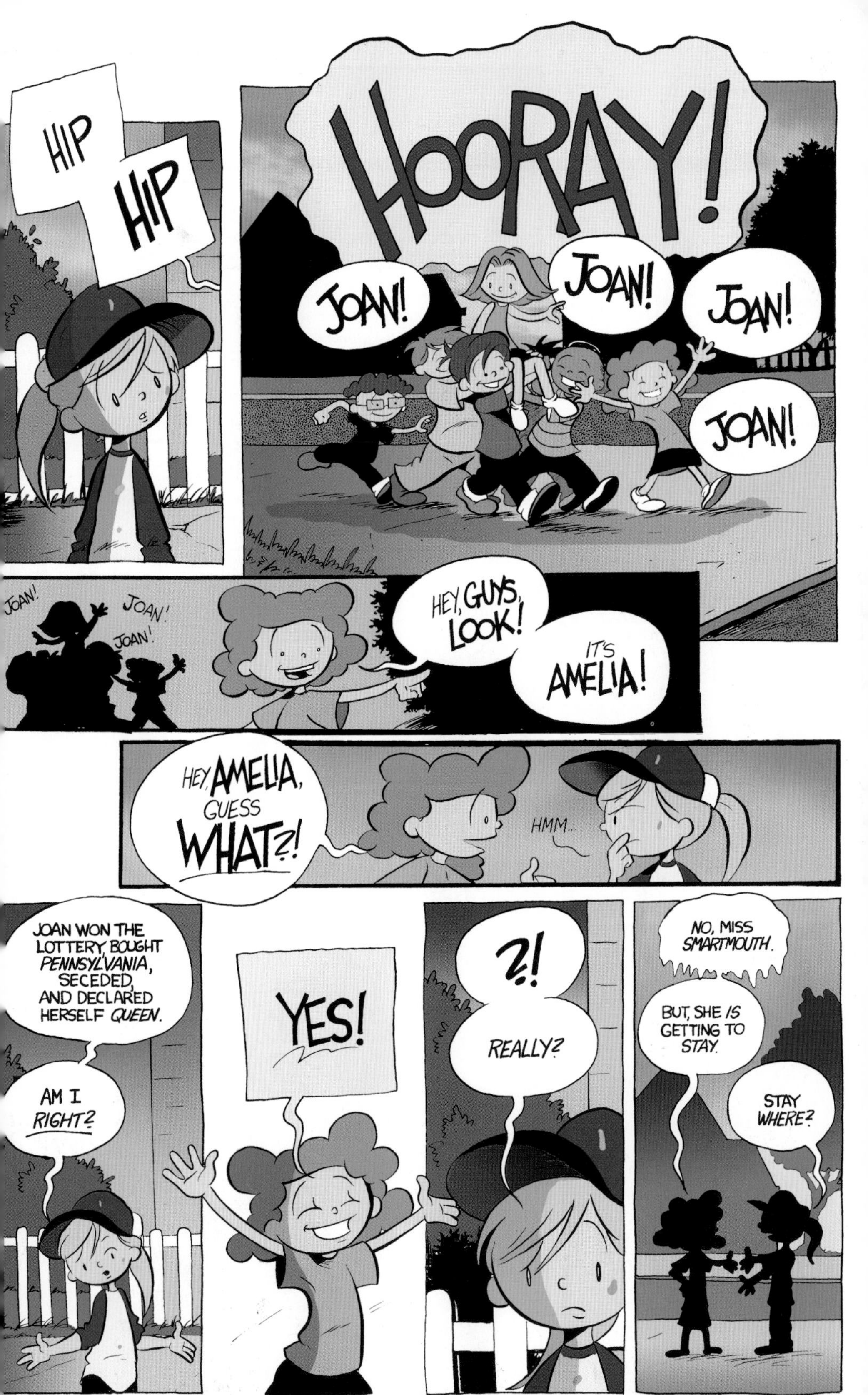
HIP
HIP
HOORAY!
JOAN!
JOAN!
JOAN!
JOAN!
JOAN!
JOAN!
JOAN!
HEY, GUYS, LOOK!
IT'S AMELIA!
HEY, AMELIA, GUESS WHAT?!
HMM...
JOAN WON THE LOTTERY, BOUGHT PENNSYLVANIA, SECEDED, AND DECLARED HERSELF QUEEN.
AM I RIGHT?
YES!
?!
REALLY?
NO, MISS SMARTMOUTH.
BUT, SHE IS GETTING TO STAY.
STAY WHERE?

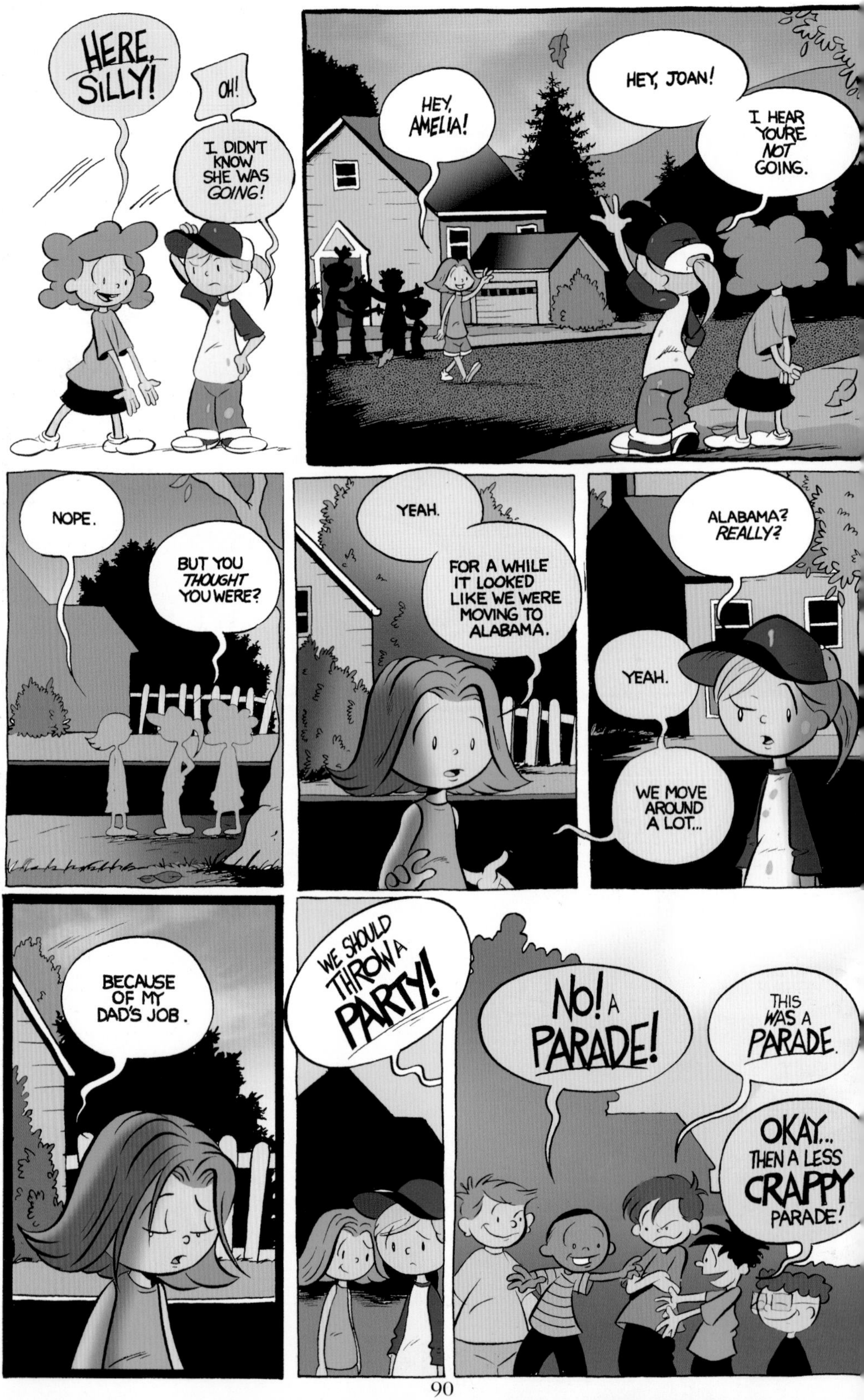
HERE, SILLY!
OH!
I DIDN'T KNOW SHE WAS GOING!
HEY, AMELIA!
HEY, JOAN!
I HEAR YOU'RE NOT GOING.
NOPE.
BUT YOU THOUGHT YOU WERE?
YEAH.
FOR A WHILE IT LOOKED LIKE WE WERE MOVING TO ALABAMA.
ALABAMA? REALLY?
YEAH.
WE MOVE AROUND A LOT...
BECAUSE OF MY DAD'S JOB.
WE SHOULD THROW A PARTY!
NO! A PARADE!
THIS WAS A PARADE.
OKAY... THEN A LESS CRAPPY PARADE!

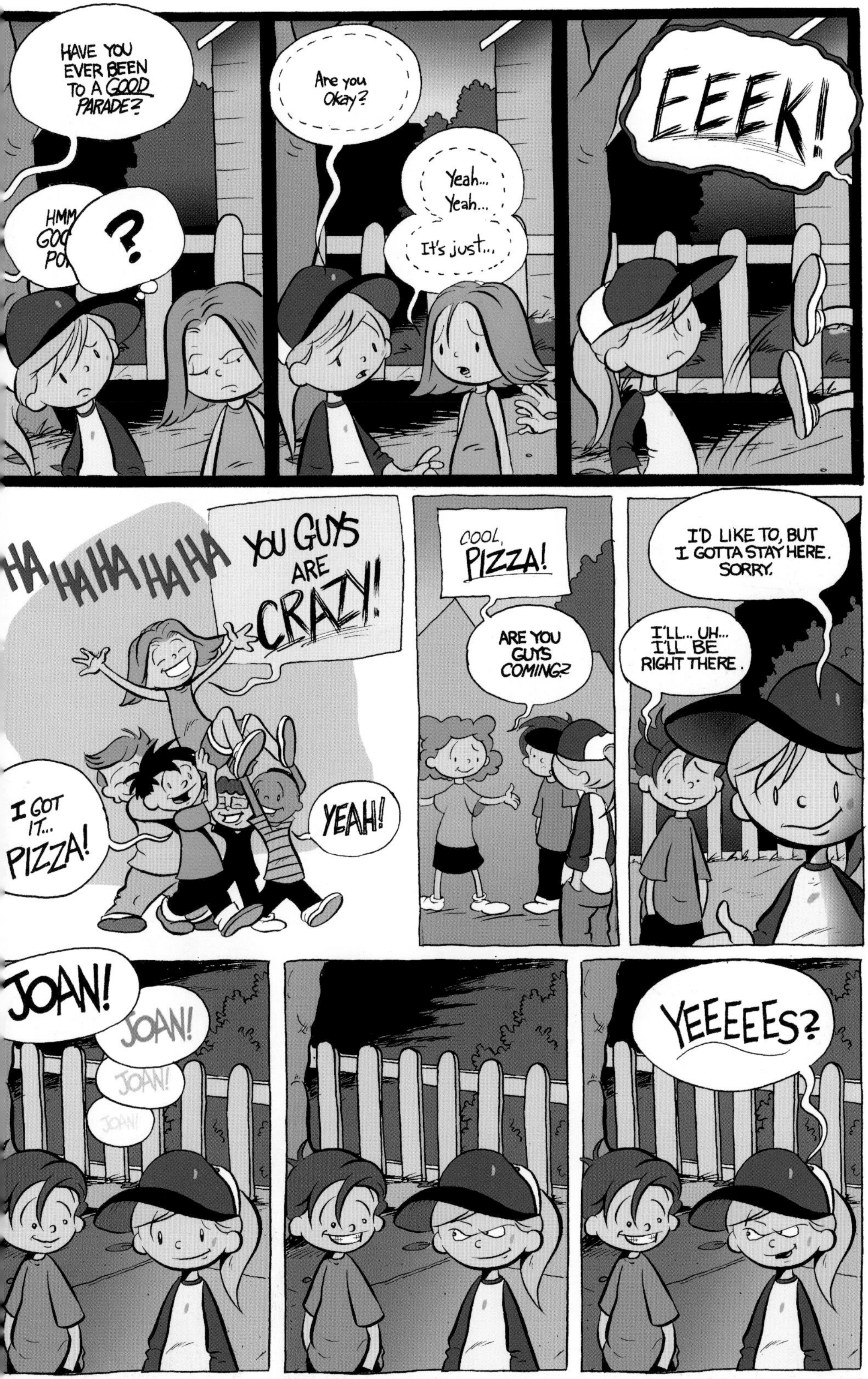
HAVE YOU EVER BEEN TO A GOOD PARADE?
?
Are you Okay?
Yeah... Yeah...
It's just...
EEEK!
HA HA HA HA HA HA
YOU GUYS ARE CRAZY!
I GOT IT... PIZZA!
YEAH!
COOL, PIZZA!
ARE YOU GUYS COMING?
I'D LIKE TO, BUT I GOTTA STAY HERE. SORRY.
I'LL... UH... I'LL BE RIGHT THERE.
JOAN!
JOAN!
JOAN!
JOAN!
YEEEEES?

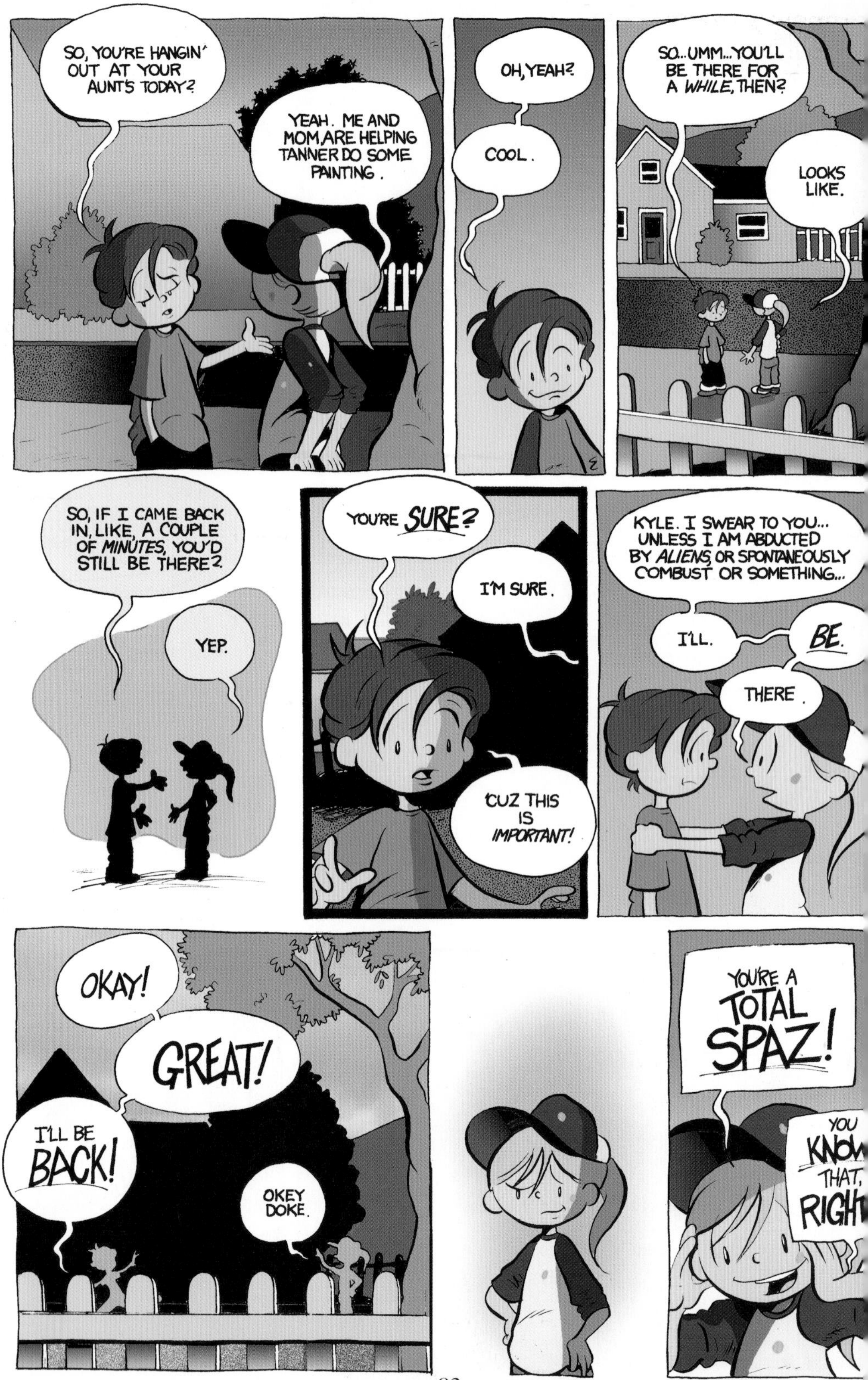
SO, YOU'RE HANGIN' OUT AT YOUR AUNT'S TODAY?
YEAH. ME AND MOM ARE HELPING TANNER DO SOME PAINTING.
OH, YEAH?
COOL.
SO...UMM...YOU'LL BE THERE FOR A WHILE, THEN?
LOOKS LIKE.
SO, IF I CAME BACK IN, LIKE, A COUPLE OF MINUTES, YOU'D STILL BE THERE?
YEP.
YOU'RE SURE?
I'M SURE.
'CUZ THIS IS IMPORTANT!
KYLE. I SWEAR TO YOU... UNLESS I AM ABDUCTED BY ALIENS, OR SPONTANEOUSLY COMBUST OR SOMETHING...
I'LL.
BE.
THERE.
OKAY!
GREAT!
I'LL BE BACK!
OKEY DOKE.
YOU'RE A TOTAL SPAZ!
YOU KNOW THAT, RIGHT

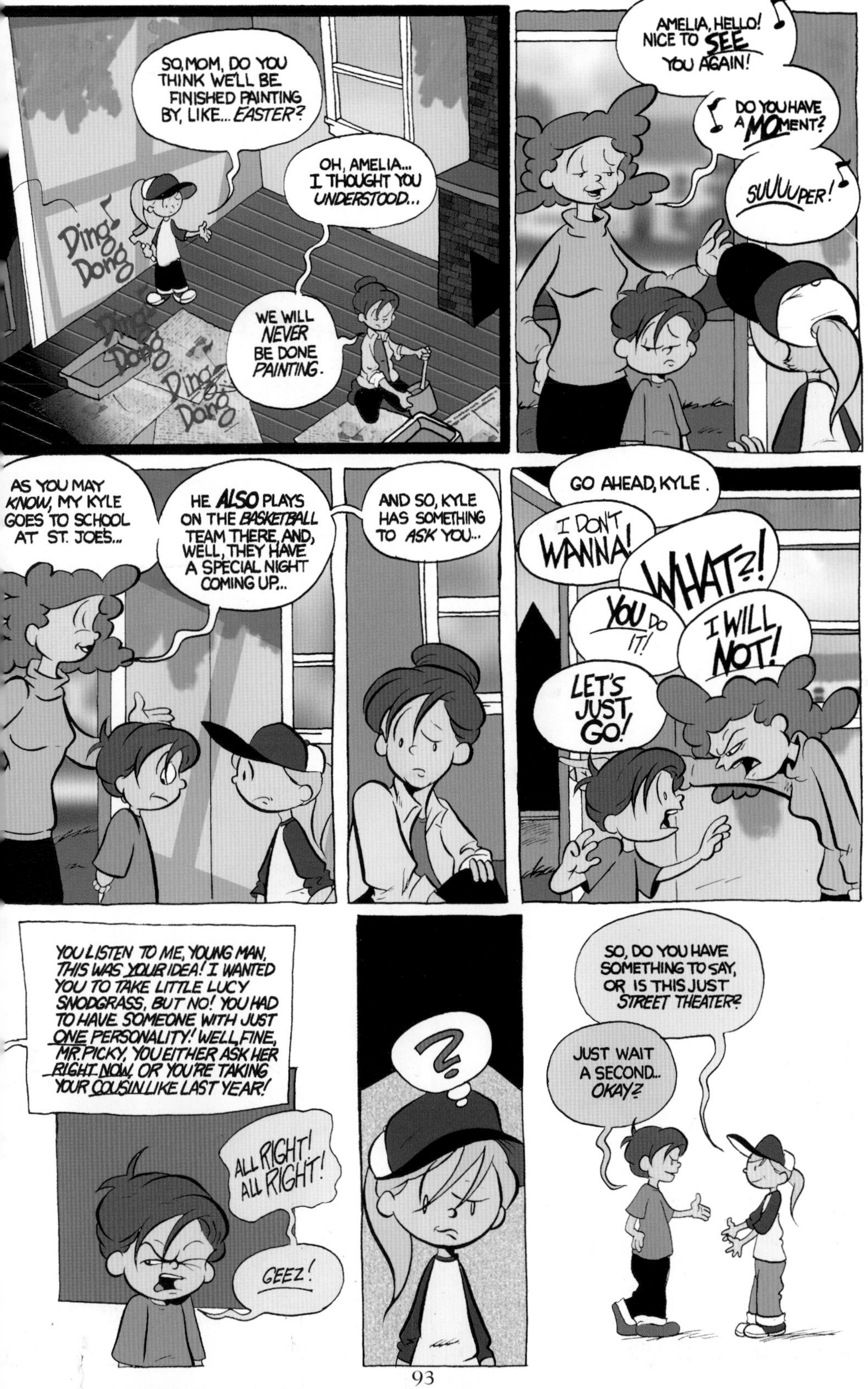

SO, MOM, DO YOU THINK WE'LL BE FINISHED PAINTING BY, LIKE... EASTER?
OH, AMELIA... I THOUGHT YOU UNDERSTOOD...
WE WILL NEVER BE DONE PAINTING.
Ding Dong
Ding Dong
Ding Dong
AMELIA, HELLO! NICE TO SEE YOU AGAIN!
DO YOU HAVE A MOMENT?
SUUUUPER!
AS YOU MAY KNOW, MY KYLE GOES TO SCHOOL AT ST. JOE'S...
HE ALSO PLAYS ON THE BASKETBALL TEAM THERE, AND, WELL, THEY HAVE A SPECIAL NIGHT COMING UP...
AND SO, KYLE HAS SOMETHING TO ASK YOU...
GO AHEAD, KYLE.
I DON'T WANNA!
WHAT?!
YOU DO IT!
I WILL NOT!
LET'S JUST GO!
YOU LISTEN TO ME, YOUNG MAN, THIS WAS YOUR IDEA! I WANTED YOU TO TAKE LITTLE LUCY SNODGRASS, BUT NO! YOU HAD TO HAVE SOMEONE WITH JUST ONE PERSONALITY! WELL, FINE, MR. PICKY, YOU EITHER ASK HER RIGHT NOW, OR YOU'RE TAKING YOUR COUSIN LIKE LAST YEAR!
ALL RIGHT! ALL RIGHT!
GEEZ!
?
SO, DO YOU HAVE SOMETHING TO SAY, OR IS THIS JUST STREET THEATER?
JUST WAIT A SECOND... OKAY?

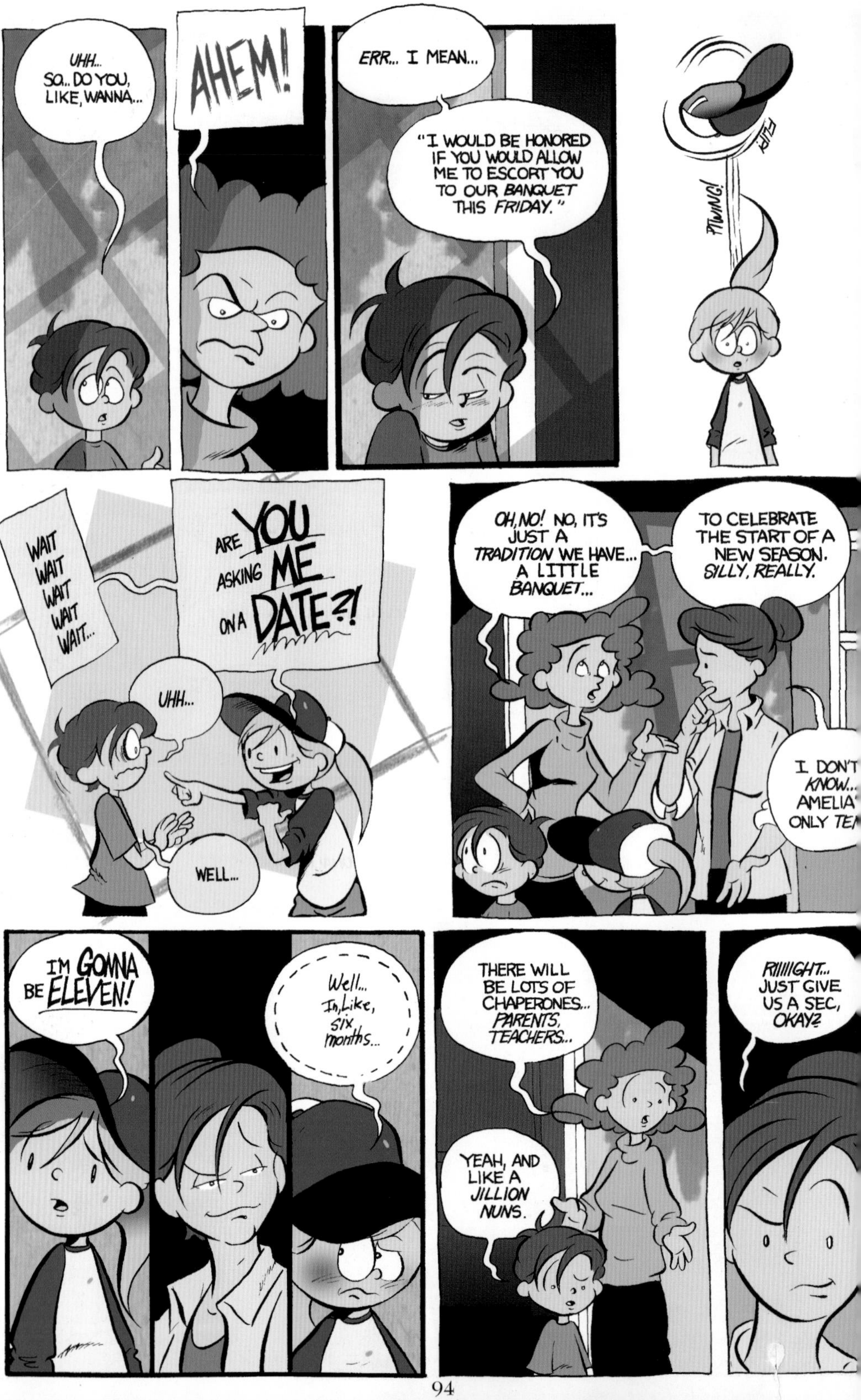
UHH... SO... DO YOU, LIKE, WANNA...
AHEM!
ERR... I MEAN...
"I WOULD BE HONORED IF YOU WOULD ALLOW ME TO ESCORT YOU TO OUR BANQUET THIS FRIDAY."
FLIP
PTWING!
WAIT WAIT WAIT WAIT WAIT...
ARE YOU ASKING ME ON A DATE?!
UHH...
WELL...
OH, NO! NO, IT'S JUST A TRADITION WE HAVE... A LITTLE BANQUET...
TO CELEBRATE THE START OF A NEW SEASON. SILLY, REALLY.
I DON'T KNOW... AMELIA ONLY TE
I'M GONNA BE ELEVEN!
Well... In, Like, six months...
THERE WILL BE LOTS OF CHAPERONES... PARENTS, TEACHERS...
YEAH, AND LIKE A JILLION NUNS.
RIIIIGHT... JUST GIVE US A SEC, OKAY?

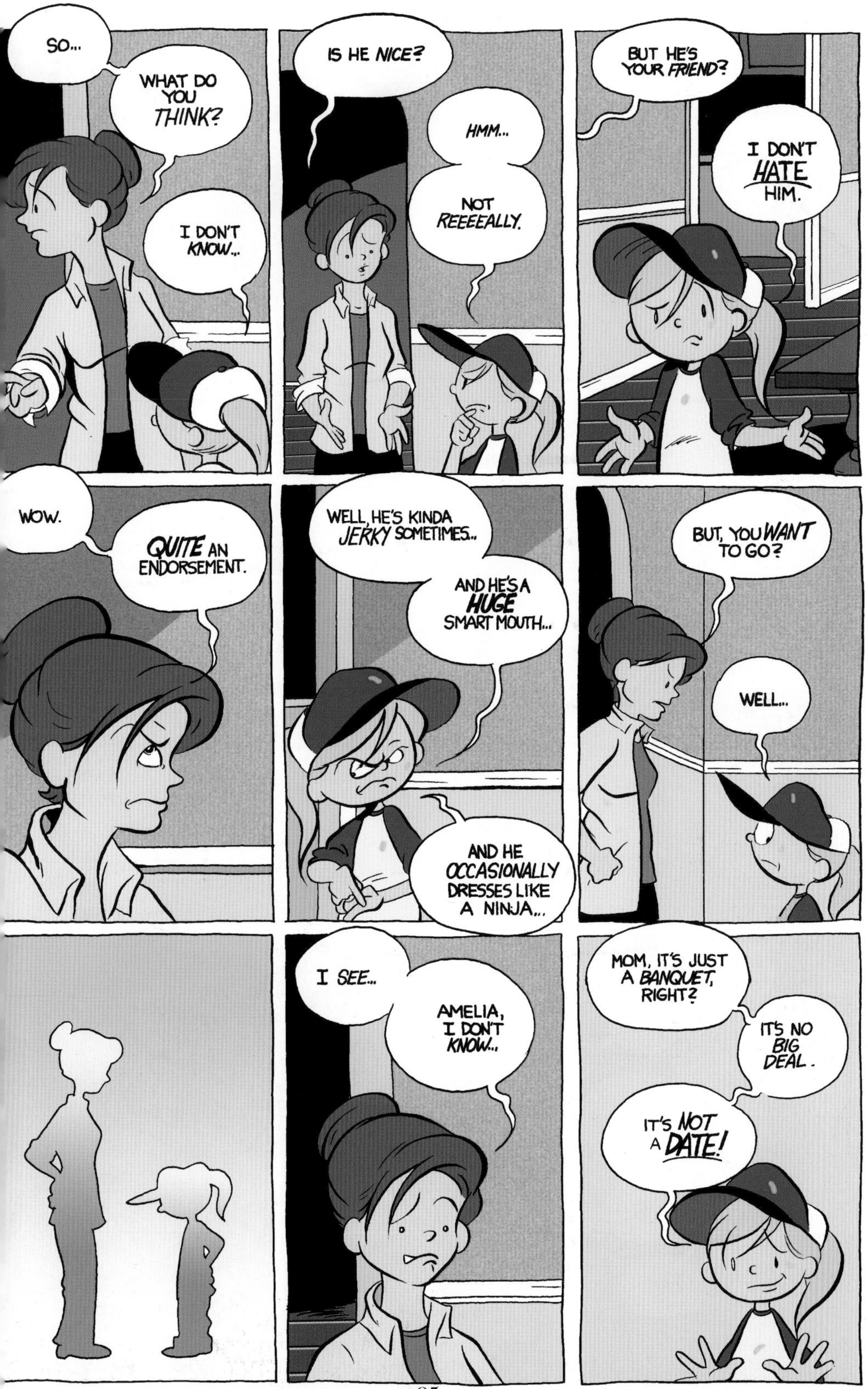
SO...
WHAT DO YOU THINK?
I DON'T KNOW...
IS HE NICE?
HMM...
NOT REEEEALLY.
BUT HE'S YOUR FRIEND?
I DON'T HATE HIM.
WOW.
QUITE AN ENDORSEMENT.
WELL, HE'S KINDA JERKY SOMETIMES...
AND HE'S A HUGE SMART MOUTH...
AND HE OCCASIONALLY DRESSES LIKE A NINJA...
BUT, YOU WANT TO GO?
WELL...
I SEE...
AMELIA, I DON'T KNOW...
MOM, IT'S JUST A BANQUET, RIGHT?
IT'S NO BIG DEAL.
IT'S NOT A DATE!

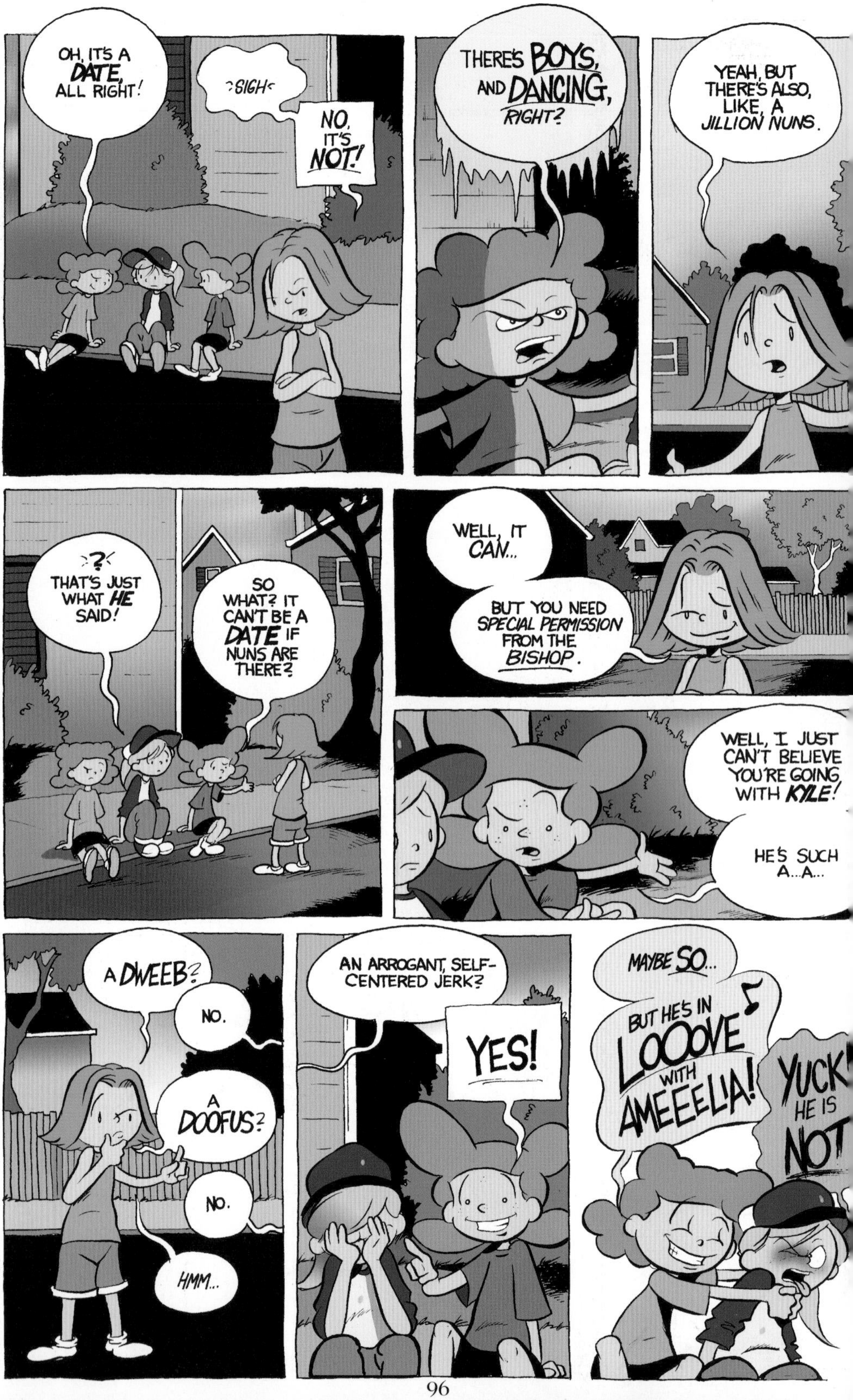
OH, IT'S A DATE, ALL RIGHT!
SIGH
NO, IT'S NOT!
THERE'S BOYS, AND DANCING, RIGHT?
YEAH, BUT THERE'S ALSO, LIKE, A JILLION NUNS.
?
THAT'S JUST WHAT HE SAID!
SO WHAT? IT CAN'T BE A DATE IF NUNS ARE THERE?
WELL, IT CAN...
BUT YOU NEED SPECIAL PERMISSION FROM THE BISHOP.
WELL, I JUST CAN'T BELIEVE YOU'RE GOING WITH KYLE!
HE'S SUCH A...A...
A DWEEB?
NO.
A DOOFUS?
NO.
HMM...
AN ARROGANT, SELF-CENTERED JERK?
YES!
MAYBE SO...
BUT HE'S IN LOOOVE WITH AMEEELIA!
YUCK! HE IS NOT

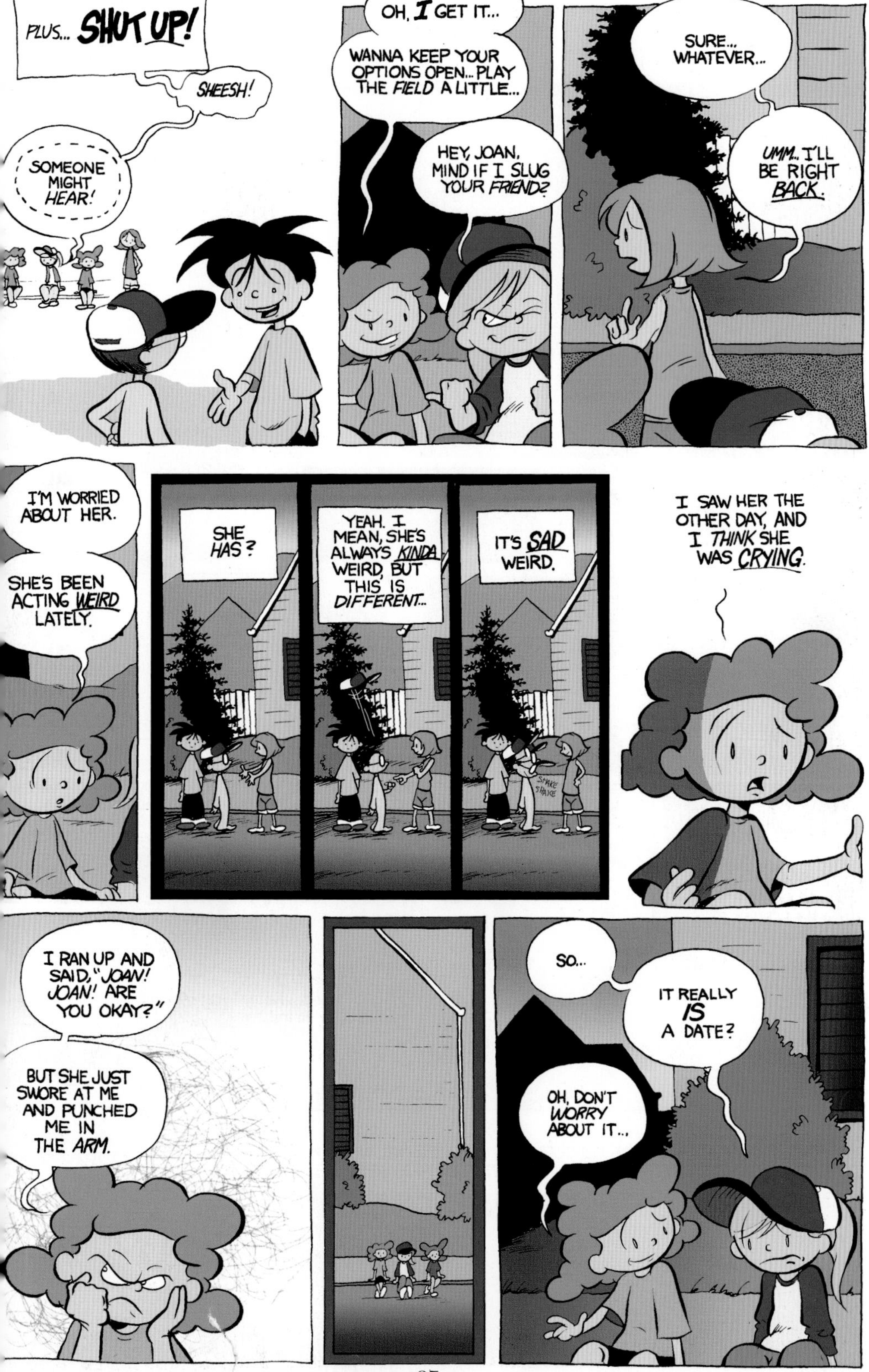
PLUS... SHUT UP!
SHEESH!
SOMEONE MIGHT HEAR!
OH, I GET IT...
WANNA KEEP YOUR OPTIONS OPEN... PLAY THE FIELD A LITTLE...
HEY, JOAN, MIND IF I SLUG YOUR FRIEND?
SURE... WHATEVER...
UMM.. I'LL BE RIGHT BACK.
I'M WORRIED ABOUT HER.
SHE'S BEEN ACTING WEIRD LATELY.
SHE HAS?
YEAH. I MEAN, SHE'S ALWAYS KINDA WEIRD, BUT THIS IS DIFFERENT...
IT'S SAD WEIRD.
SHAKE SHAKE
I SAW HER THE OTHER DAY, AND I THINK SHE WAS CRYING.
I RAN UP AND SAID, "JOAN! JOAN! ARE YOU OKAY?"
BUT SHE JUST SWORE AT ME AND PUNCHED ME IN THE ARM.
SO...
IT REALLY IS A DATE?
OH, DON'T WORRY ABOUT IT...

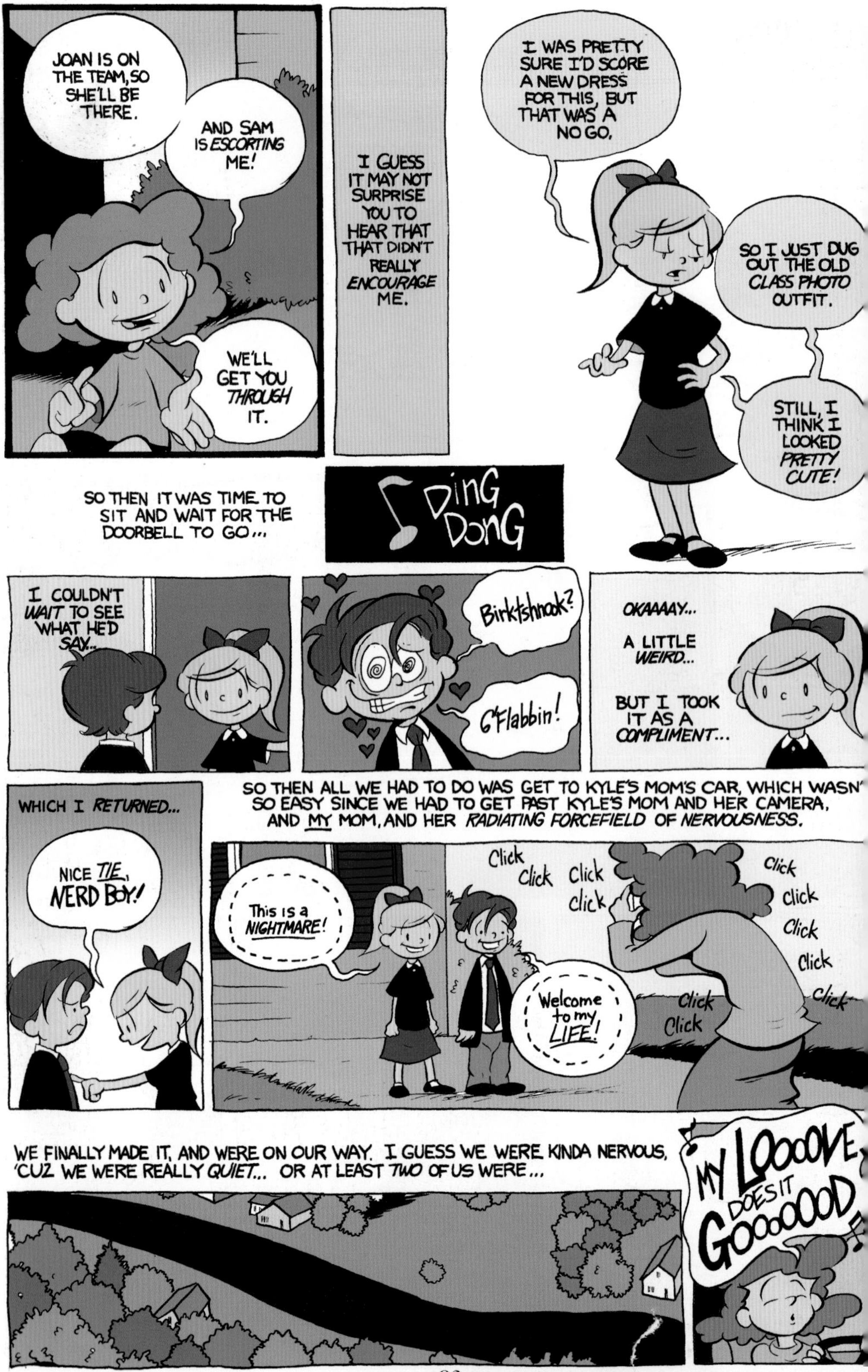
JOAN IS ON THE TEAM, SO SHE'LL BE THERE.
AND SAM IS ESCORTING ME!
WE'LL GET YOU THROUGH IT.
I GUESS IT MAY NOT SURPRISE YOU TO HEAR THAT THAT DIDN'T REALLY ENCOURAGE ME.
I WAS PRETTY SURE I'D SCORE A NEW DRESS FOR THIS, BUT THAT WAS A NO GO.
SO I JUST DUG OUT THE OLD CLASS PHOTO OUTFIT.
STILL, I THINK I LOOKED PRETTY CUTE!
SO THEN IT WAS TIME TO SIT AND WAIT FOR THE DOORBELL TO GO...
DING DONG
I COULDN'T WAIT TO SEE WHAT HE'D SAY...
Birktshnook?
G'Flabbin!
OKAAAAY...
A LITTLE WEIRD...
BUT I TOOK IT AS A COMPLIMENT...
WHICH I RETURNED...
NICE TIE, NERD BOY!
SO THEN ALL WE HAD TO DO WAS GET TO KYLE'S MOM'S CAR, WHICH WASN' SO EASY SINCE WE HAD TO GET PAST KYLE'S MOM AND HER CAMERA, AND MY MOM, AND HER RADIATING FORCEFIELD OF NERVOUSNESS.
This is a NIGHTMARE!
Welcome to my LIFE!
Click Click Click Click Click Click Click Click Click Click Click
WE FINALLY MADE IT, AND WERE ON OUR WAY. I GUESS WE WERE KINDA NERVOUS, 'CUZ WE WERE REALLY QUIET... OR AT LEAST TWO OF US WERE...
MY LOOOOVE DOES IT GOOOOOOD

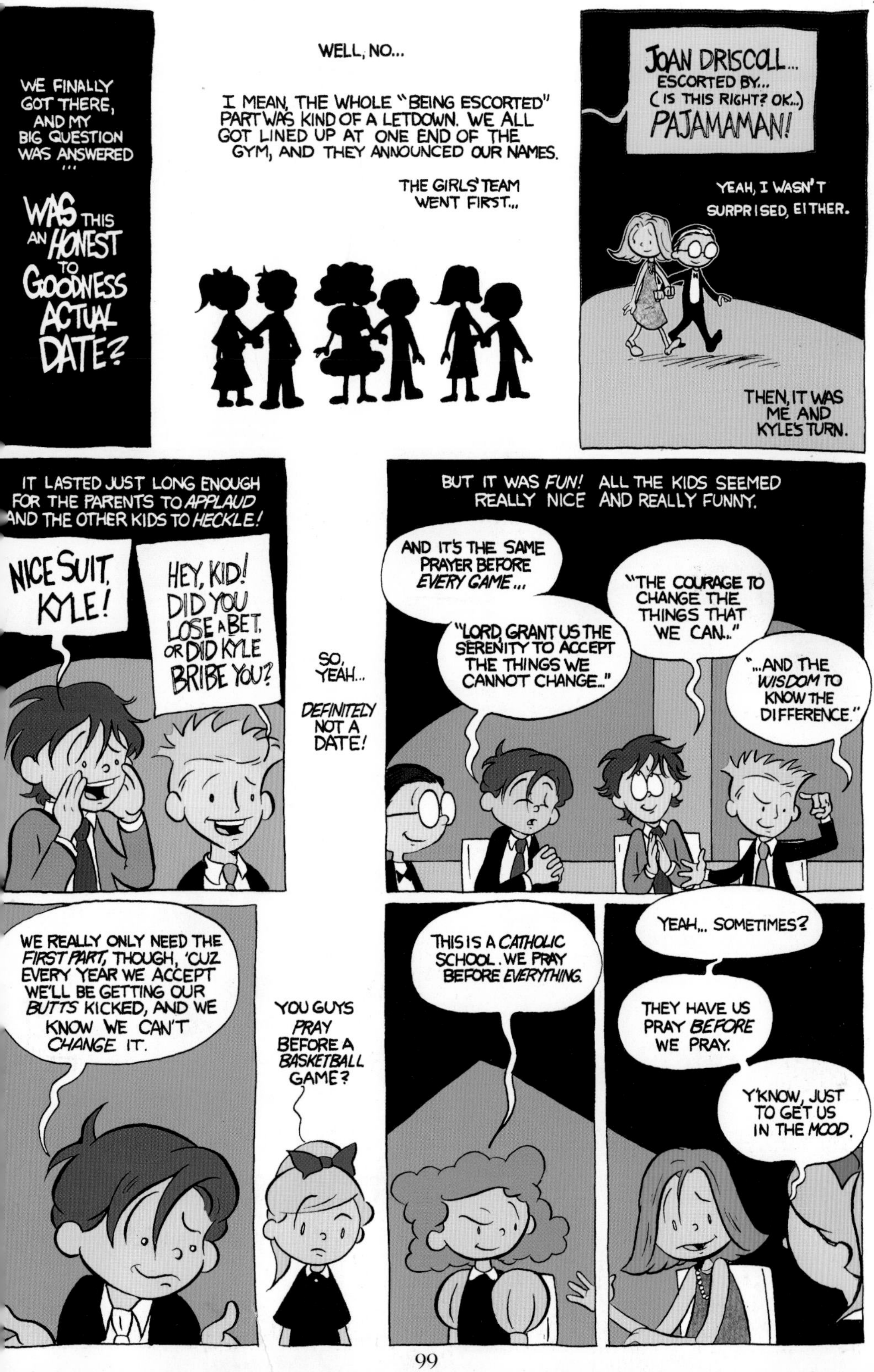

WE FINALLY GOT THERE, AND MY BIG QUESTION WAS ANSWERED ...
WAS THIS AN HONEST TO GOODNESS ACTUAL DATE?
WELL, NO...
I MEAN, THE WHOLE "BEING ESCORTED" PART WAS KIND OF A LETDOWN. WE ALL GOT LINED UP AT ONE END OF THE GYM, AND THEY ANNOUNCED OUR NAMES.
THE GIRLS' TEAM WENT FIRST...
JOAN DRISCOLL... ESCORTED BY... (IS THIS RIGHT? OK...) PAJAMAMAN!
YEAH, I WASN'T SURPRISED, EITHER.
THEN, IT WAS ME AND KYLE'S TURN.
IT LASTED JUST LONG ENOUGH FOR THE PARENTS TO APPLAUD AND THE OTHER KIDS TO HECKLE!
NICE SUIT, KYLE!
HEY, KID! DID YOU LOSE A BET, OR DID KYLE BRIBE YOU?
SO, YEAH...
DEFINITELY NOT A DATE!
BUT IT WAS FUN! ALL THE KIDS SEEMED REALLY NICE AND REALLY FUNNY.
AND IT'S THE SAME PRAYER BEFORE EVERY GAME...
"LORD, GRANT US THE SERENITY TO ACCEPT THE THINGS WE CANNOT CHANGE..."
"THE COURAGE TO CHANGE THE THINGS THAT WE CAN..."
"...AND THE WISDOM TO KNOW THE DIFFERENCE."
WE REALLY ONLY NEED THE FIRST PART, THOUGH, 'CUZ EVERY YEAR WE ACCEPT WE'LL BE GETTING OUR BUTTS KICKED, AND WE KNOW WE CAN'T CHANGE IT.
YOU GUYS PRAY BEFORE A BASKETBALL GAME?
THIS IS A CATHOLIC SCHOOL. WE PRAY BEFORE EVERYTHING.
YEAH... SOMETIMES?
THEY HAVE US PRAY BEFORE WE PRAY.
Y'KNOW, JUST TO GET US IN THE MOOD.

SO, YEAH... IT WAS *DEFINITELY FUN!*

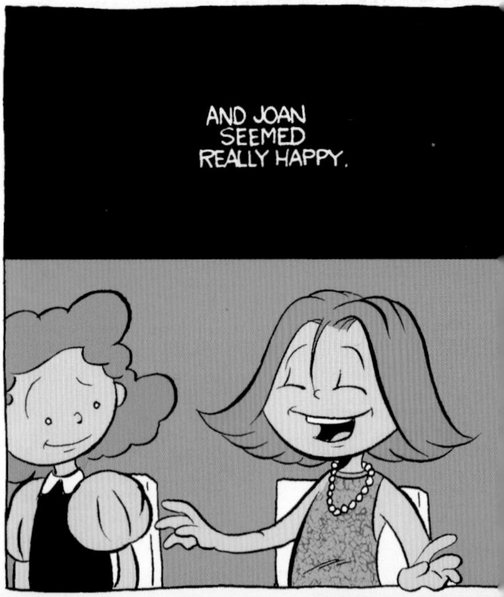
AND JOAN SEEMED REALLY HAPPY.

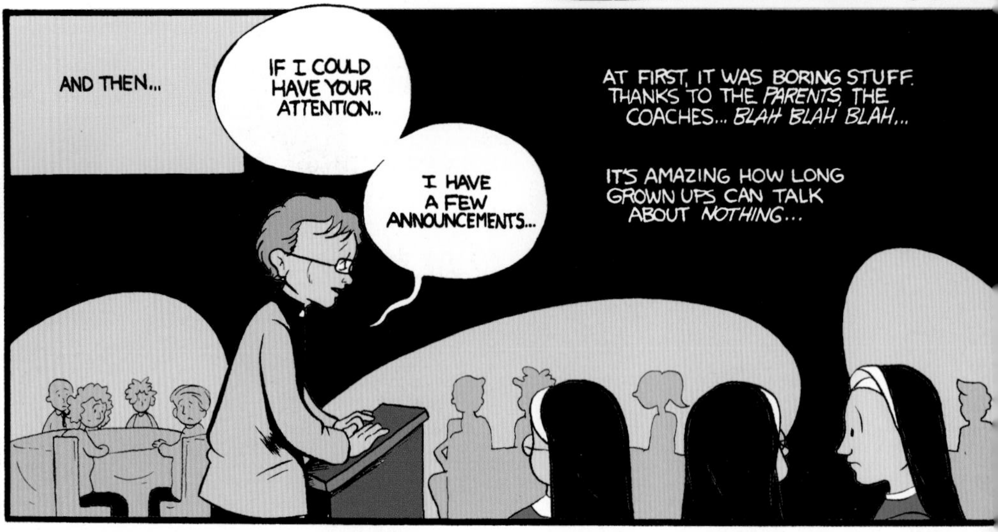
AND THEN...
IF I COULD HAVE YOUR ATTENTION...
I HAVE A FEW ANNOUNCEMENTS...
AT FIRST, IT WAS BORING STUFF. THANKS TO THE *PARENTS,* THE COACHES... *BLAH BLAH BLAH...*
IT'S AMAZING HOW LONG GROWN UPS CAN TALK ABOUT *NOTHING...*

BUT THEN HE ASKED SOMEONE NAMED CAPTAIN DRISCOLL TO STAND.

IT WAS JOAN'S DAD.

HE WAS WEARING AN ARMY UNIFORM... A REAL FANCY ONE.

HE LOOKED IMPRESSIVE.

LIKE AN ACTION FIGURE.

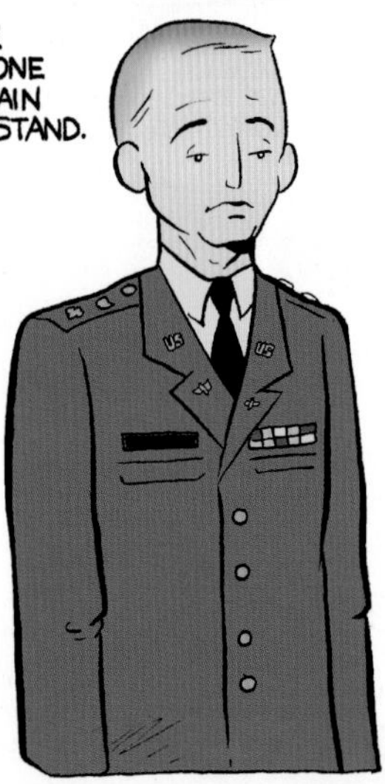

NO, THAT'S STUPID, NOT AN ACTION FIGURE... LIKE...

I DON'T KNOW... JUST IMPRESSIVE.

ANYWAY, THE PRIEST STARTED TALKING ABOUT ALL MISTER... ERR... CAPTAIN DRISCOLL HAD DONE FOR THE SCHOOL...

AND HOW HARD IT WAS GOING TO BE...

HOW *HARD...*

TO HAVE TO SAY GOODBYE.

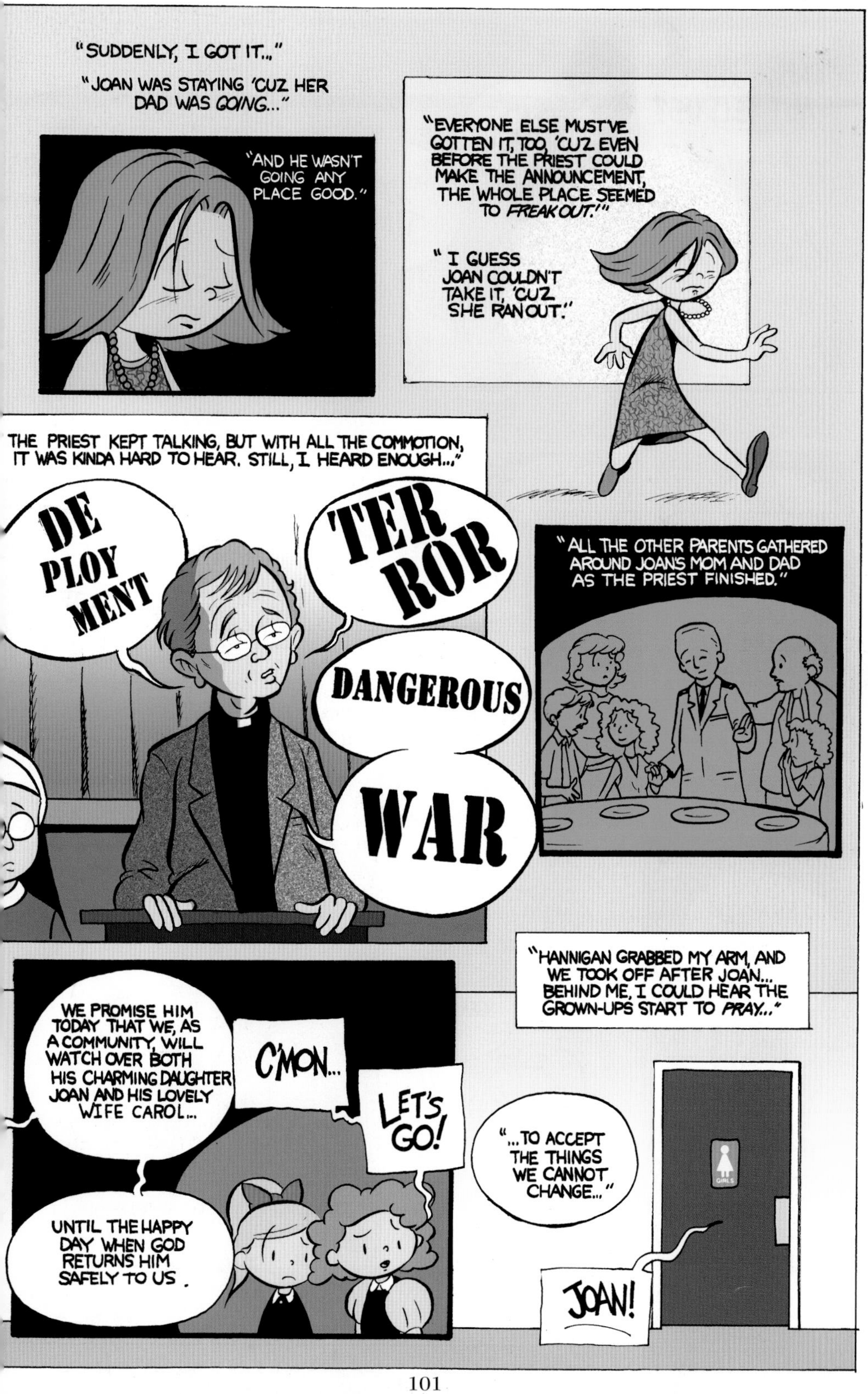
"SUDDENLY, I GOT IT..."
"JOAN WAS STAYING 'CUZ HER DAD WAS GOING..."
"AND HE WASN'T GOING ANY PLACE GOOD."
"EVERYONE ELSE MUST'VE GOTTEN IT, TOO, 'CUZ EVEN BEFORE THE PRIEST COULD MAKE THE ANNOUNCEMENT, THE WHOLE PLACE SEEMED TO FREAK OUT!"
"I GUESS JOAN COULDN'T TAKE IT, 'CUZ SHE RAN OUT."
THE PRIEST KEPT TALKING, BUT WITH ALL THE COMMOTION, IT WAS KINDA HARD TO HEAR. STILL, I HEARD ENOUGH..."
DE PLOY MENT
TER ROR
DANGEROUS
WAR
"ALL THE OTHER PARENTS GATHERED AROUND JOAN'S MOM AND DAD AS THE PRIEST FINISHED."
"HANNIGAN GRABBED MY ARM, AND WE TOOK OFF AFTER JOAN... BEHIND ME, I COULD HEAR THE GROWN-UPS START TO PRAY..."
WE PROMISE HIM TODAY THAT WE, AS A COMMUNITY, WILL WATCH OVER BOTH HIS CHARMING DAUGHTER JOAN AND HIS LOVELY WIFE CAROL...
C'MON...
LET'S GO!
UNTIL THE HAPPY DAY WHEN GOD RETURNS HIM SAFELY TO US.
"...TO ACCEPT THE THINGS WE CANNOT CHANGE..."
GIRLS
JOAN!

102

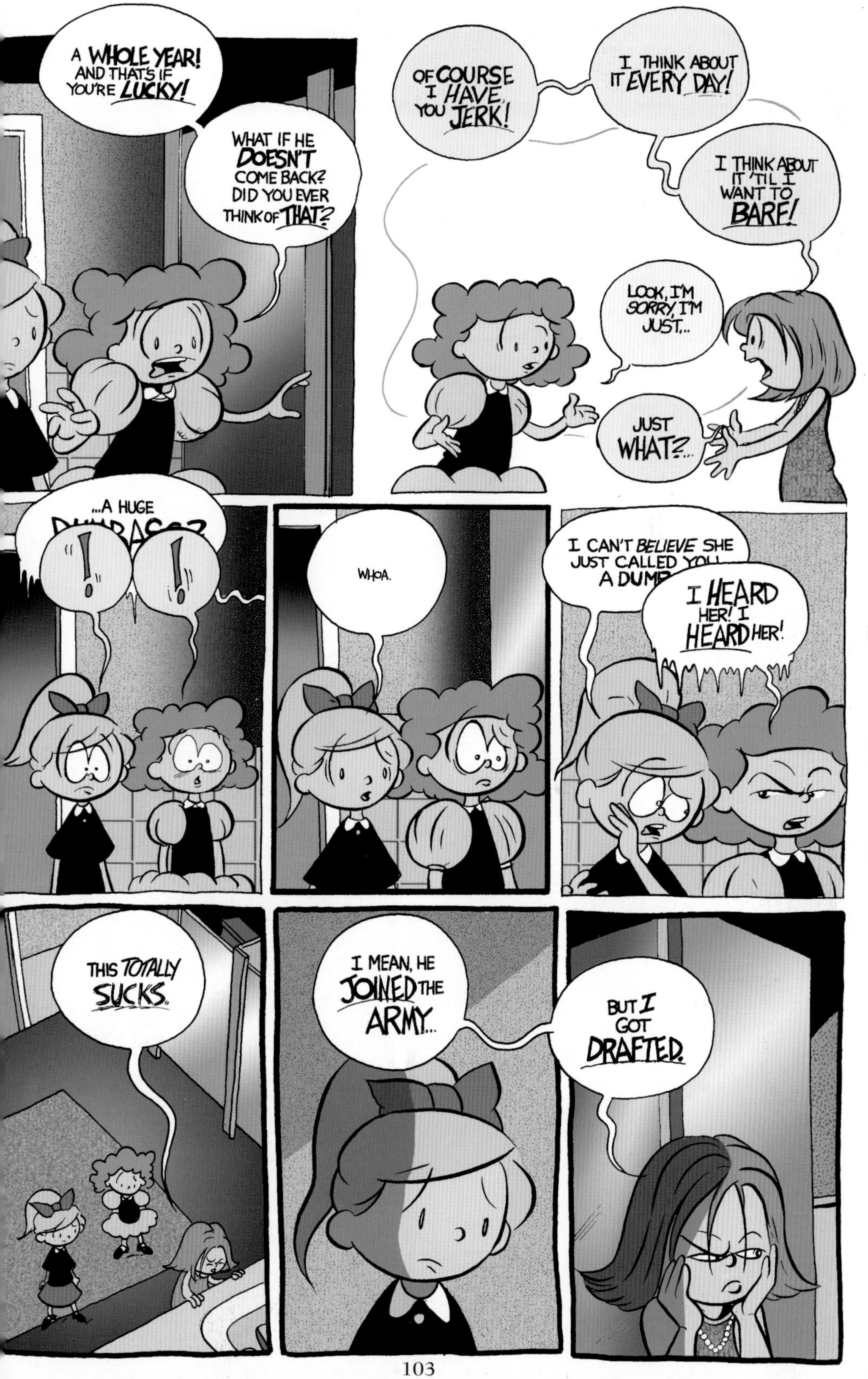
A WHOLE YEAR! AND THAT'S IF YOU'RE LUCKY!
WHAT IF HE DOESN'T COME BACK? DID YOU EVER THINK OF THAT?
OF COURSE I HAVE, YOU JERK!
I THINK ABOUT IT EVERY DAY!
I THINK ABOUT IT 'TIL I WANT TO BARF!
LOOK, I'M SORRY, I'M JUST...
JUST WHAT?...
...A HUGE
!
!
WHOA.
I CAN'T BELIEVE SHE JUST CALLED YOU A DUMB
I HEARD HER! I HEARD HER!
THIS TOTALLY SUCKS.
I MEAN, HE JOINED THE ARMY...
BUT I GOT DRAFTED.

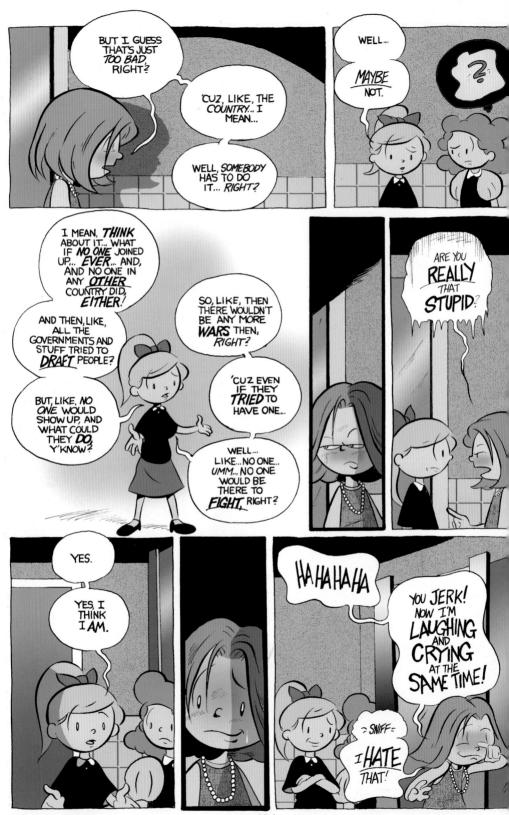

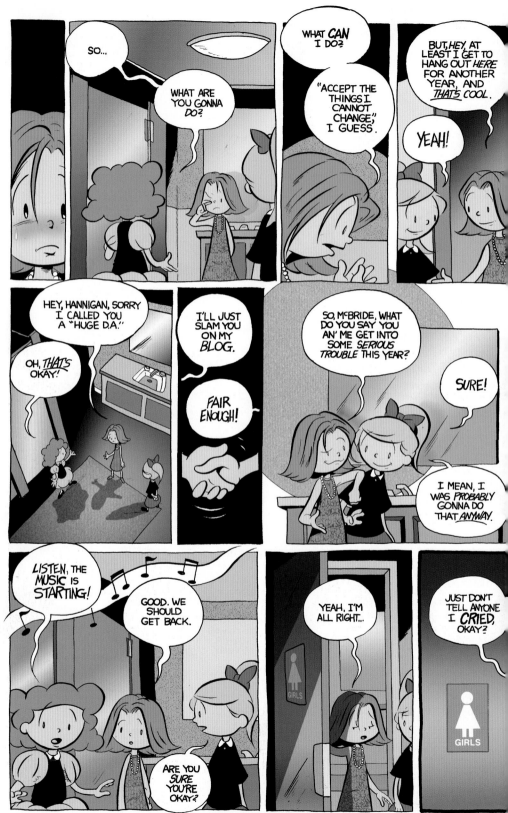

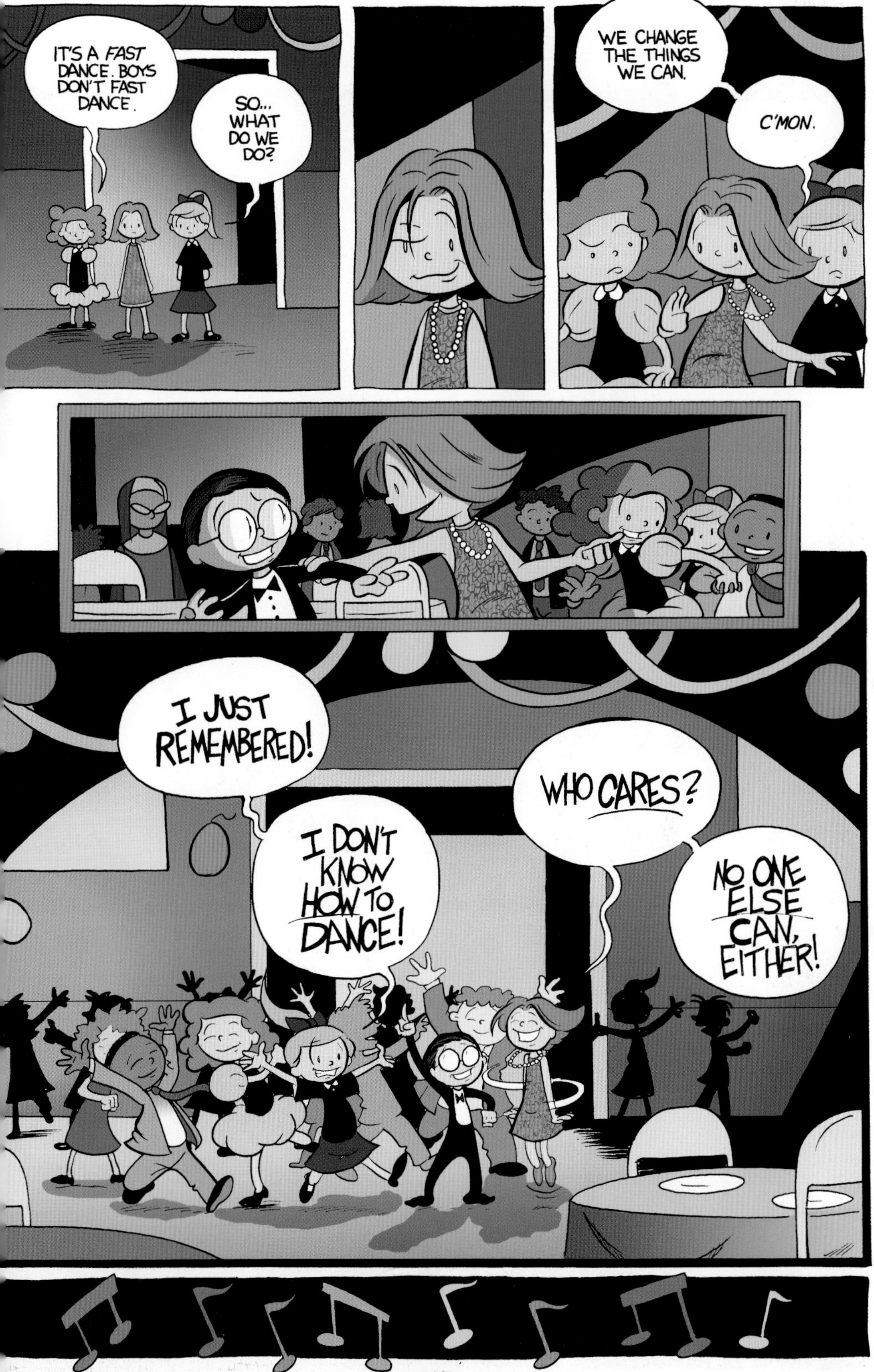
IT'S A *FAST* DANCE. BOYS DON'T FAST DANCE.
SO... WHAT DO WE DO?
WE CHANGE THE THINGS WE CAN.
C'MON.
I JUST REMEMBERED!
I DON'T KNOW HOW TO DANCE!
WHO CARES?
NO ONE ELSE CAN, EITHER!

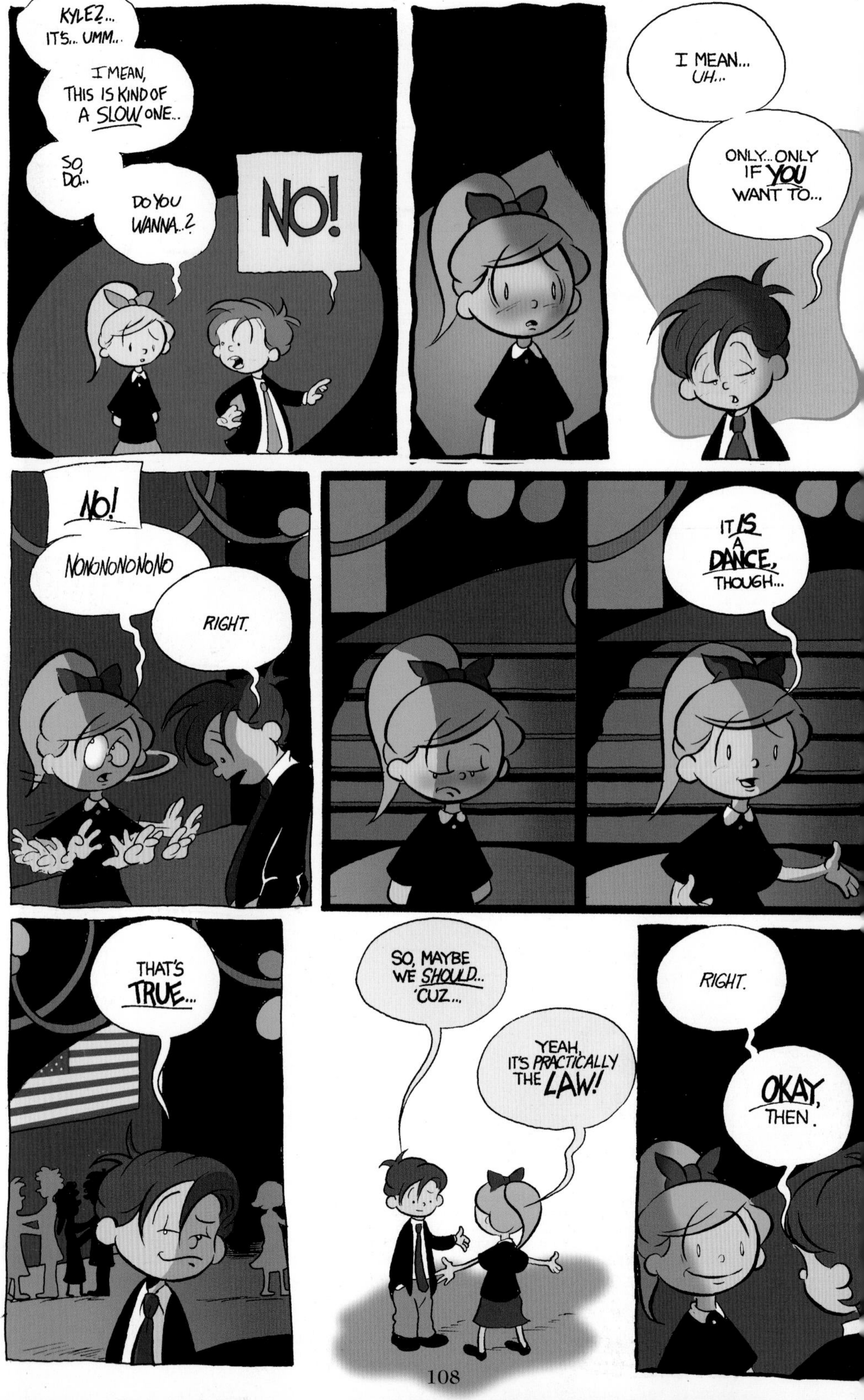
KYLE?... IT'S... UMM...
I MEAN, THIS IS KIND OF A SLOW ONE...
SO, DO...
DO YOU WANNA...?
NO!
I MEAN... UH...
ONLY... ONLY IF YOU WANT TO...
NO!
NONONONONONO
RIGHT.
IT IS A DANCE, THOUGH...
THAT'S TRUE...
SO, MAYBE WE SHOULD... 'CUZ...
YEAH, IT'S PRACTICALLY THE LAW!
RIGHT.
OKAY, THEN.

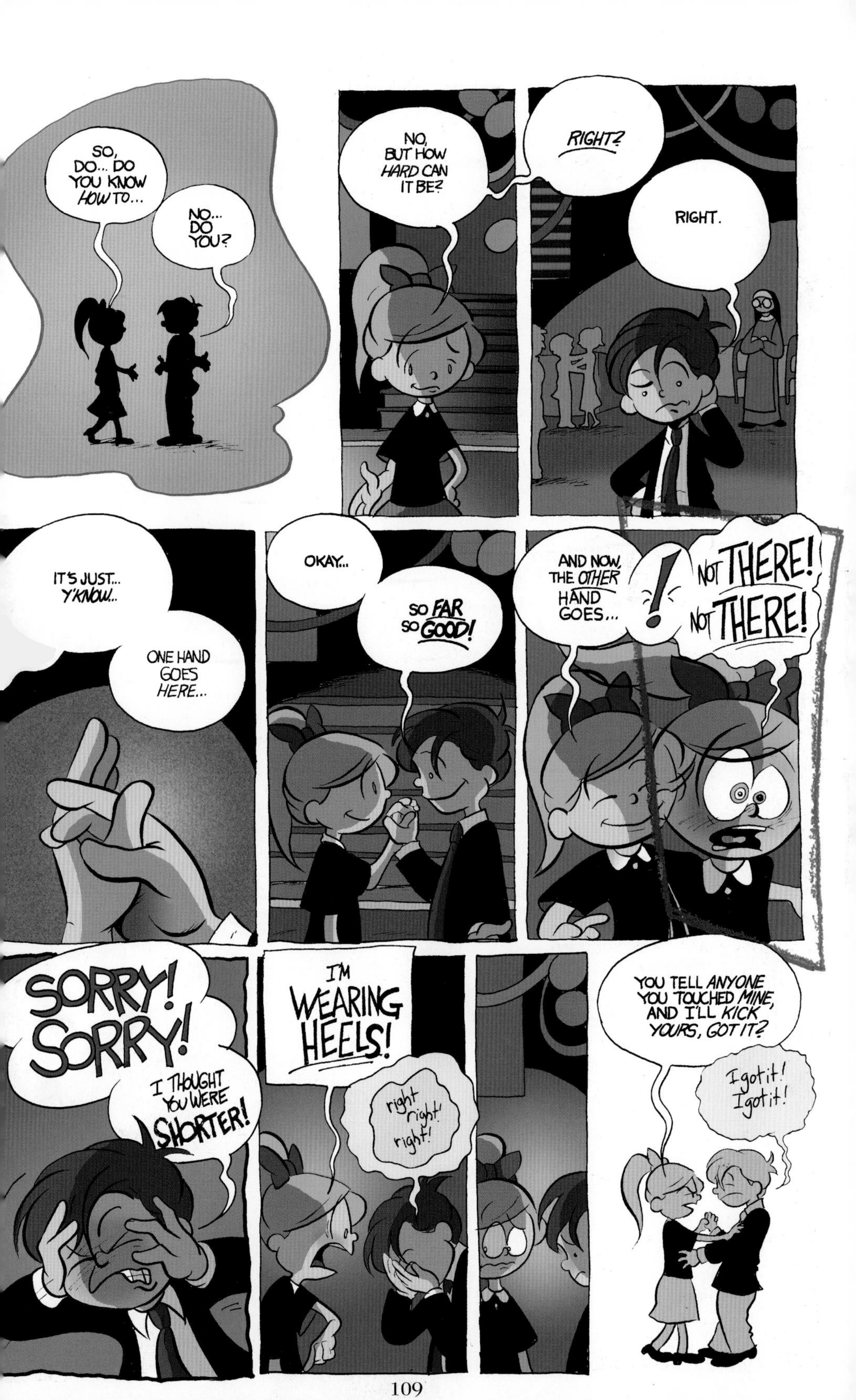

SO, DO... DO YOU KNOW HOW TO...
NO... DO YOU?
NO, BUT HOW HARD CAN IT BE?
RIGHT?
RIGHT.
IT'S JUST... Y'KNOW...
ONE HAND GOES HERE...
OKAY...
SO FAR SO GOOD!
AND NOW, THE OTHER HAND GOES...
!
NOT THERE! NOT THERE!
SORRY! SORRY!
I THOUGHT YOU WERE SHORTER!
I'M WEARING HEELS!
right right! right!
YOU TELL ANYONE YOU TOUCHED MINE, AND I'LL KICK YOURS, GOT IT?
I got it! I got it!

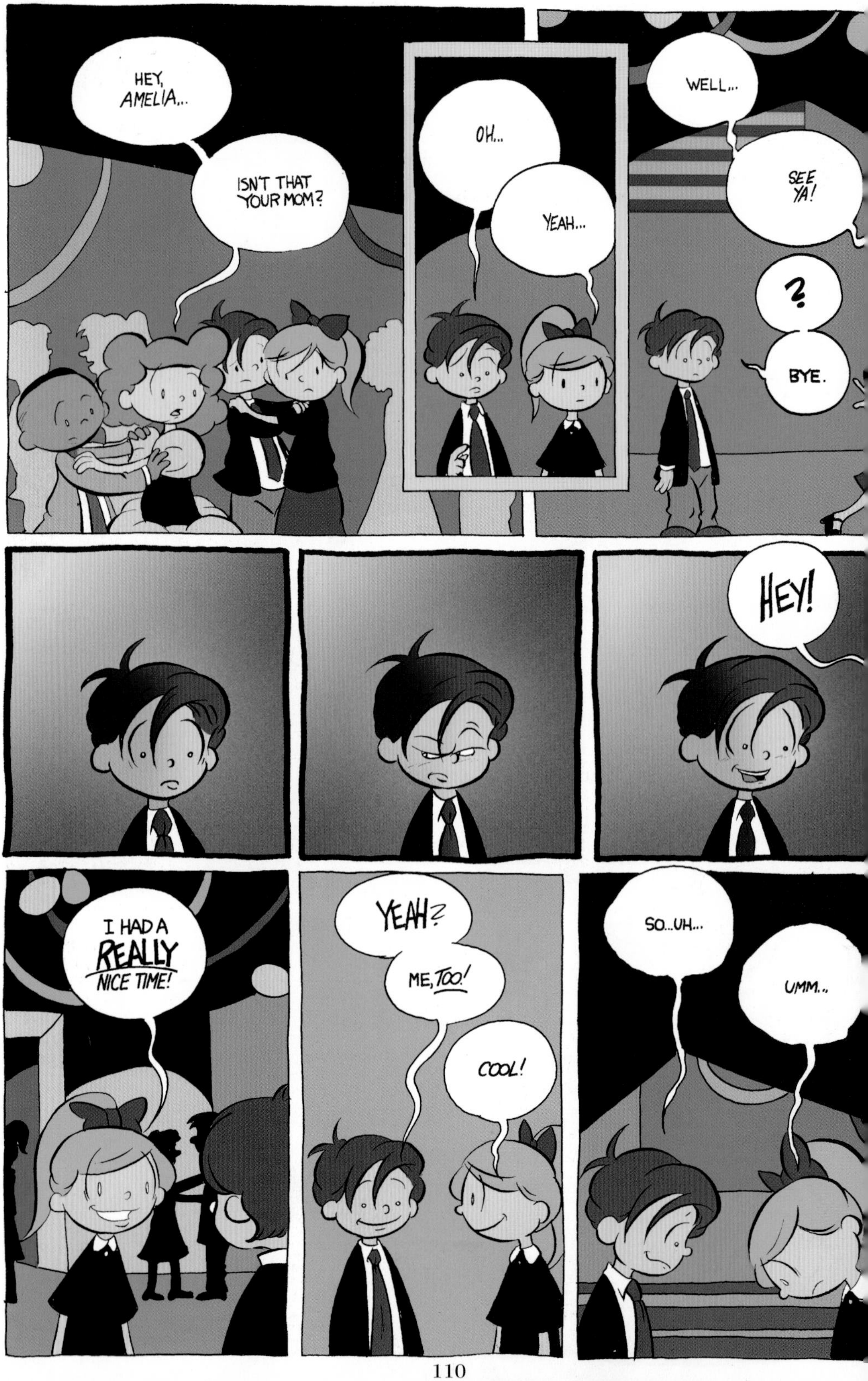
HEY, AMELIA...
ISN'T THAT YOUR MOM?
OH...
YEAH...
WELL...
SEE YA!
?
BYE.
HEY!
I HAD A REALLY NICE TIME!
YEAH?
ME, TOO!
COOL!
SO...UH...
UMM...

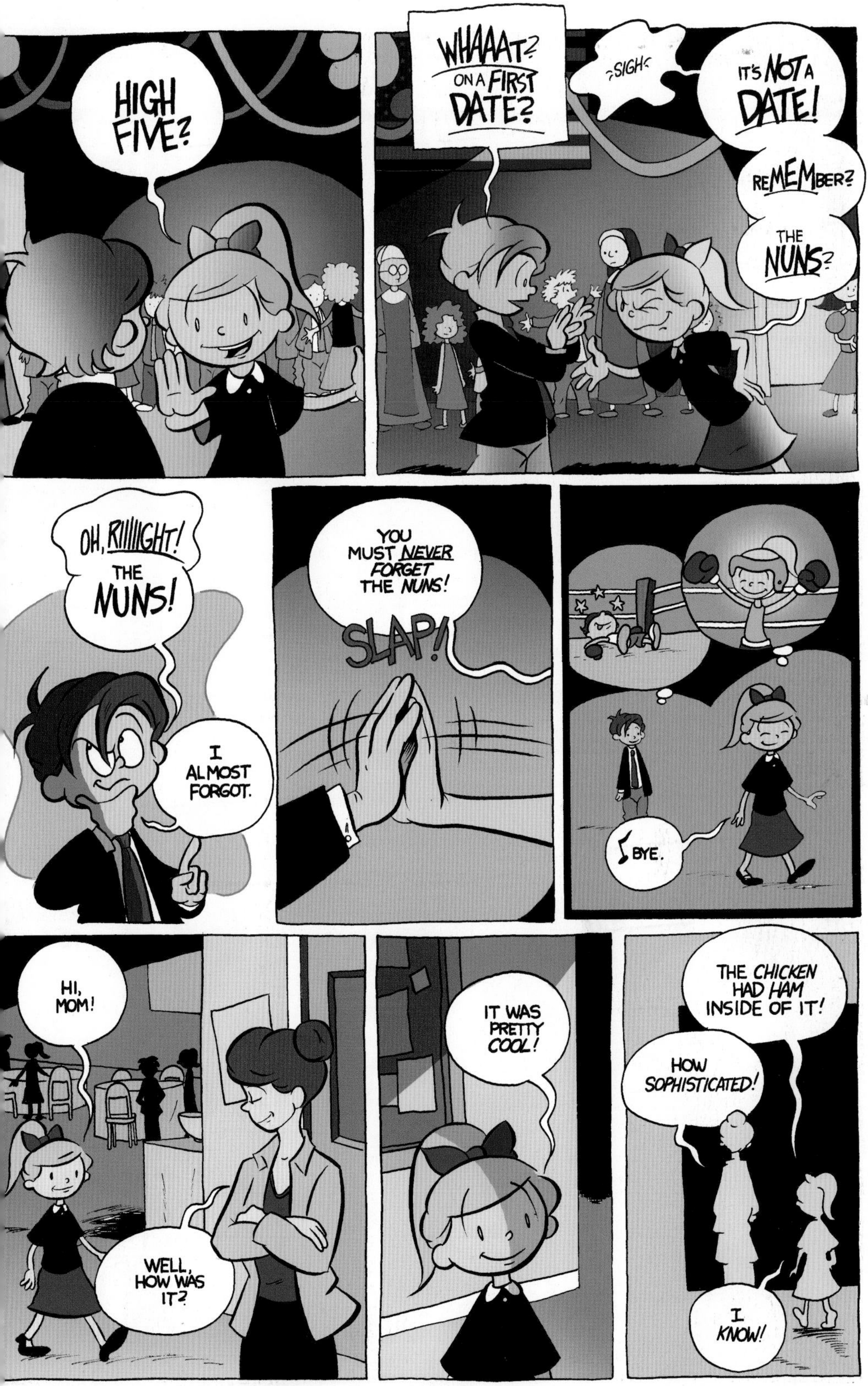
HIGH FIVE?
WHAAAT? ON A FIRST DATE?
SIGH
IT'S NOT A DATE!
REMEMBER?
THE NUNS?
OH, RIIIIGHT! THE NUNS!
I ALMOST FORGOT.
YOU MUST NEVER FORGET THE NUNS!
SLAP!
BYE.
HI, MOM!
WELL, HOW WAS IT?
IT WAS PRETTY COOL!
THE CHICKEN HAD HAM INSIDE OF IT!
HOW SOPHISTICATED!
I KNOW!

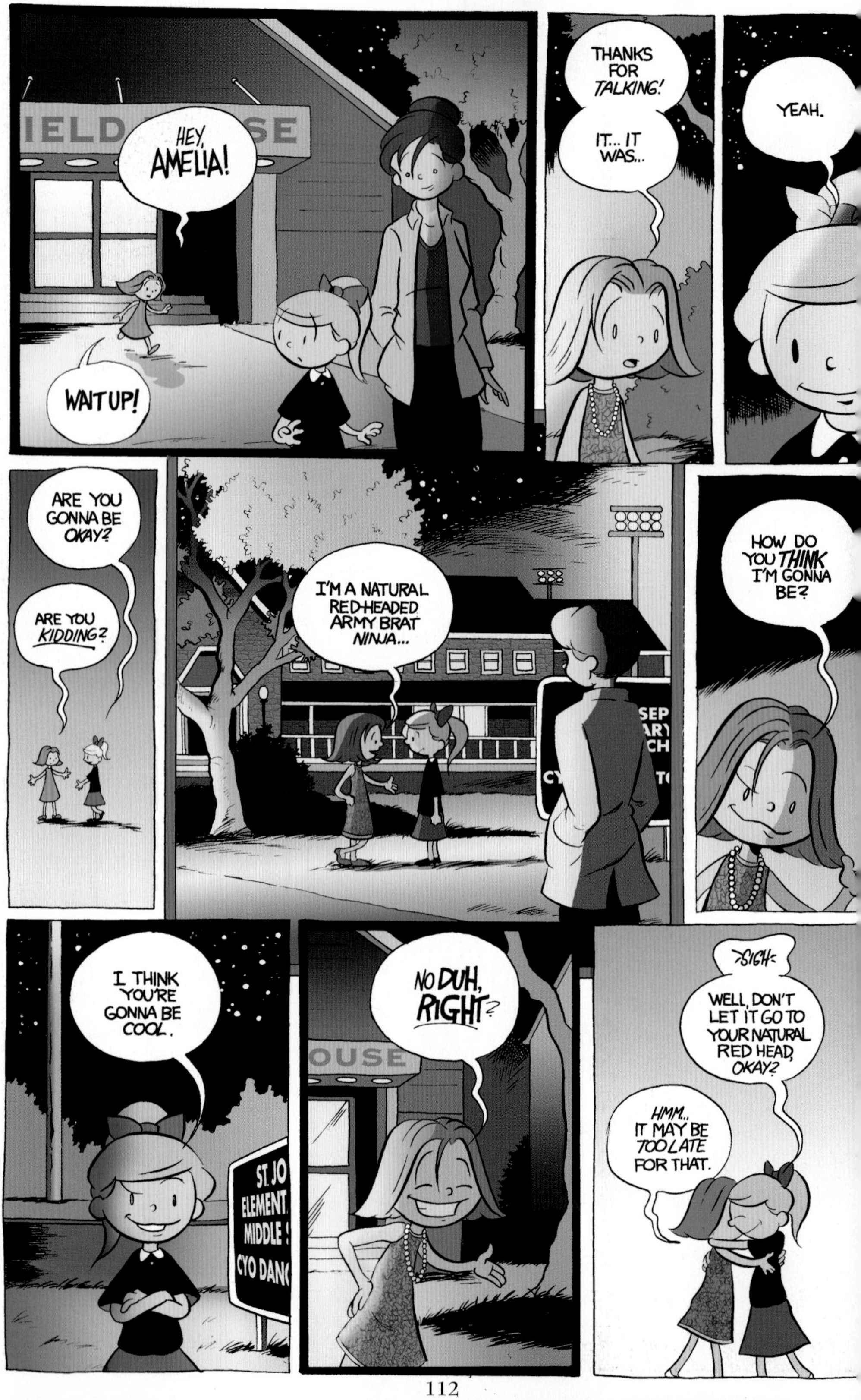
HEY, AMELIA!
WAIT UP!
THANKS FOR TALKING!
IT... IT WAS...
YEAH.
ARE YOU GONNA BE OKAY?
ARE YOU KIDDING?
I'M A NATURAL RED-HEADED ARMY BRAT NINJA...
HOW DO YOU THINK I'M GONNA BE?
I THINK YOU'RE GONNA BE COOL.
ST. JO
ELEMENT
MIDDLE S
CYO DANC
NO DUH, RIGHT?
SIGH
WELL, DON'T LET IT GO TO YOUR NATURAL RED HEAD, OKAY?
HMM... IT MAY BE TOO LATE FOR THAT.

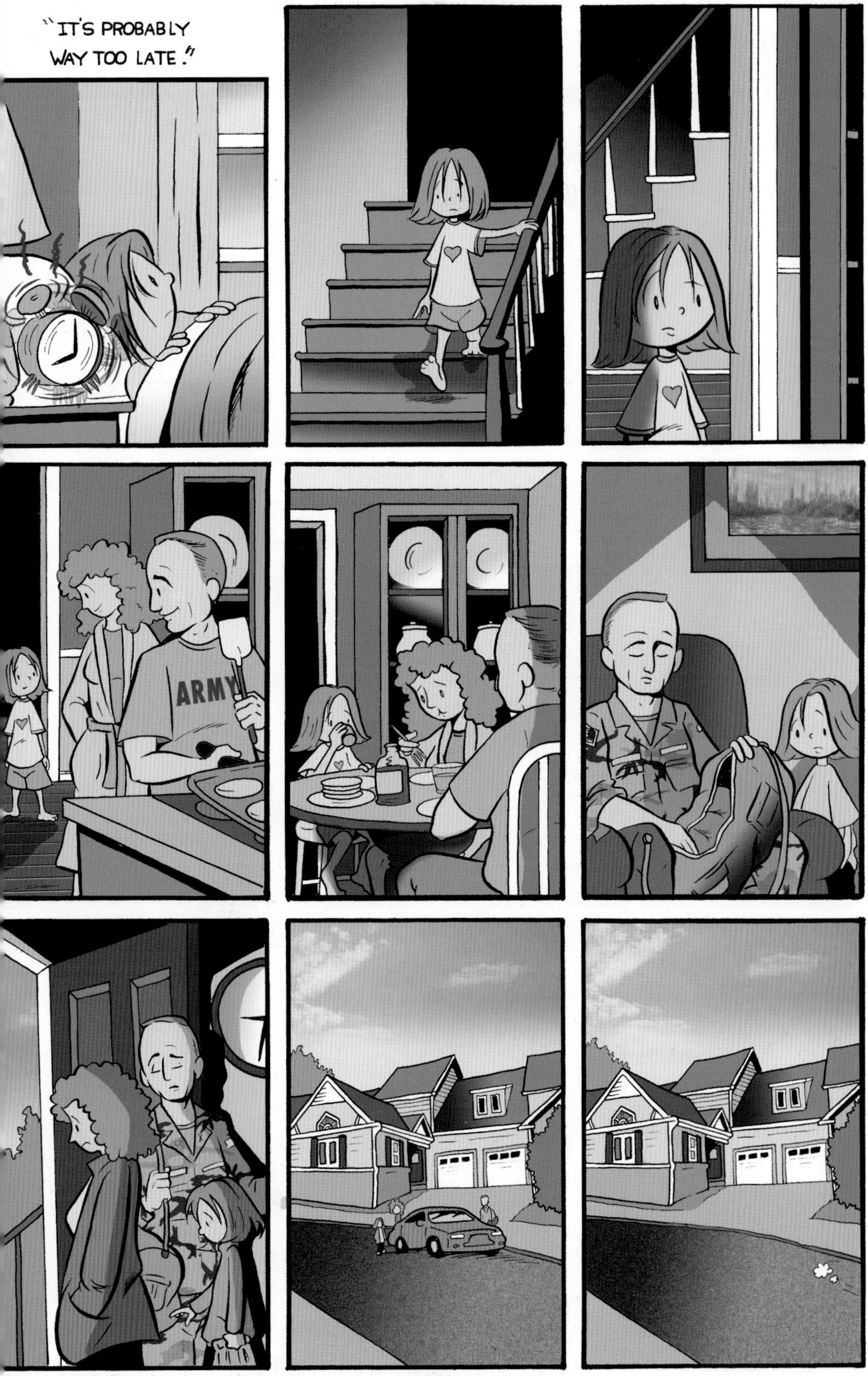
"IT'S PROBABLY WAY TOO LATE."
ARMY

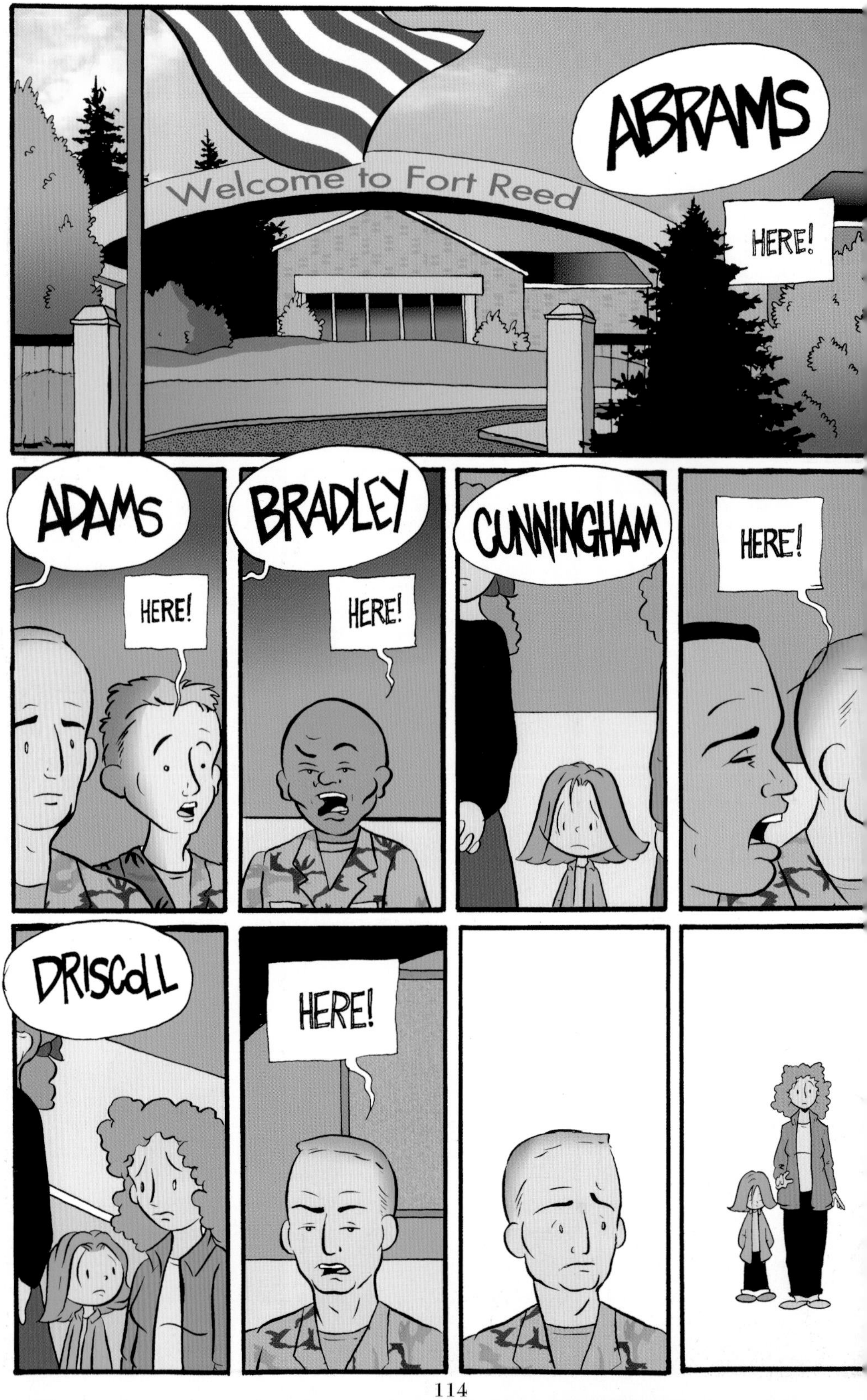
Welcome to Fort Reed
ABRAMS
HERE!
ADAMS
HERE!
BRADLEY
HERE!
CUNNINGHAM
HERE!
DRISCOLL
HERE!

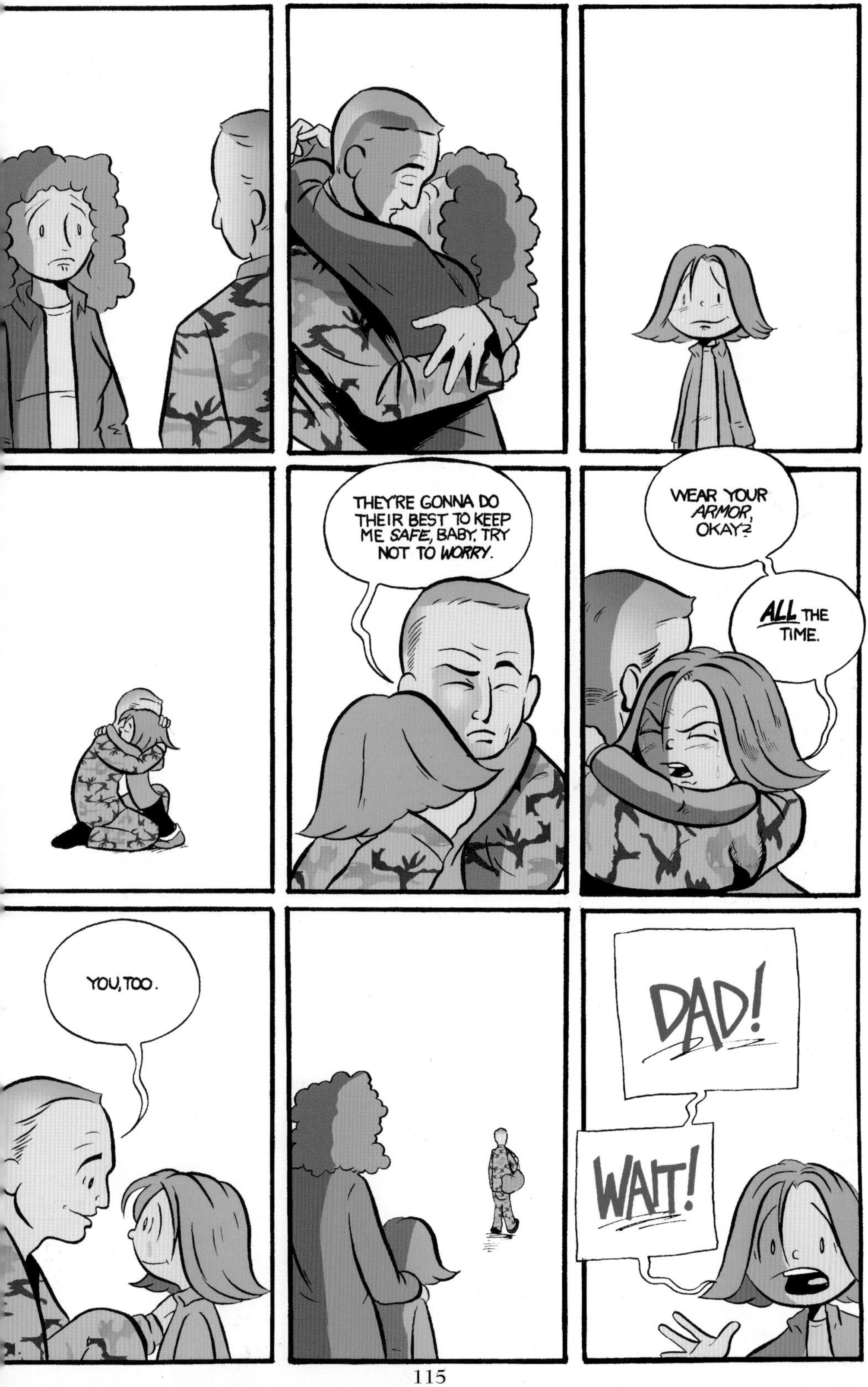

THEY'RE GONNA DO THEIR BEST TO KEEP ME SAFE, BABY. TRY NOT TO WORRY.
WEAR YOUR ARMOR, OKAY?
ALL THE TIME.
YOU, TOO.
DAD!
WAIT!

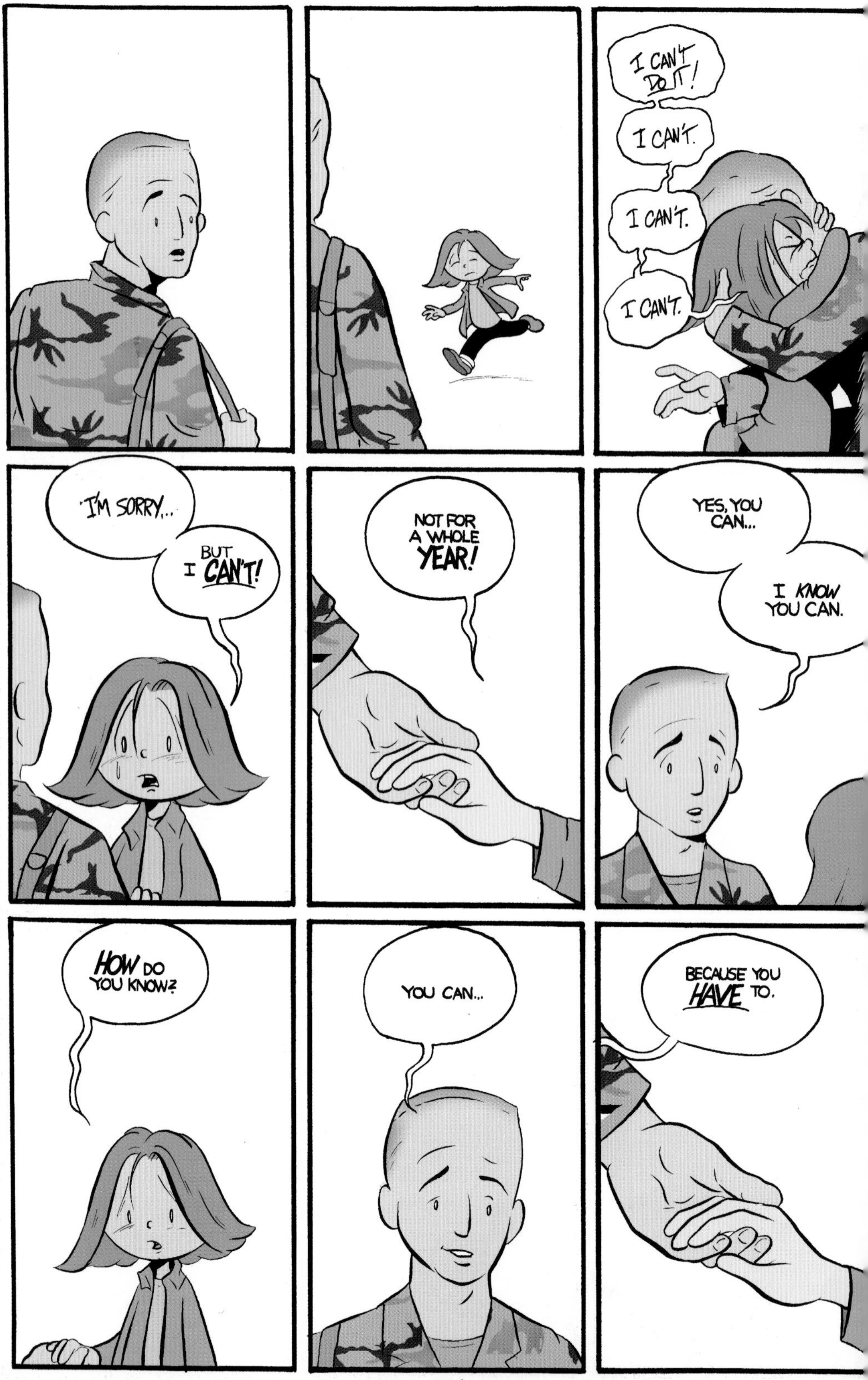
I CAN'T DO IT!
I CAN'T.
I CAN'T.
I CAN'T.
I'M SORRY...
BUT I CAN'T!
NOT FOR A WHOLE YEAR!
YES, YOU CAN...
I KNOW YOU CAN.
HOW DO YOU KNOW?
YOU CAN...
BECAUSE YOU HAVE TO.

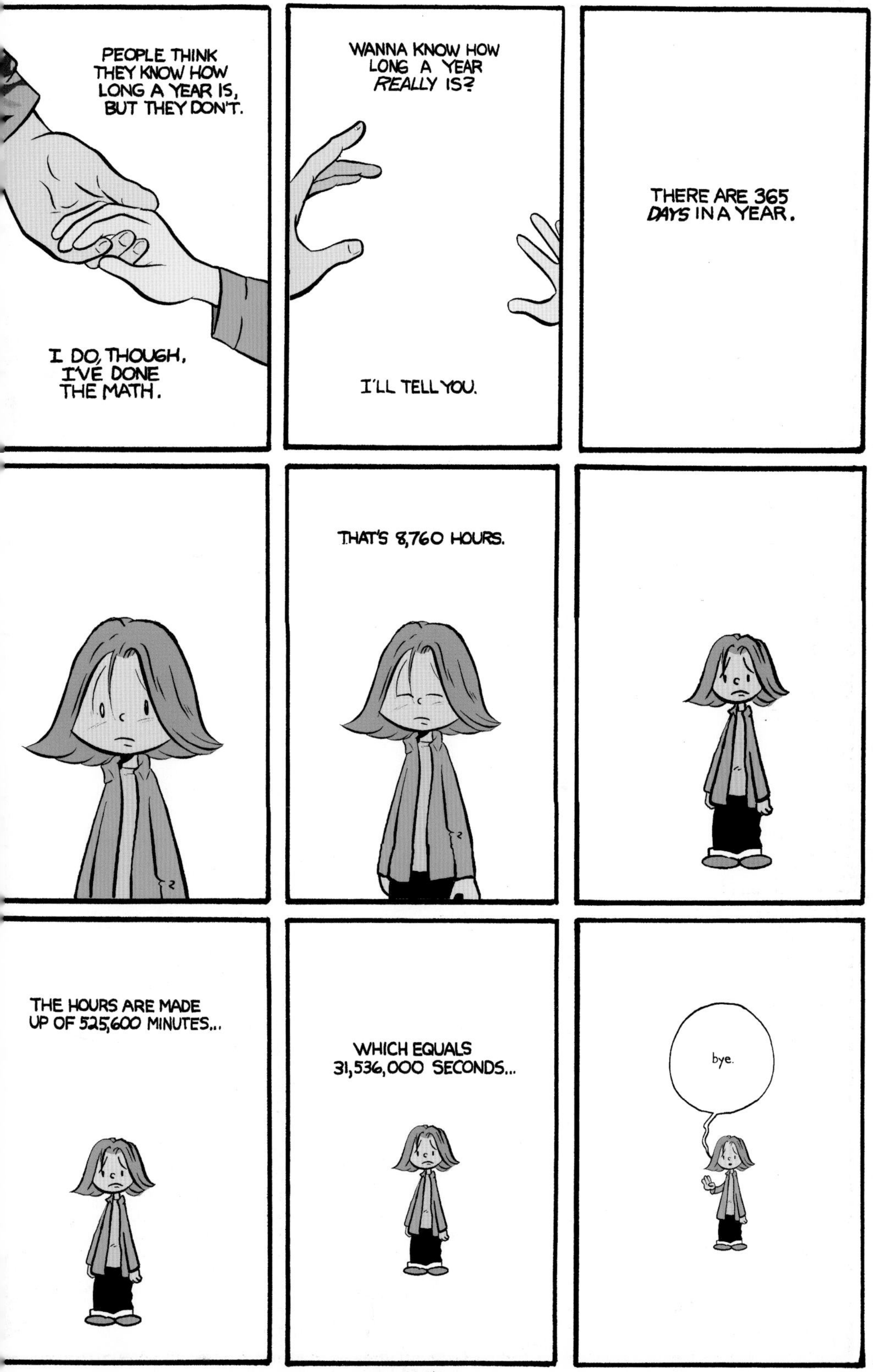
PEOPLE THINK THEY KNOW HOW LONG A YEAR IS, BUT THEY DON'T.
I DO, THOUGH. I'VE DONE THE MATH.
WANNA KNOW HOW LONG A YEAR *REALLY* IS?
I'LL TELL YOU.
THERE ARE 365 *DAYS* IN A YEAR.
THAT'S 8,760 HOURS.
THE HOURS ARE MADE UP OF 525,600 MINUTES...
WHICH EQUALS 31,536,000 SECONDS...
bye.

ONE- ONE THOUSAND...

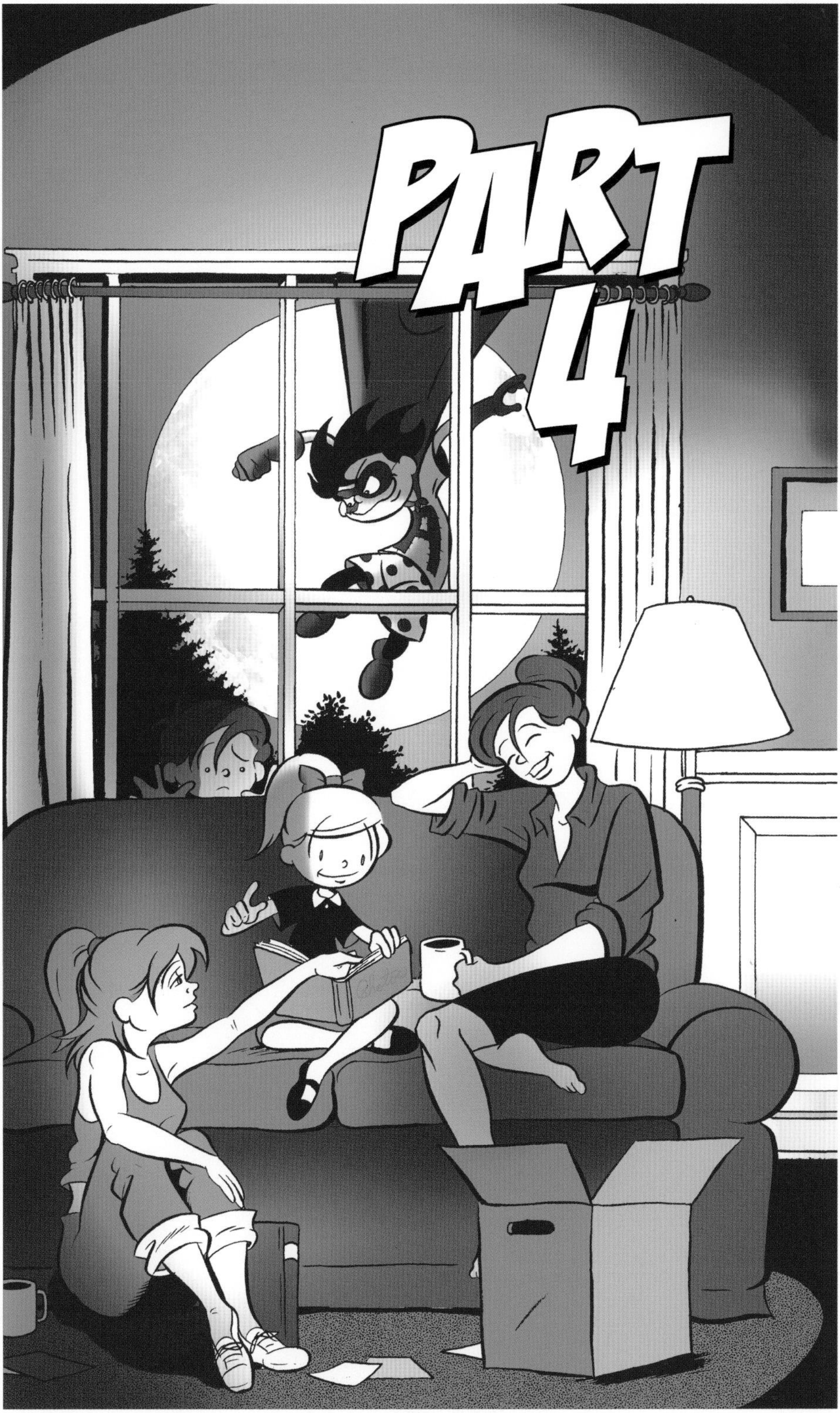
PART 4

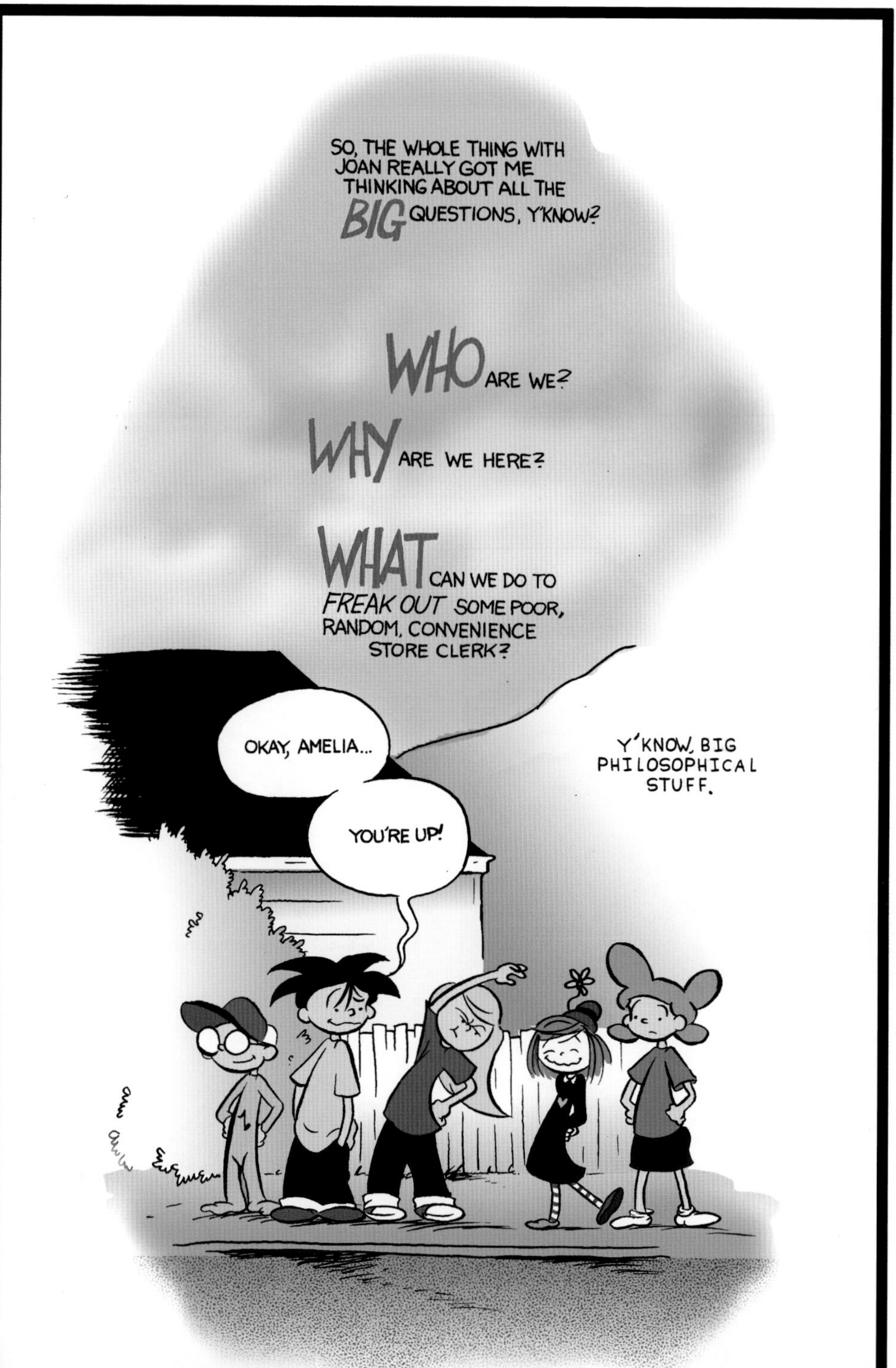
SO, THE WHOLE THING WITH JOAN REALLY GOT ME THINKING ABOUT ALL THE BIG QUESTIONS, Y'KNOW?
WHO ARE WE?
WHY ARE WE HERE?
WHAT CAN WE DO TO FREAK OUT SOME POOR, RANDOM, CONVENIENCE STORE CLERK?
OKAY, AMELIA...
YOU'RE UP!
Y'KNOW, BIG PHILOSOPHICAL STUFF.

"WHEN the PasT is a PRESENT"

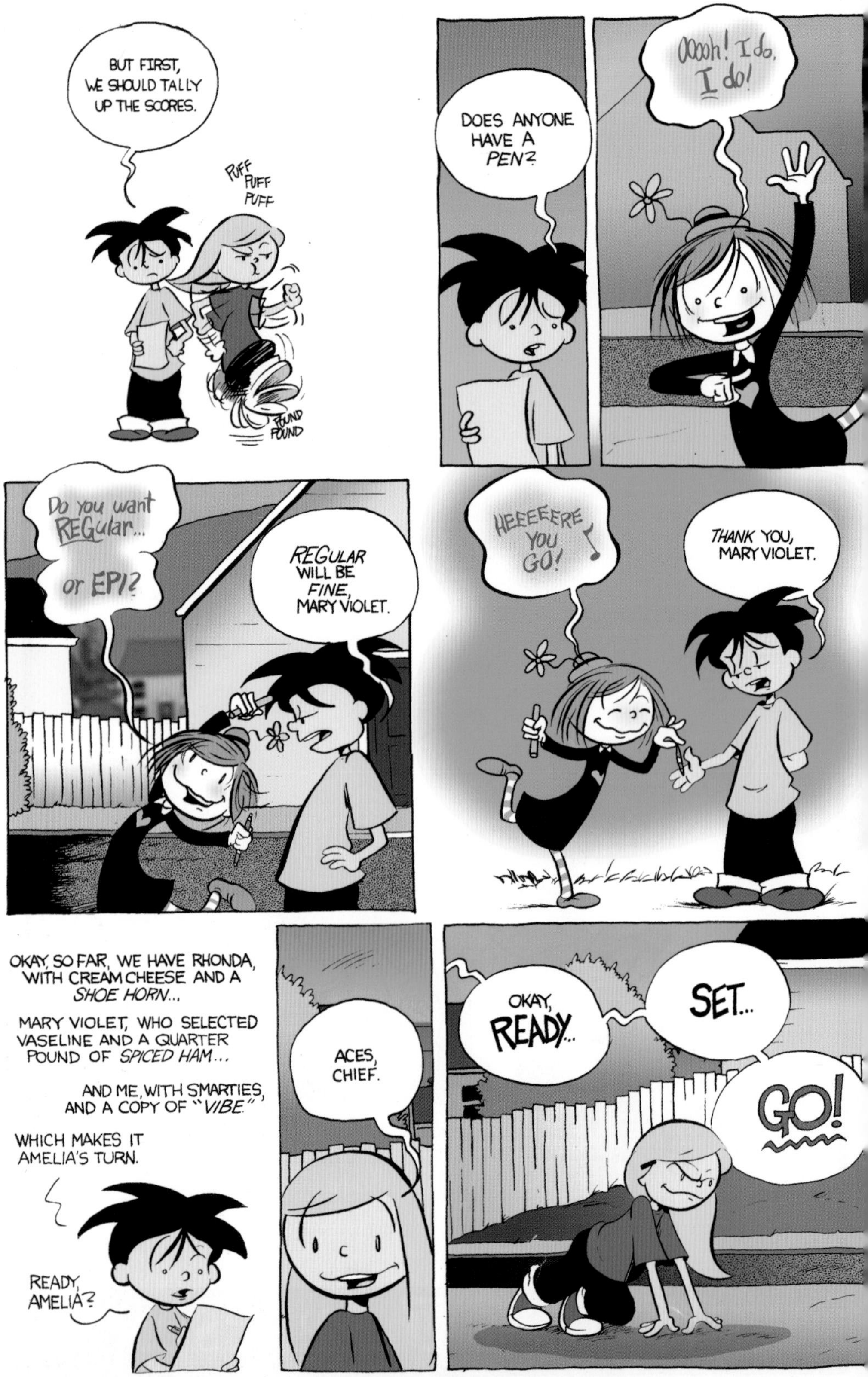

BUT FIRST, WE SHOULD TALLY UP THE SCORES.
PUFF PUFF PUFF
POUND POUND
DOES ANYONE HAVE A PEN?
Ooooh! I do. I do!
Do you want REGular... or EPI?
REGULAR WILL BE FINE, MARY VIOLET.
HEEEEERE YOU GO!
THANK YOU, MARY VIOLET.
OKAY, SO FAR, WE HAVE RHONDA, WITH CREAM CHEESE AND A SHOE HORN...
MARY VIOLET, WHO SELECTED VASELINE AND A QUARTER POUND OF SPICED HAM...
AND ME, WITH SMARTIES, AND A COPY OF "VIBE."
WHICH MAKES IT AMELIA'S TURN.
READY, AMELIA?
ACES, CHIEF.
OKAY, READY...
SET...
GO!

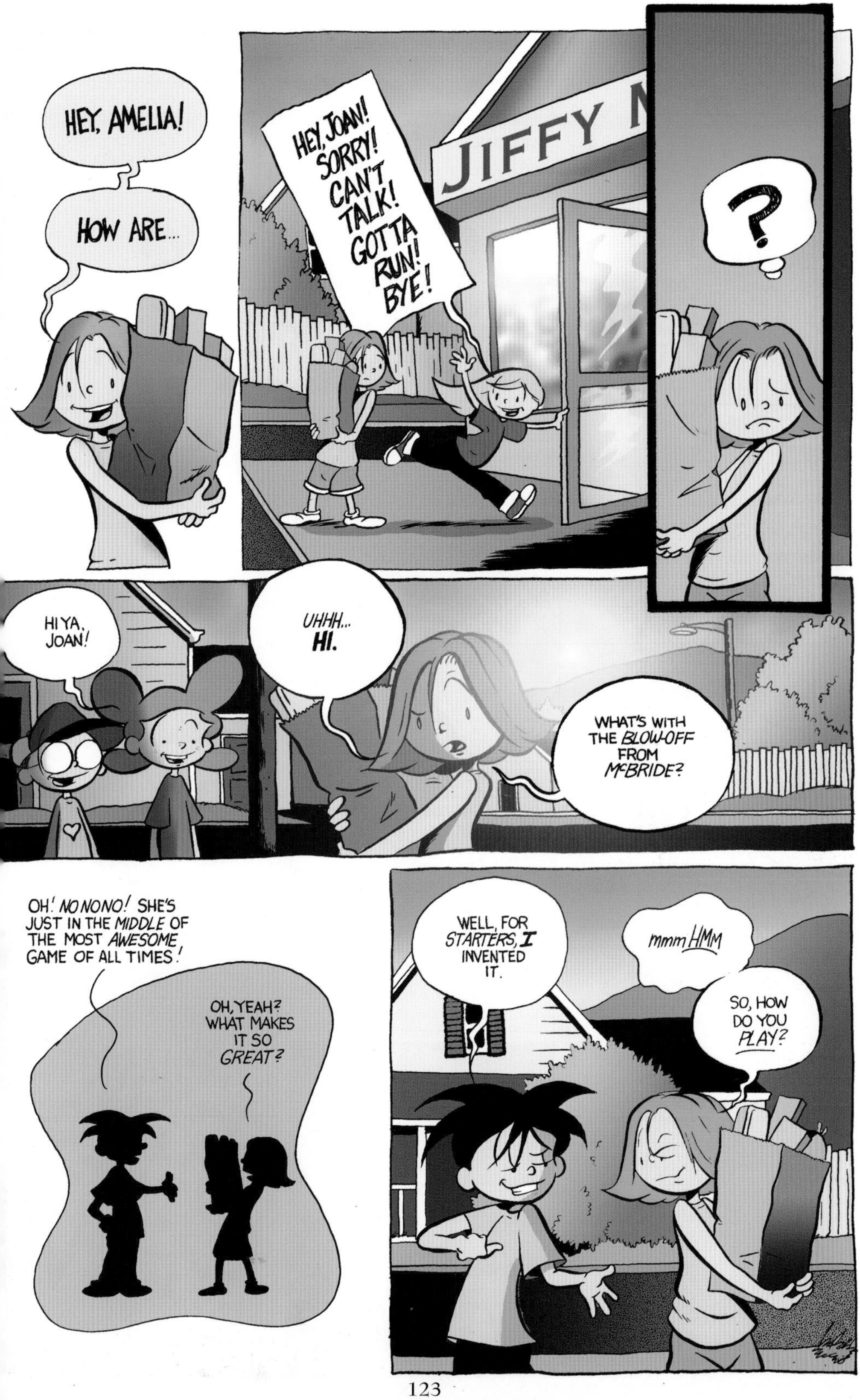
HEY, AMELIA!
HOW ARE...
HEY, JOAN! SORRY! CAN'T TALK! GOTTA RUN! BYE!
JIFFY M
?
HI YA, JOAN!
UHHH... HI.
WHAT'S WITH THE BLOW-OFF FROM McBRIDE?
OH! NO NO NO! SHE'S JUST IN THE MIDDLE OF THE MOST AWESOME GAME OF ALL TIMES!
OH, YEAH? WHAT MAKES IT SO GREAT?
WELL, FOR STARTERS, I INVENTED IT.
mmm HMM
SO, HOW DO YOU PLAY?

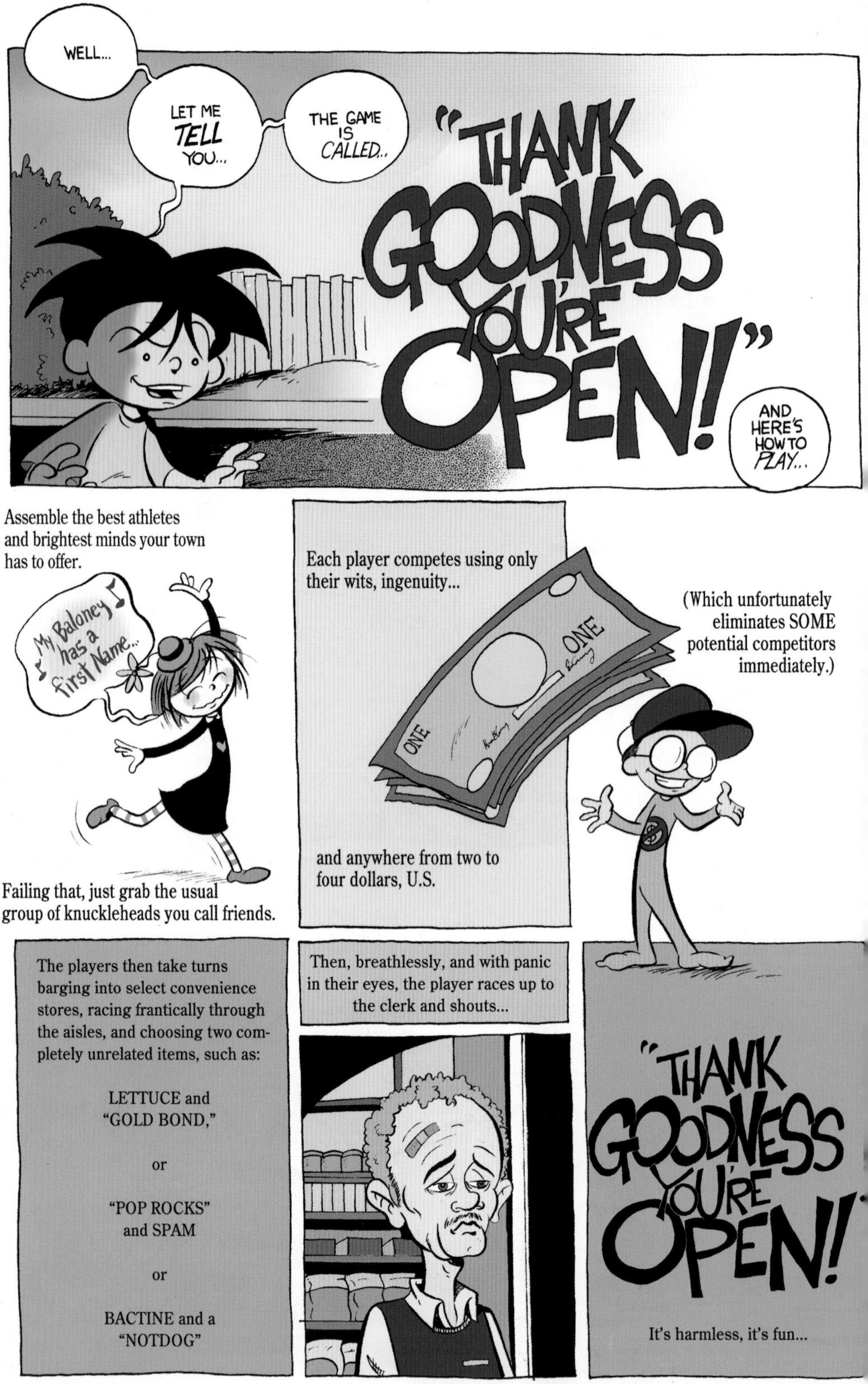
WELL...
LET ME TELL YOU...
THE GAME IS CALLED...
"THANK GOODNESS YOU'RE OPEN!"
AND HERE'S HOW TO PLAY...
Assemble the best athletes and brightest minds your town has to offer.
My Baloney has a first Name...
Failing that, just grab the usual group of knuckleheads you call friends.
Each player competes using only their wits, ingenuity...
ONE
ONE
and anywhere from two to four dollars, U.S.
(Which unfortunately eliminates SOME potential competitors immediately.)
The players then take turns barging into select convenience stores, racing frantically through the aisles, and choosing two completely unrelated items, such as:
LETTUCE and "GOLD BOND,"
or
"POP ROCKS" and SPAM
or
BACTINE and a "NOTDOG"
Then, breathlessly, and with panic in their eyes, the player races up to the clerk and shouts...
"THANK GOODNESS YOU'RE OPEN!
It's harmless, it's fun...

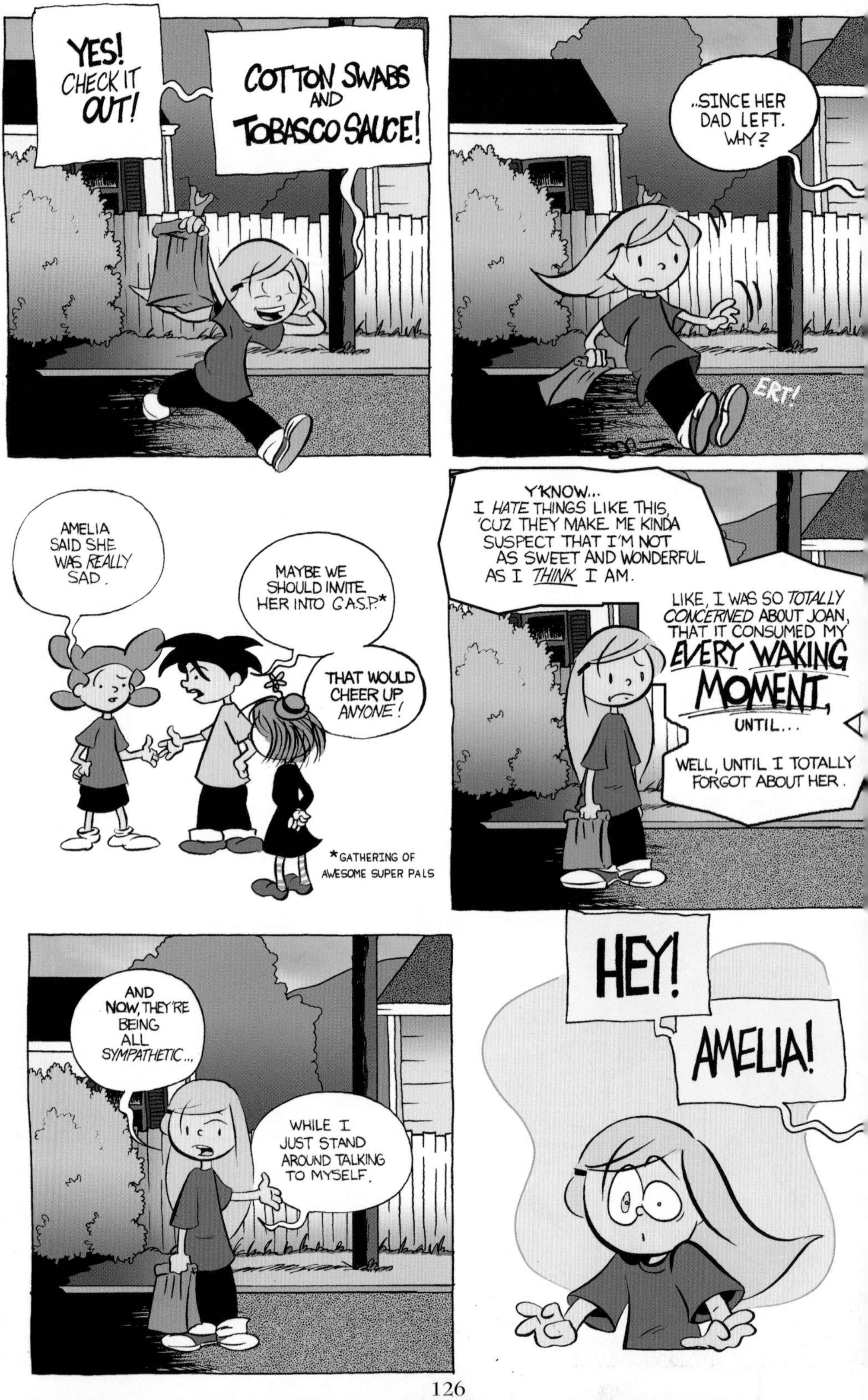

YES! CHECK IT OUT!
COTTON SWABS AND TOBASCO SAUCE!
..SINCE HER DAD LEFT. WHY?
ERT!
AMELIA SAID SHE WAS *REALLY* SAD.
MAYBE WE SHOULD INVITE HER INTO G.A.S.P.*
THAT WOULD CHEER UP *ANYONE*!
*GATHERING OF AWESOME SUPER PALS
Y'KNOW... I *HATE* THINGS LIKE THIS, 'CUZ THEY MAKE ME KINDA SUSPECT THAT I'M NOT AS SWEET AND WONDERFUL AS I *THINK* I AM.
LIKE, I WAS SO *TOTALLY CONCERNED* ABOUT JOAN, THAT IT CONSUMED MY **EVERY WAKING MOMENT**, UNTIL...
WELL, UNTIL I TOTALLY FORGOT ABOUT HER.
AND NOW, THEY'RE BEING ALL *SYMPATHETIC*...
WHILE I JUST STAND AROUND TALKING TO MYSELF.
HEY!
AMELIA!

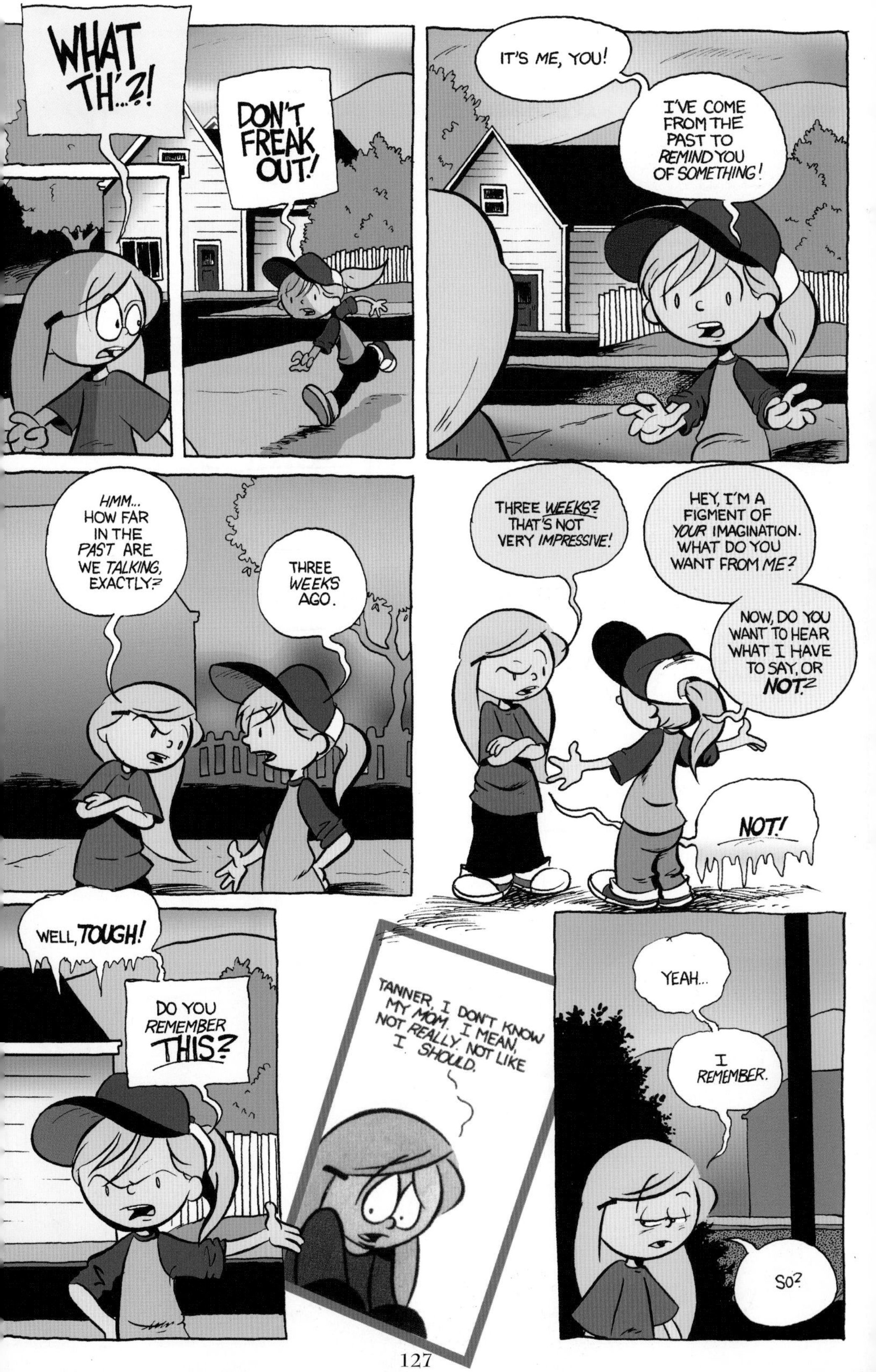
WHAT TH'...?!
DON'T FREAK OUT!
IT'S ME, YOU!
I'VE COME FROM THE PAST TO REMIND YOU OF SOMETHING!
HMM... HOW FAR IN THE PAST ARE WE TALKING, EXACTLY?
THREE WEEKS AGO.
THREE WEEKS? THAT'S NOT VERY IMPRESSIVE!
HEY, I'M A FIGMENT OF YOUR IMAGINATION. WHAT DO YOU WANT FROM ME?
NOW, DO YOU WANT TO HEAR WHAT I HAVE TO SAY, OR NOT?
NOT!
WELL, TOUGH!
DO YOU REMEMBER THIS?
TANNER, I DON'T KNOW MY MOM. I MEAN, NOT REALLY. NOT LIKE I SHOULD.
YEAH...
I REMEMBER.
SO?

128

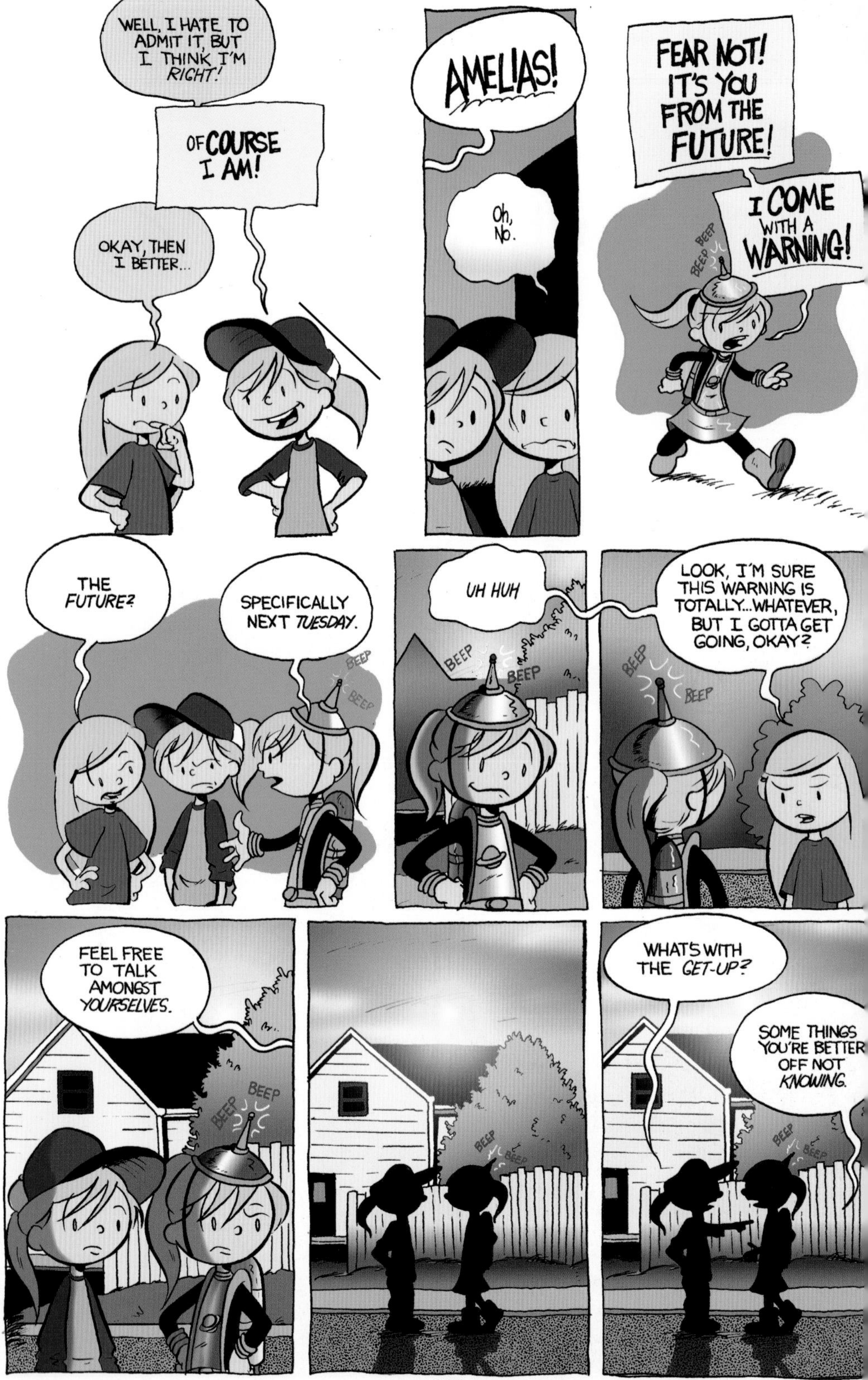
WELL, I HATE TO ADMIT IT, BUT I THINK I'M *RIGHT*!
OF COURSE I AM!
OKAY, THEN I BETTER...
AMELIAS!
Oh, No.
FEAR NOT! IT'S YOU FROM THE FUTURE!
I COME WITH A WARNING!
BEEP BEEP
THE *FUTURE*?
SPECIFICALLY NEXT *TUESDAY*.
BEEP BEEP
UH HUH
BEEP BEEP
LOOK, I'M SURE THIS WARNING IS TOTALLY...WHATEVER, BUT I GOTTA GET GOING, OKAY?
BEEP BEEP
FEEL FREE TO TALK AMONGST *YOURSELVES*.
BEEP BEEP
BEEP BEEP
WHAT'S WITH THE *GET-UP*?
SOME THINGS YOU'RE BETTER OFF NOT *KNOWING*.
BEEP BEEP

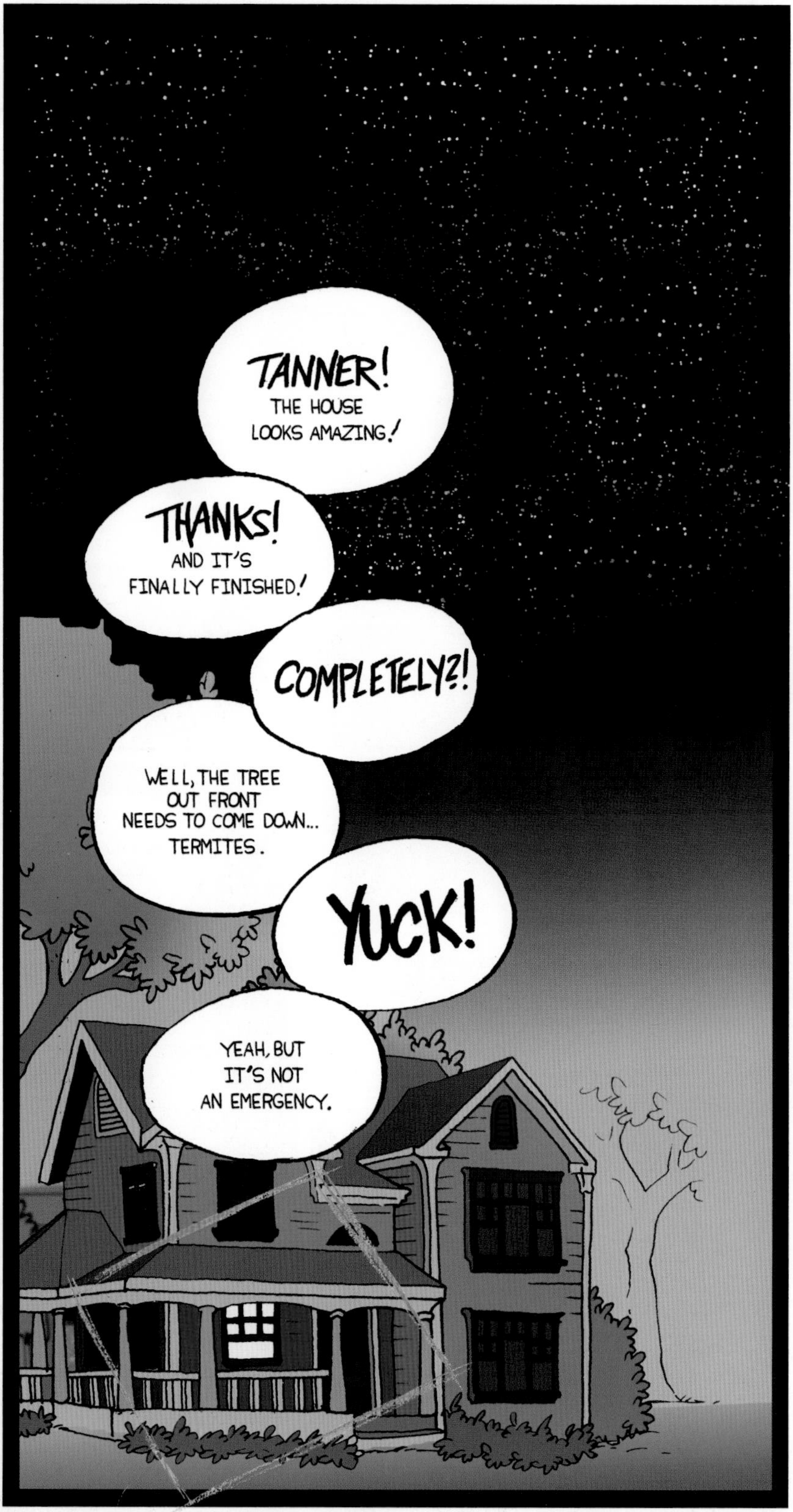
TANNER! THE HOUSE LOOKS AMAZING!
THANKS! AND IT'S FINALLY FINISHED!
COMPLETELY?!
WELL, THE TREE OUT FRONT NEEDS TO COME DOWN... TERMITES.
YUCK!
YEAH, BUT IT'S NOT AN EMERGENCY.

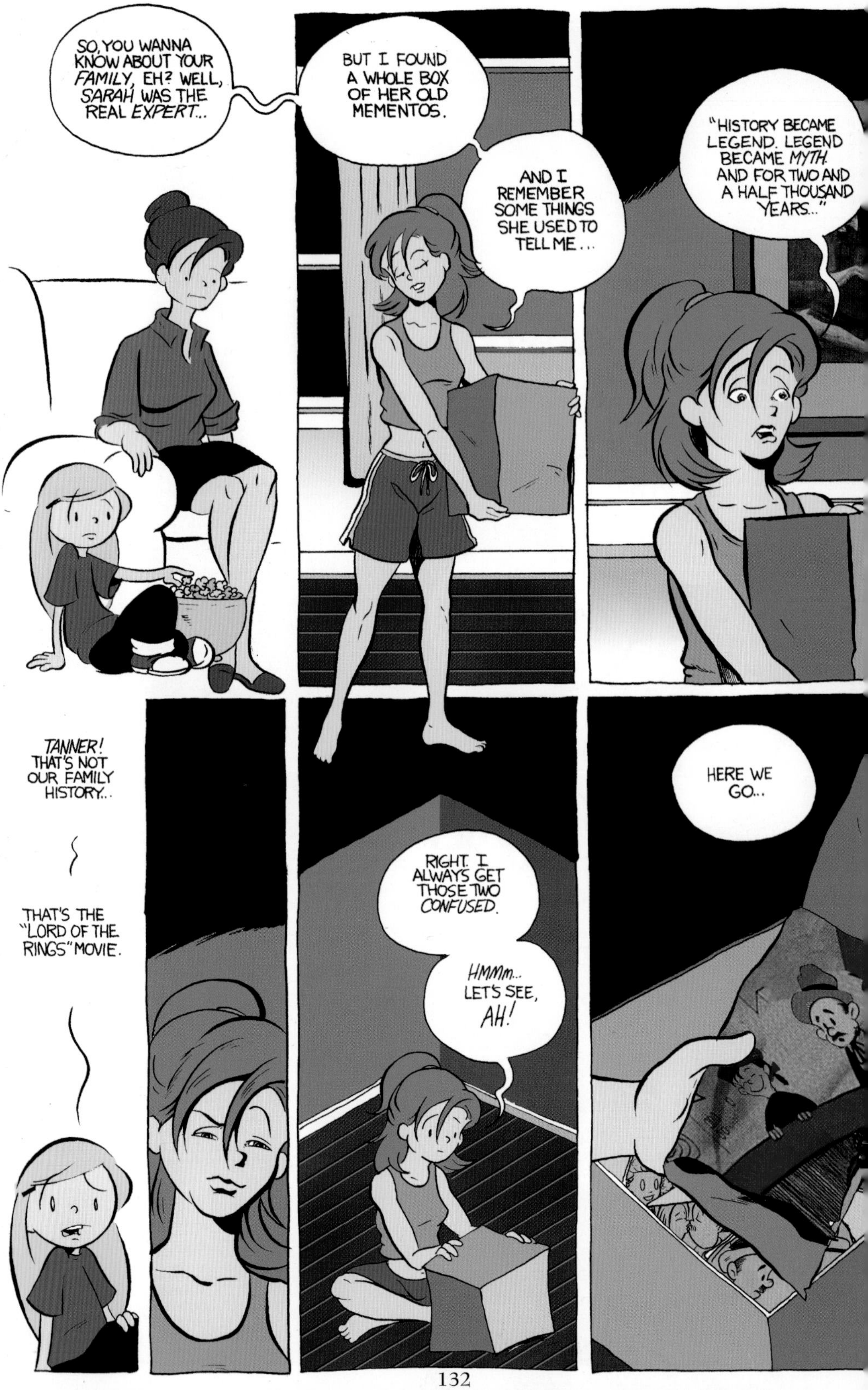
SO, YOU WANNA KNOW ABOUT YOUR FAMILY, EH? WELL, SARAH WAS THE REAL EXPERT...
BUT I FOUND A WHOLE BOX OF HER OLD MEMENTOS.
AND I REMEMBER SOME THINGS SHE USED TO TELL ME...
"HISTORY BECAME LEGEND. LEGEND BECAME MYTH. AND FOR TWO AND A HALF THOUSAND YEARS..."
TANNER! THAT'S NOT OUR FAMILY HISTORY...
THAT'S THE "LORD OF THE RINGS" MOVIE.
RIGHT. I ALWAYS GET THOSE TWO CONFUSED.
HMMM... LET'S SEE, AH!
HERE WE GO...

ARTHUR T. FLETCHER ARRIVES IN U.S.A.

Joined by new bride Louise.

We don't know much about the Clark side of the family, and if you want to know about the Irish McBrides you'll have to ask your dad.

But we know a lot about your grandmother's family, the Fletchers.

Arthur T. Fletcher grew up in England, the youngest child of George and Delores Fletcher. Now there were only two things Arthur wanted in the whole world: to marry his childhood sweetheart Louise and to move to America.

Unfortunately his entire family hated both Louise and the U.S. and made Arthur swear an oath that he would stay put and stay single (or at least marry someone more suitable).

So Arthur did what he believed was most sensible. He waited until everyone else in his family croaked and then did what he wanted.

So, as one century faded into the next, Arthur and Louise arrived in America.

FLETCHER'S FOLLIES

FLETCHER BUYS WIFE GIFT

Neighbors thrown into jealous rage.

Eventually the couple found themselves in Indiana, where a distant cousin of Louise owned a farm. Arthur was so happy to be in the land of his dreams and so grateful for the patience and devotion Louise had showed him that he bought her a present – a simple, delicate, and beautiful locket.

Louise kept the locket for the next 30 years until, on the day of her only son John's wedding, she passed it on to his bride Edna.

Now, Arthur had long since acquired his own farm, so John and Edna stayed on helping. By now, he and Edna had three children of their own: Jerome, Sarah, and Grace.

But try as he might, John just wasn't a farmer. So on the day of his tenth wedding anniversary, John Fletcher opened the "Family Valley General Store." No one but Edna believed it would succeed. Even John himself doubted it.

But somehow, against unbelievable odds, it did. It thrived through depression and war.

It even outlived John himself. It's still there today.

Unfortunately, during all the chaos and commotion of building the store, Edna lost the locket. Even though she searched and searched it never turned up.

One day, years after it was lost, Sarah found the locket in a field behind the store. She had no idea of the object's significance. It was weeks before she discovered that the little heart charm opened and she found a picture of her parents' wedding inside.

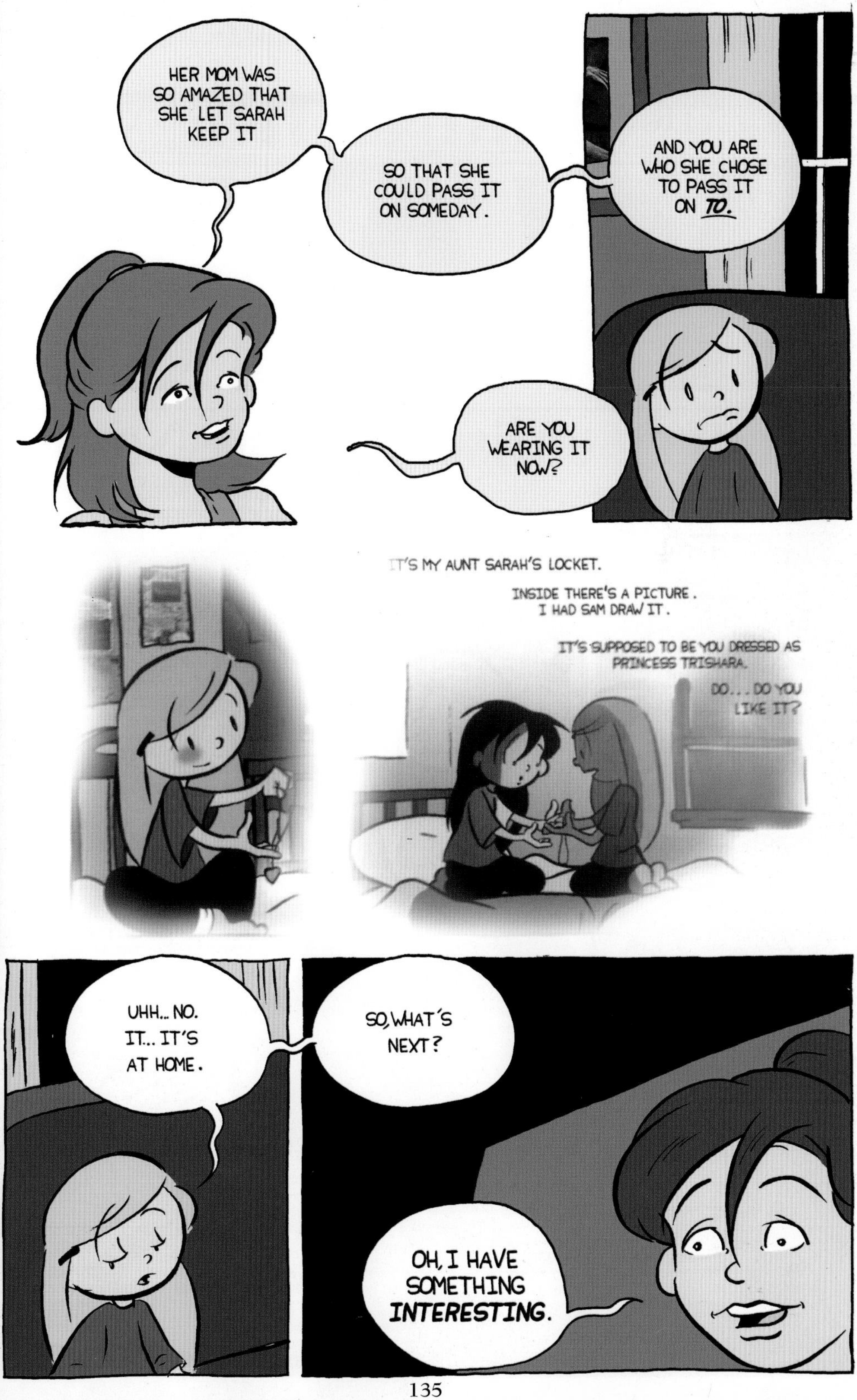
HER MOM WAS SO AMAZED THAT SHE LET SARAH KEEP IT
SO THAT SHE COULD PASS IT ON SOMEDAY.
AND YOU ARE WHO SHE CHOSE TO PASS IT ON TO.
ARE YOU WEARING IT NOW?
IT'S MY AUNT SARAH'S LOCKET.
INSIDE THERE'S A PICTURE. I HAD SAM DRAW IT.
IT'S SUPPOSED TO BE YOU DRESSED AS PRINCESS TRISHARA.
DO... DO YOU LIKE IT?
UHH... NO. IT... IT'S AT HOME.
SO, WHAT'S NEXT?
OH, I HAVE SOMETHING INTERESTING.

CONNERTON EDITION

EXTRA **DURING THE** EXTRA

WAR!

Jerry enlisted in the Navy.

The oldest of the three children, Jerry, was just eighteen when he joined up. He got stationed on a destroyer, the USS Gainard. He never talked much about the war, but he would sometimes tell this one story.... One night, while on patrol in the Pacific, the alarm sounded that another ship, the Wadsworth, had been hit and was on fire and sinking fast. The Gainard was called to rescue the crew and Jerry was one of the men hauling injured sailors off the Wadsworth to safety on the Gainard.

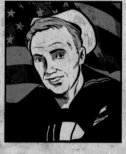

I don't know why the one incident stuck in Jerry's mind more than any other, but it was really the only war story he ever told.

Anyway, one Christmas your father and I had a big dinner with both sides of the family at our place in New York. When Jerry met your grandfather McBride and found out that he too was an ex-Navy man, he told his story. The look on your grandfather's face was pure amazement. He was one of the injured men that Jerry had pulled to safety. We couldn't believe that all those years after the fact, these two men were reconnected through us.

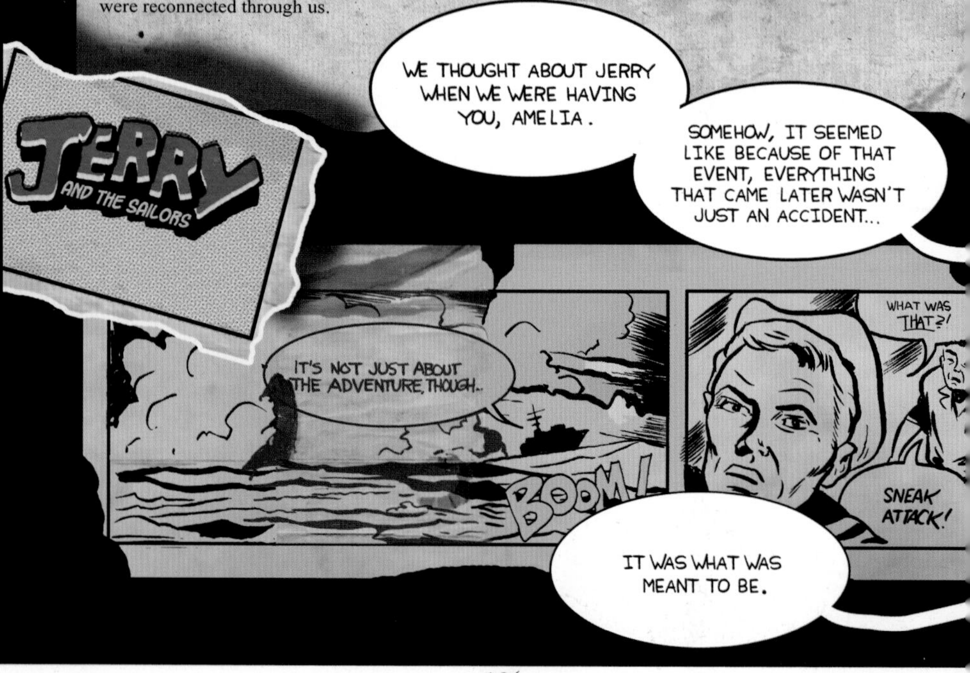

WE THOUGHT ABOUT JERRY WHEN WE WERE HAVING YOU, AMELIA.
SOMEHOW, IT SEEMED LIKE BECAUSE OF THAT EVENT, EVERYTHING THAT CAME LATER WASN'T JUST AN ACCIDENT...
JERRY AND THE SAILORS
IT'S NOT JUST ABOUT THE ADVENTURE, THOUGH...
BOOM!
WHAT WAS THAT?!
SNEAK ATTACK!
IT WAS WHAT WAS MEANT TO BE.

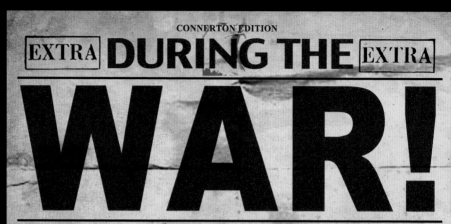

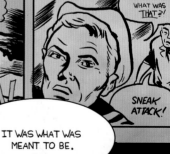

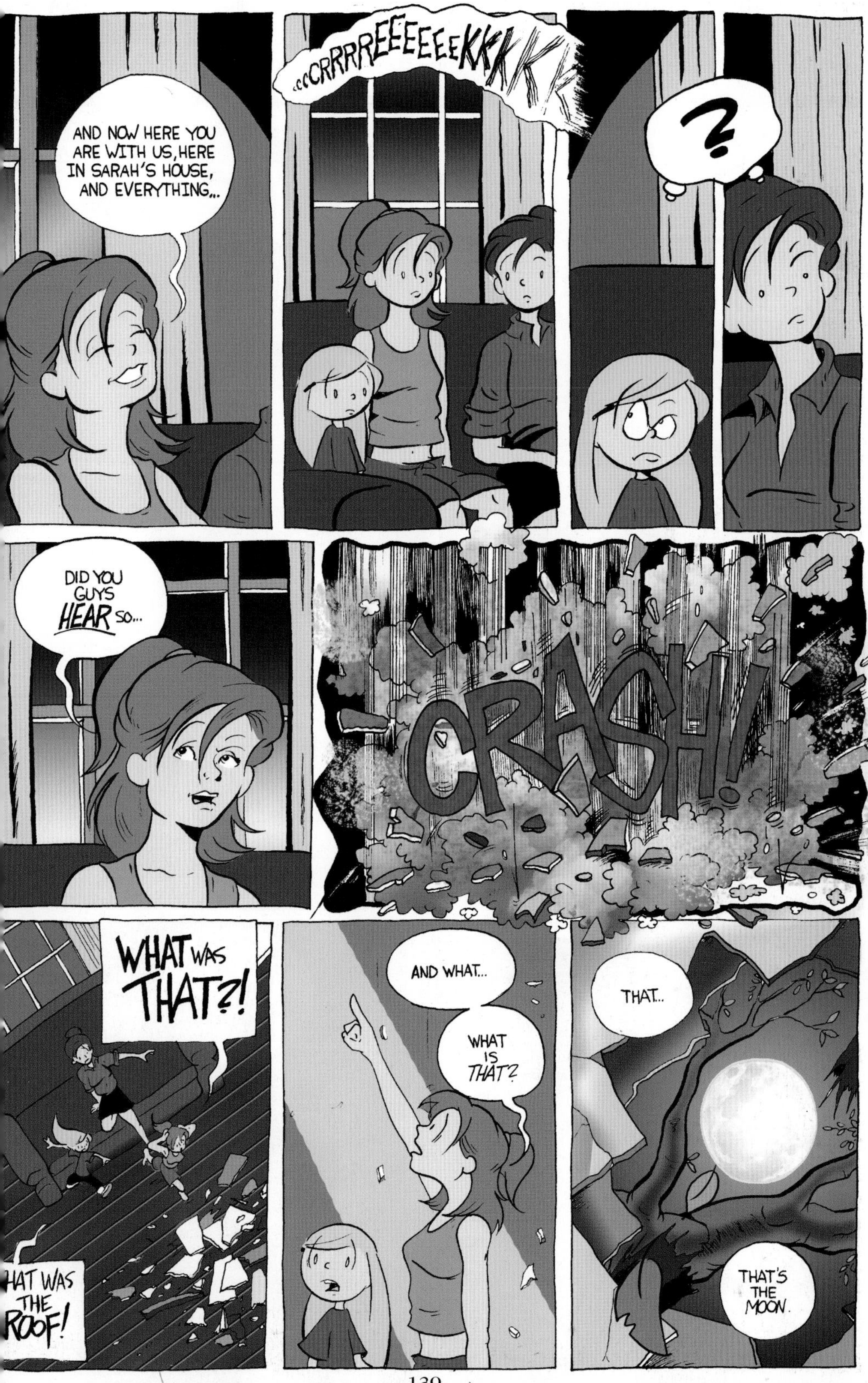
AND NOW HERE YOU ARE WITH US, HERE IN SARAH'S HOUSE, AND EVERYTHING...
cccCRRRREEEEEEEKKKKK
?
DID YOU GUYS HEAR SO...
CRASH!
WHAT WAS THAT?!
HAT WAS THE ROOF!
AND WHAT...
WHAT IS THAT?
THAT..
THAT'S THE MOON.

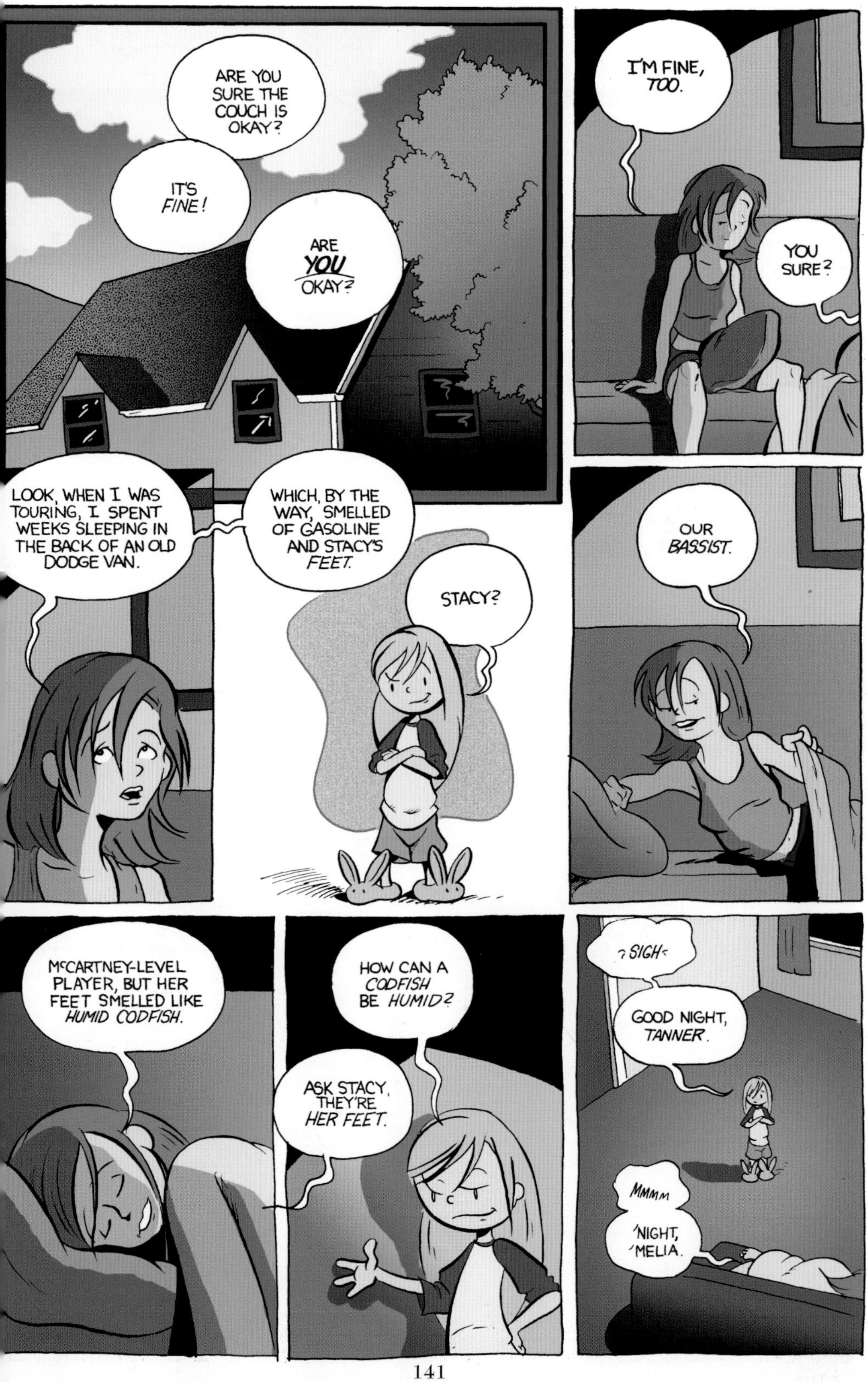
ARE YOU SURE THE COUCH IS OKAY?
IT'S FINE!
ARE YOU OKAY?
I'M FINE, TOO.
YOU SURE?
LOOK, WHEN I WAS TOURING, I SPENT WEEKS SLEEPING IN THE BACK OF AN OLD DODGE VAN.
WHICH, BY THE WAY, SMELLED OF GASOLINE AND STACY'S FEET.
STACY?
OUR BASSIST.
McCARTNEY-LEVEL PLAYER, BUT HER FEET SMELLED LIKE HUMID CODFISH.
HOW CAN A CODFISH BE HUMID?
ASK STACY, THEY'RE HER FEET.
SIGH
GOOD NIGHT, TANNER.
MMMM
'NIGHT, 'MELIA.

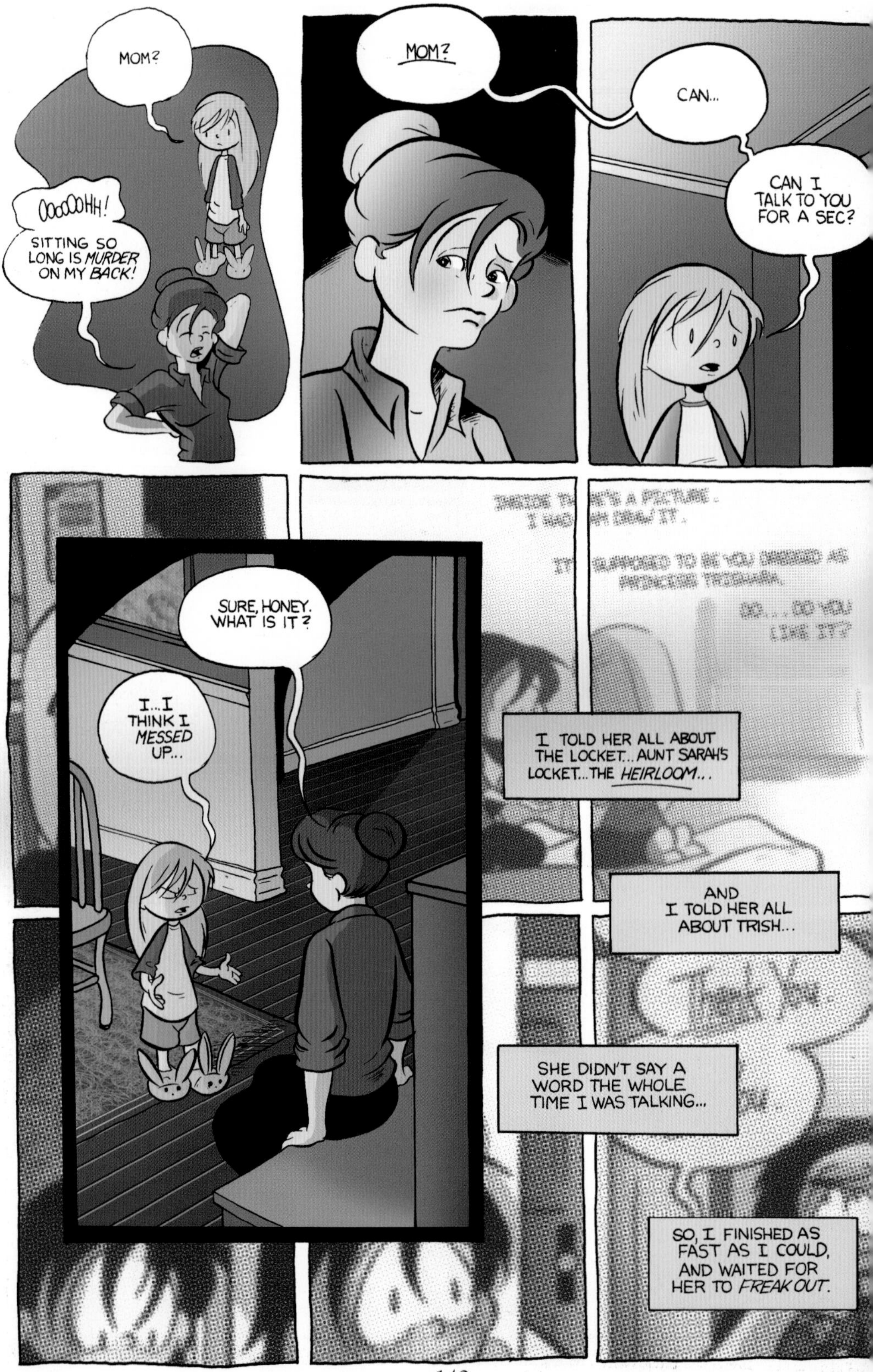

MOM?
OOOOOOHH!
SITTING SO LONG IS *MURDER* ON MY *BACK*!
MOM?
CAN...
CAN I TALK TO YOU FOR A SEC?
SURE, HONEY. WHAT IS IT?
I...I THINK I *MESSED* UP...
I TOLD HER ALL ABOUT THE LOCKET... AUNT SARAH'S LOCKET... THE *HEIRLOOM*...
AND I TOLD HER ALL ABOUT TRISH...
SHE DIDN'T SAY A WORD THE WHOLE TIME I WAS TALKING...
SO, I FINISHED AS FAST AS I COULD, AND WAITED FOR HER TO *FREAK OUT*.

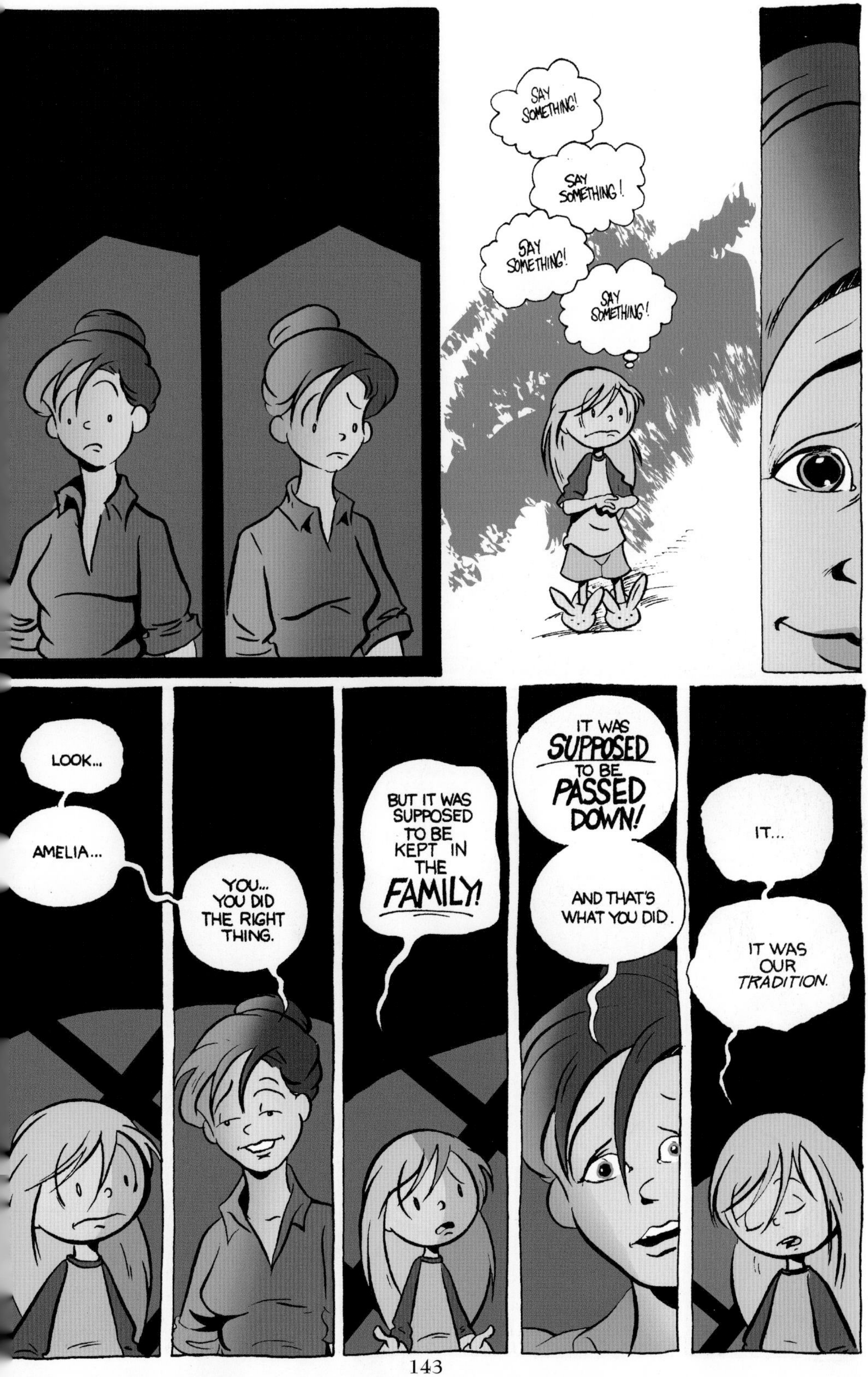
SAY SOMETHING!
SAY SOMETHING!
SAY SOMETHING!
SAY SOMETHING!
LOOK...
AMELIA...
YOU... YOU DID THE RIGHT THING.
BUT IT WAS SUPPOSED TO BE KEPT IN THE FAMILY!
IT WAS SUPPOSED TO BE PASSED DOWN!
AND THAT'S WHAT YOU DID.
IT...
IT WAS OUR TRADITION.

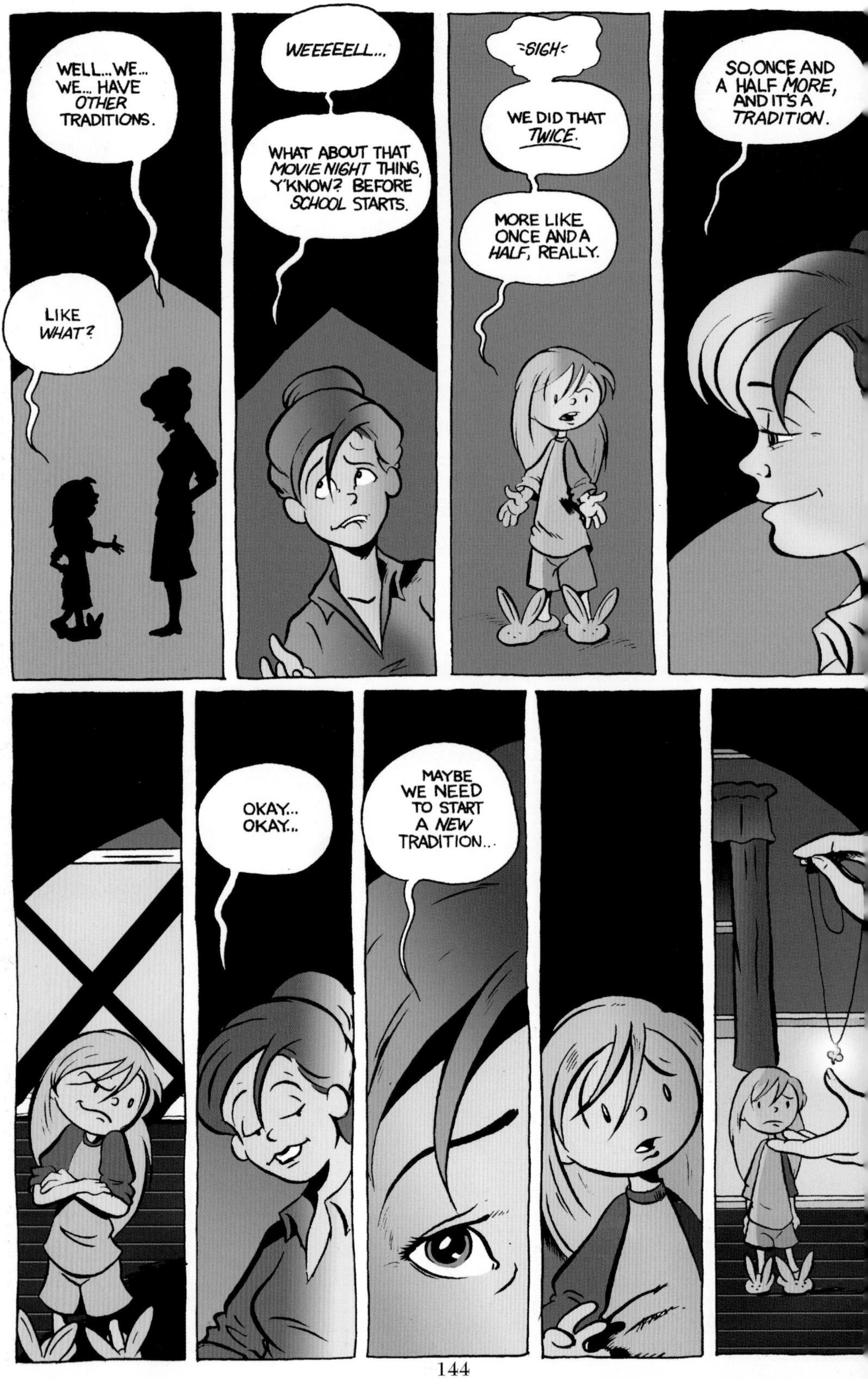
WELL... WE... WE... HAVE OTHER TRADITIONS.
LIKE WHAT?
WEEEEELL...
WHAT ABOUT THAT MOVIE NIGHT THING, Y'KNOW? BEFORE SCHOOL STARTS.
=SIGH=
WE DID THAT TWICE.
MORE LIKE ONCE AND A HALF, REALLY.
SO, ONCE AND A HALF MORE, AND IT'S A TRADITION.
OKAY... OKAY...
MAYBE WE NEED TO START A NEW TRADITION...

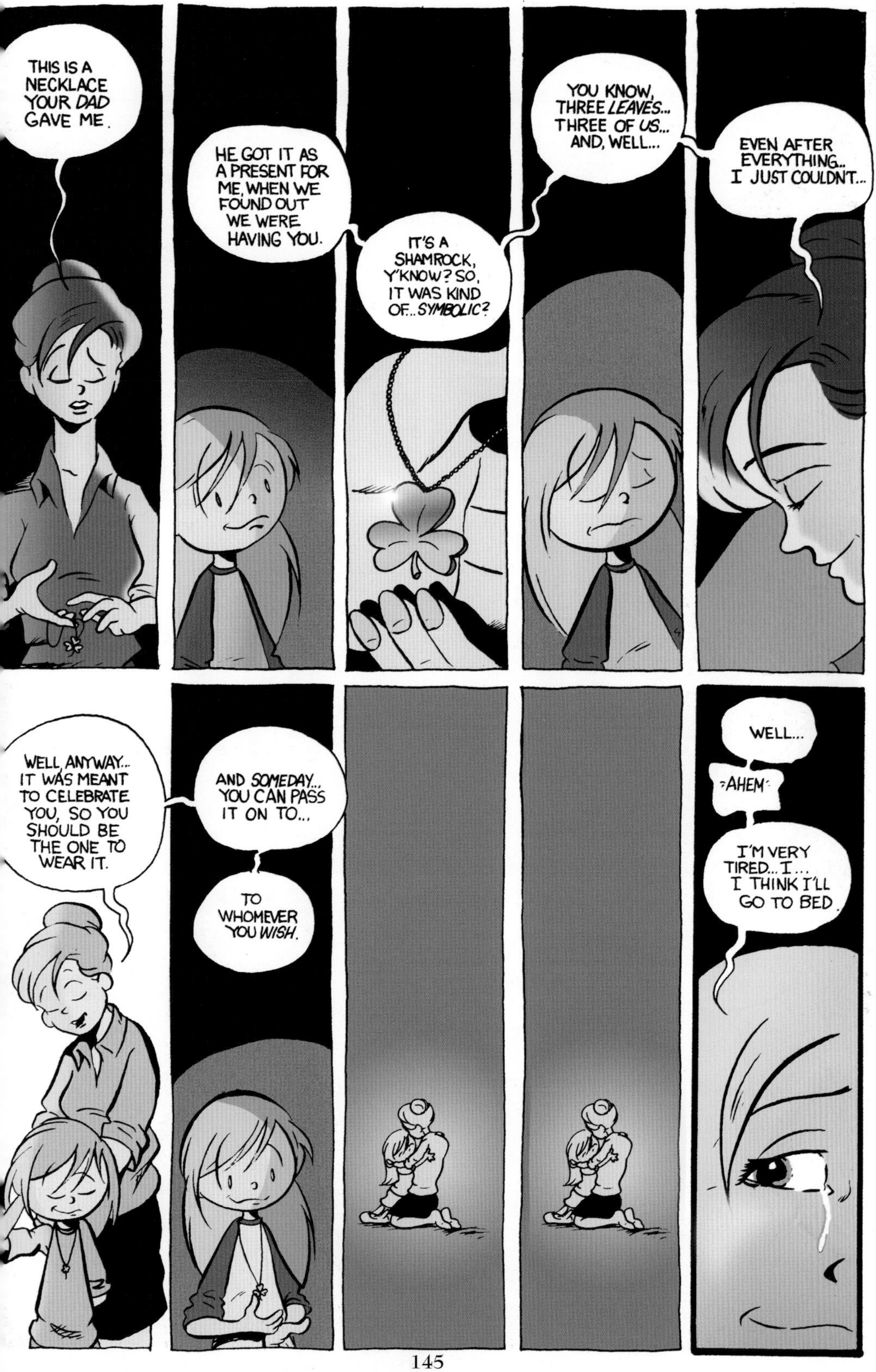
THIS IS A NECKLACE YOUR *DAD* GAVE ME.
HE GOT IT AS A PRESENT FOR ME, WHEN WE FOUND OUT WE WERE HAVING YOU.
IT'S A SHAMROCK, Y'KNOW? SO, IT WAS KIND OF... *SYMBOLIC?*
YOU KNOW, THREE *LEAVES*... THREE OF *US*... AND, WELL...
EVEN AFTER EVERYTHING... I JUST COULDN'T...
WELL, ANYWAY... IT WAS MEANT TO CELEBRATE YOU, SO YOU SHOULD BE THE ONE TO WEAR IT.
AND *SOMEDAY*... YOU CAN PASS IT ON TO...
TO WHOMEVER YOU *WISH*.
WELL...
AHEM
I'M VERY TIRED... I... I THINK I'LL GO TO BED.

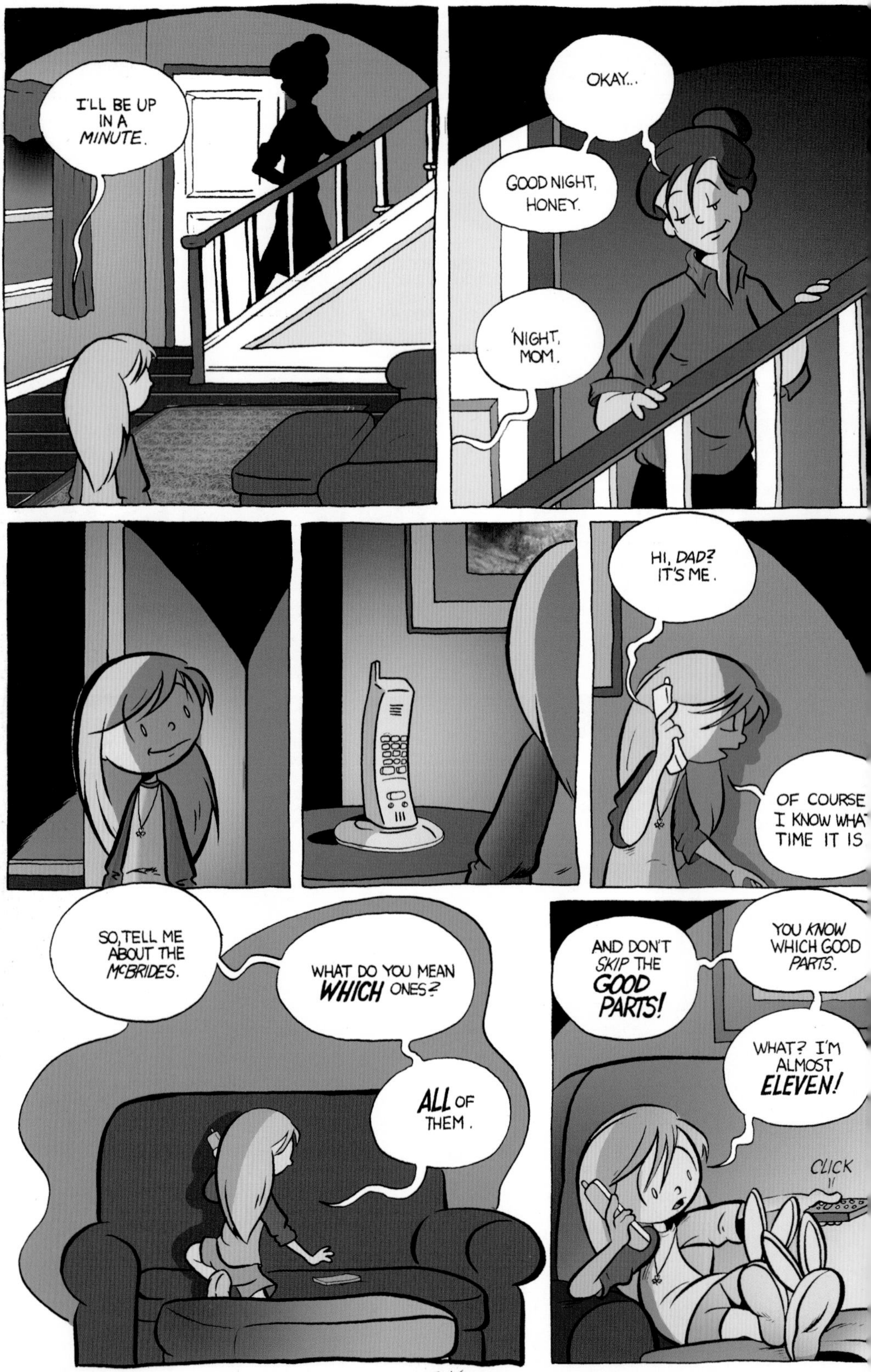
I'LL BE UP IN A *MINUTE*.
OKAY...
GOOD NIGHT, HONEY.
'NIGHT, MOM.
HI, *DAD?* IT'S ME.
OF COURSE I KNOW WHAT TIME IT IS
SO, TELL ME ABOUT THE *McBRIDES*.
WHAT DO YOU MEAN **WHICH** ONES?
ALL OF THEM.
AND DON'T *SKIP* THE **GOOD PARTS!**
YOU *KNOW* WHICH GOOD *PARTS*.
WHAT? I'M ALMOST **ELEVEN!**
CLICK

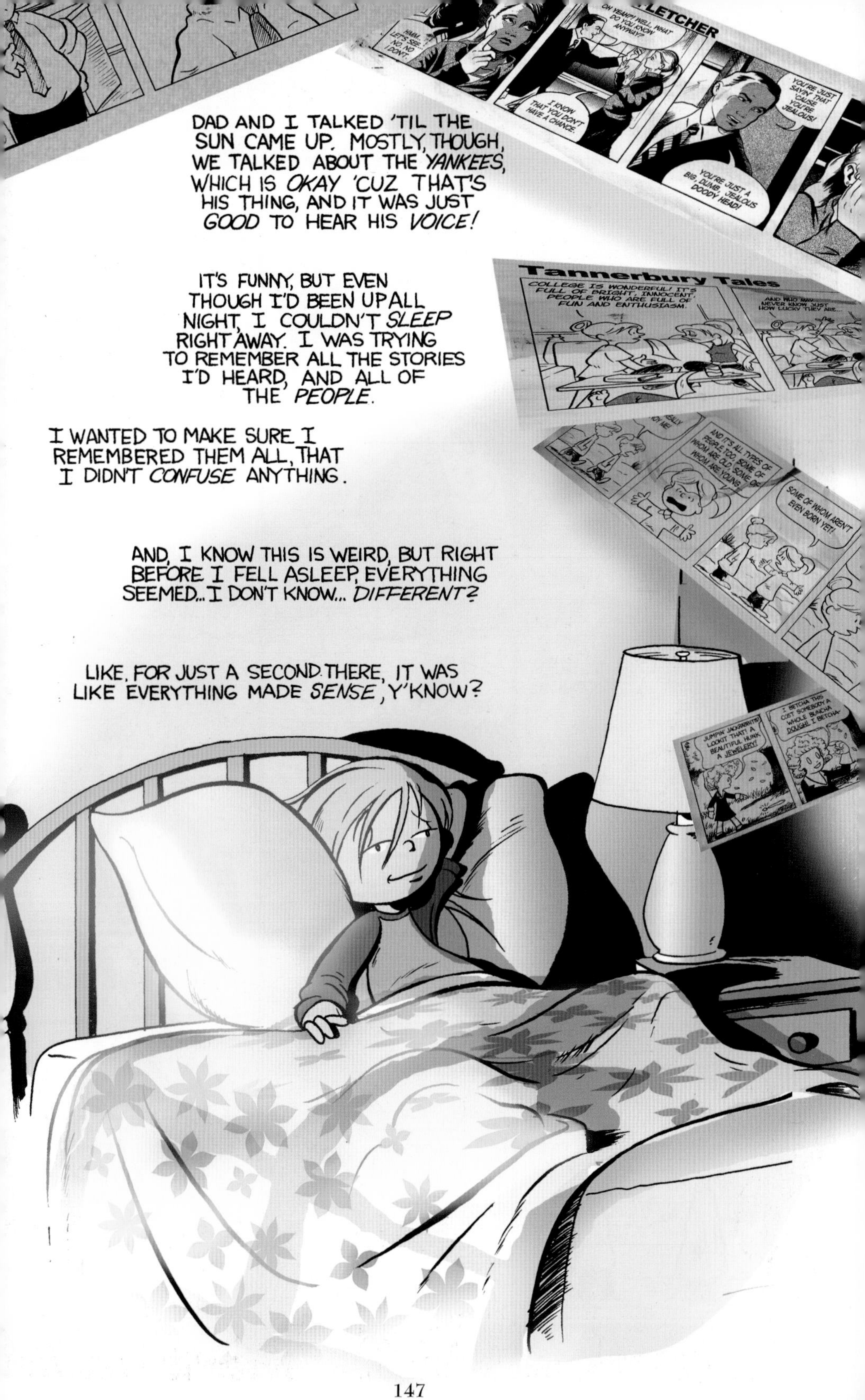

DAD AND I TALKED 'TIL THE SUN CAME UP. MOSTLY, THOUGH, WE TALKED ABOUT THE *YANKEES*, WHICH IS *OKAY* 'CUZ THAT'S HIS THING, AND IT WAS JUST *GOOD* TO HEAR HIS *VOICE!*

IT'S FUNNY, BUT EVEN THOUGH I'D BEEN UP ALL NIGHT, I COULDN'T *SLEEP* RIGHT AWAY. I WAS TRYING TO REMEMBER ALL THE STORIES I'D HEARD, AND ALL OF THE *PEOPLE.*

I WANTED TO MAKE SURE I REMEMBERED THEM ALL, THAT I DIDN'T *CONFUSE* ANYTHING.

AND, I KNOW THIS IS WEIRD, BUT RIGHT BEFORE I FELL ASLEEP, EVERYTHING SEEMED... I DON'T KNOW... *DIFFERENT?*

LIKE, FOR JUST A SECOND THERE, IT WAS LIKE EVERYTHING MADE *SENSE*, Y'KNOW?

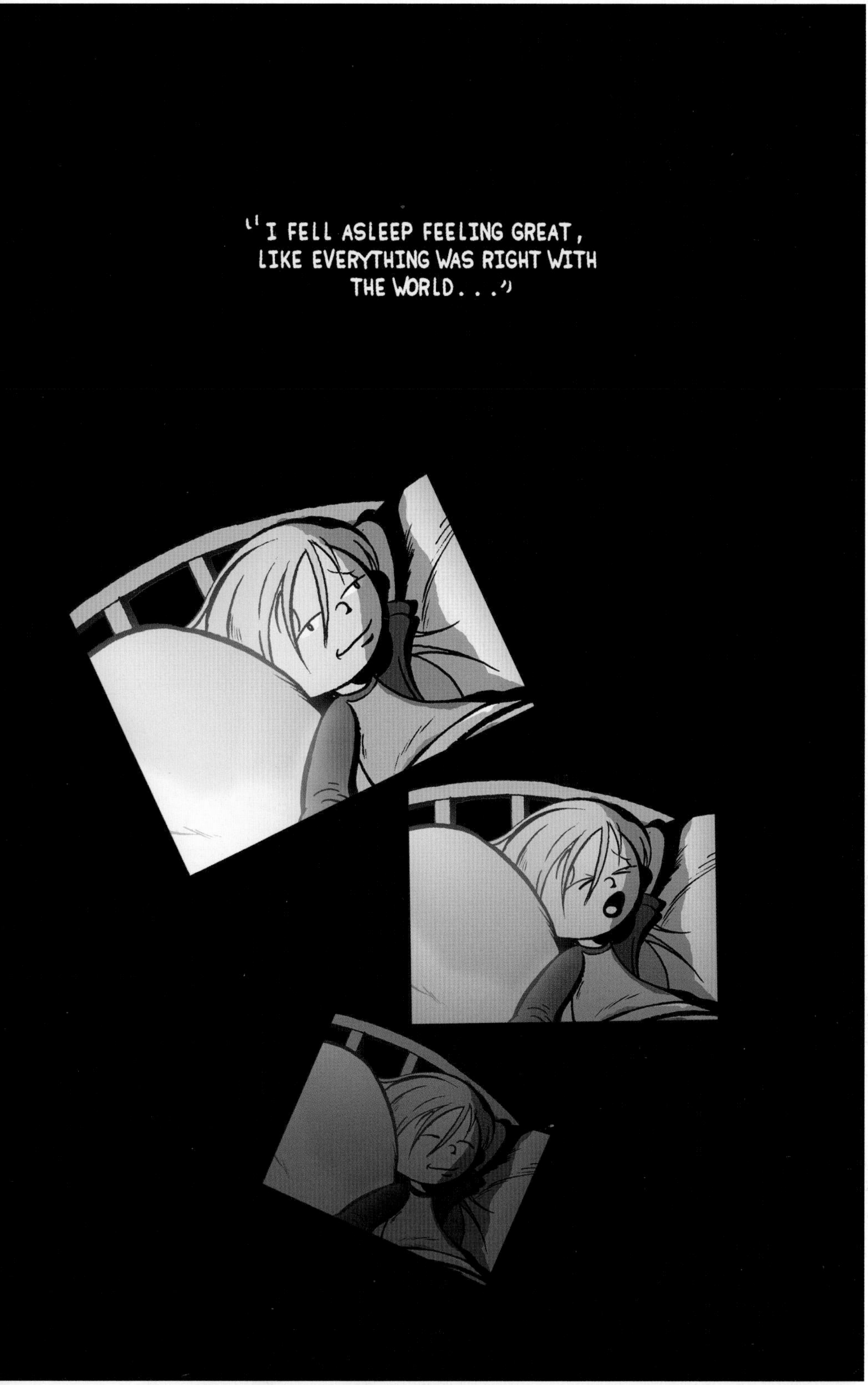
"I FELL ASLEEP FEELING GREAT, LIKE EVERYTHING WAS RIGHT WITH THE WORLD..."

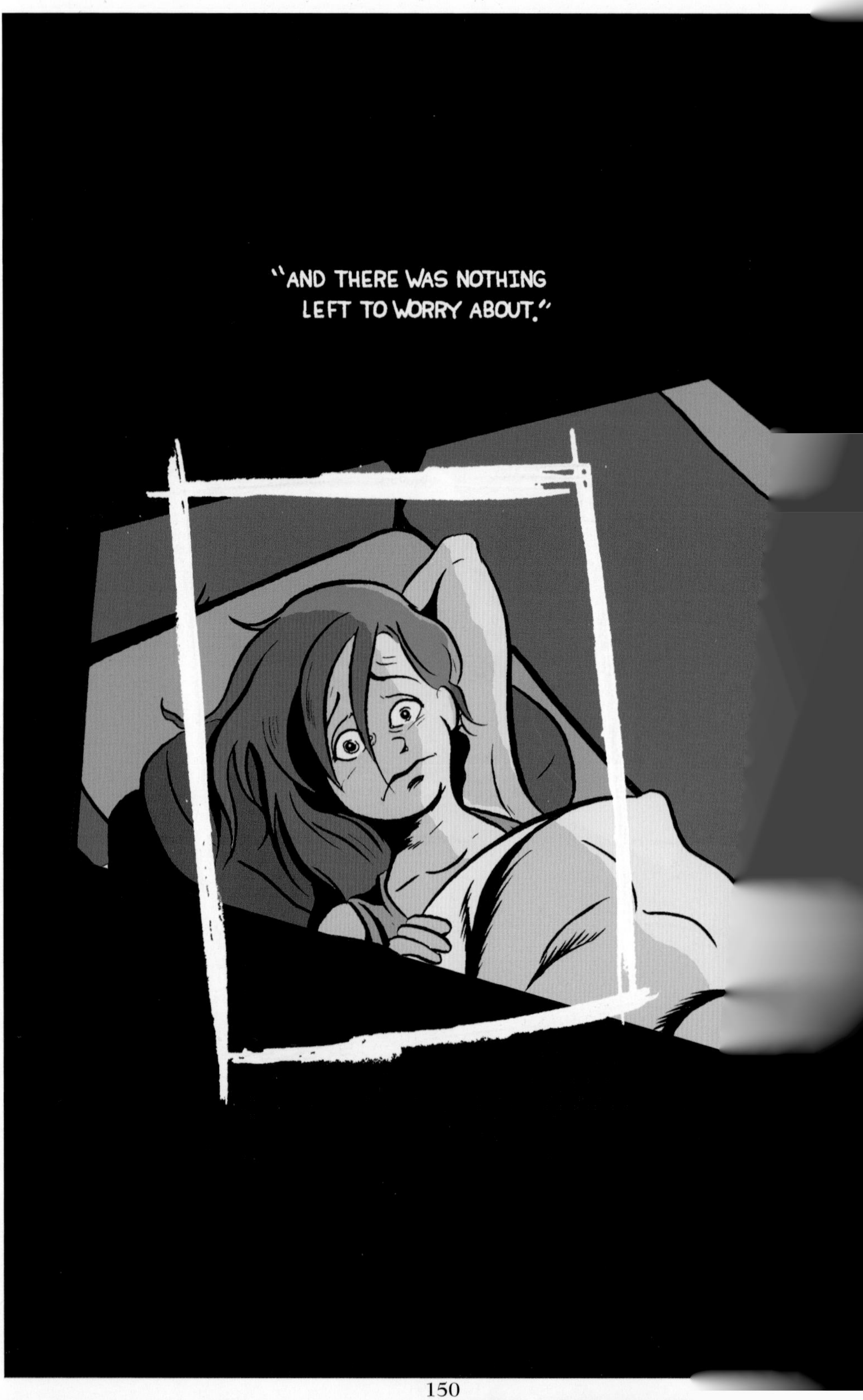
"AND THERE WAS NOTHING LEFT TO WORRY ABOUT."

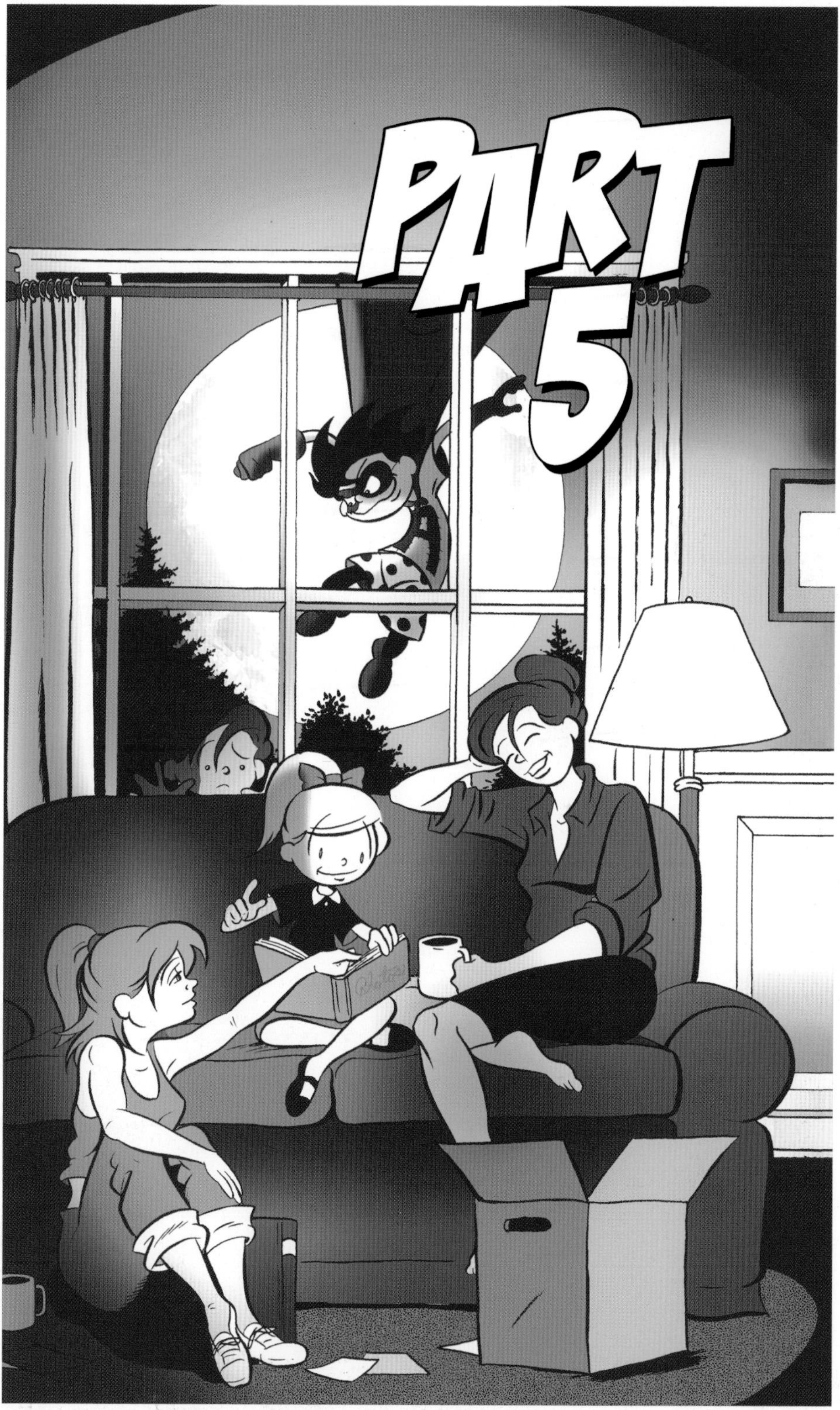
PART 5

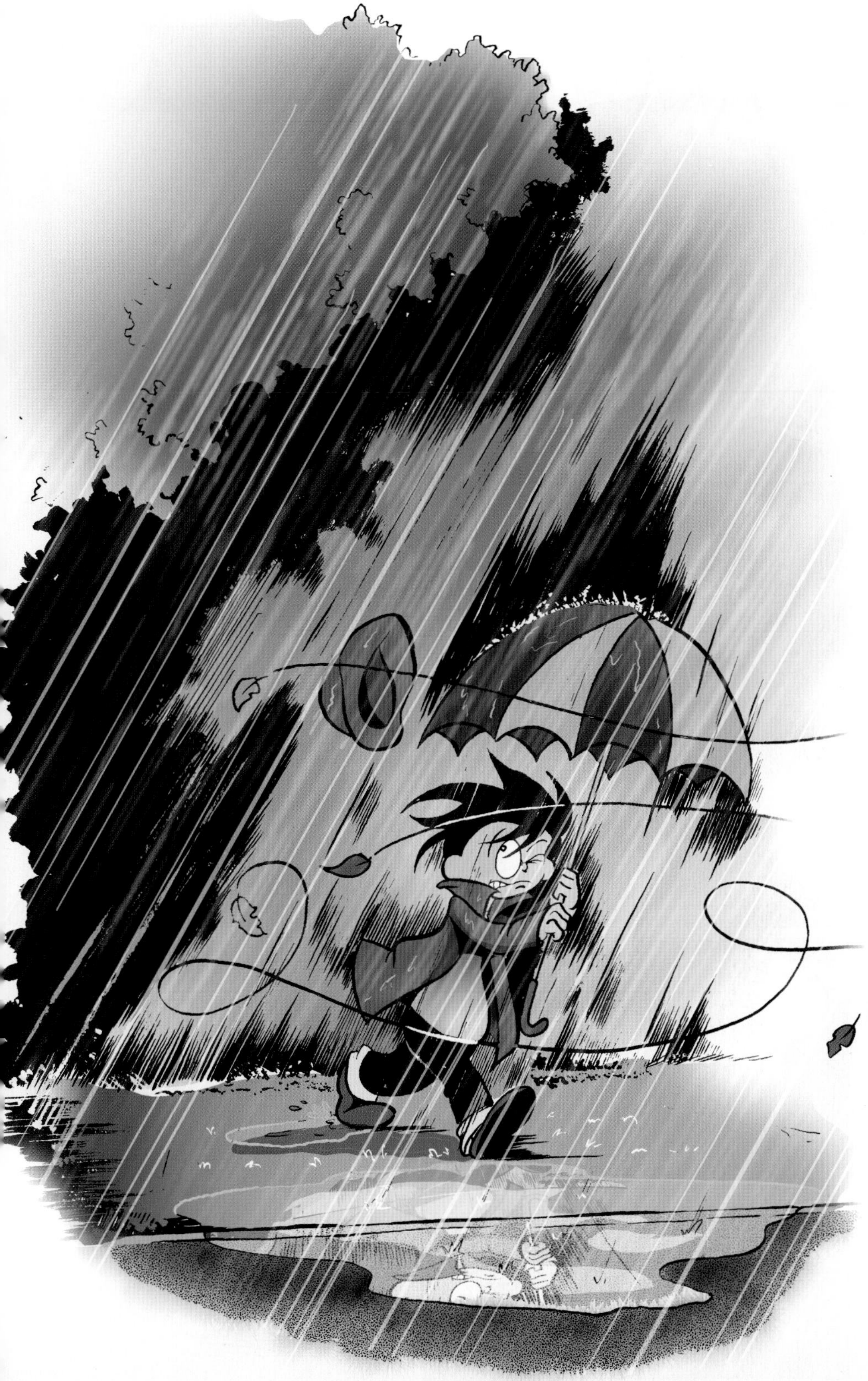

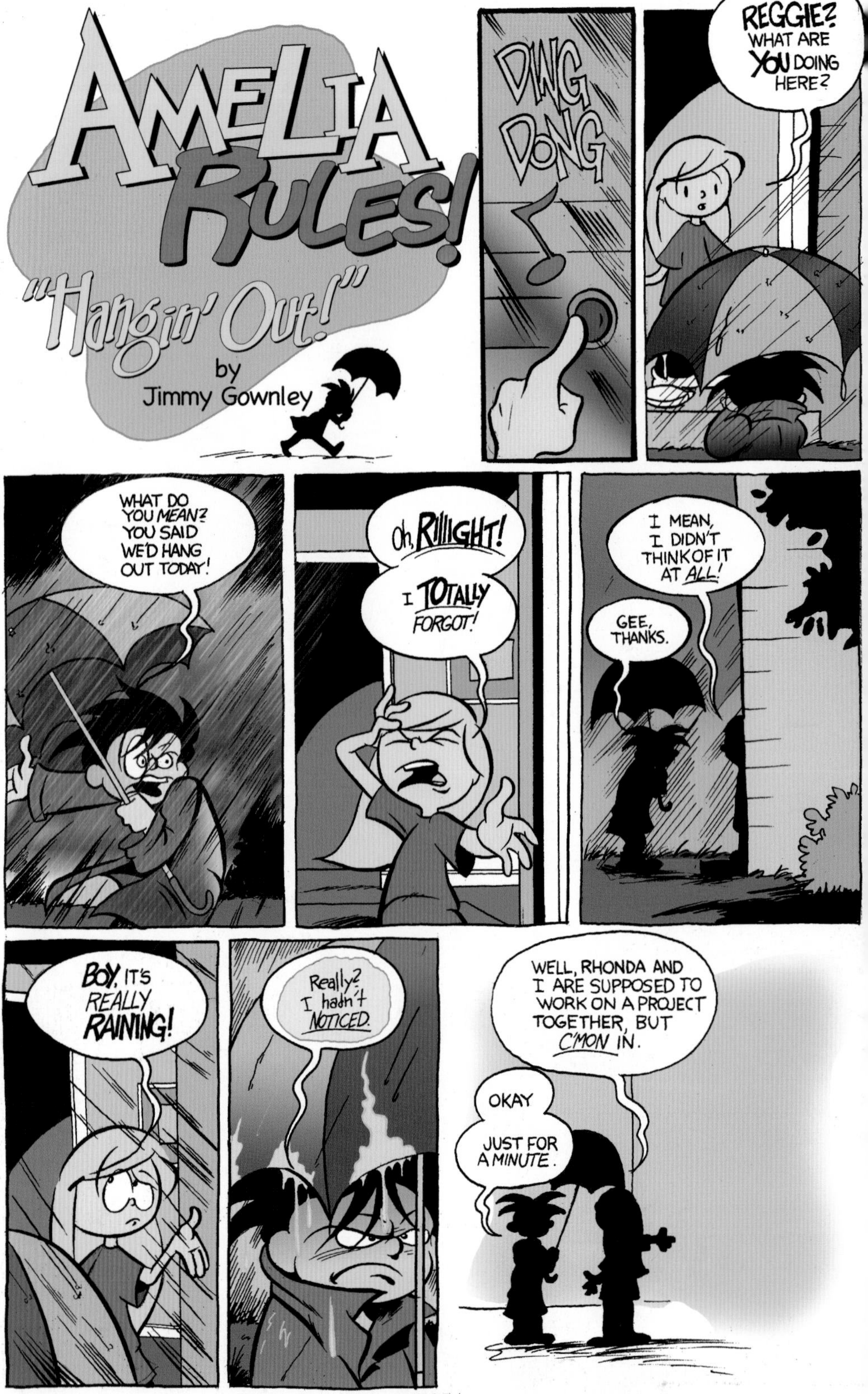
AMELIA RULES!
"Hangin' Out!"
by
Jimmy Gownley
DING DONG
REGGIE? WHAT ARE YOU DOING HERE?
WHAT DO YOU MEAN? YOU SAID WE'D HANG OUT TODAY!
Oh, RIIIIGHT!
I TOTALLY FORGOT!
I MEAN, I DIDN'T THINK OF IT AT ALL!
GEE, THANKS.
BOY, IT'S REALLY RAINING!
Really? I hadn't NOTICED.
WELL, RHONDA AND I ARE SUPPOSED TO WORK ON A PROJECT TOGETHER, BUT C'MON IN.
OKAY
JUST FOR A MINUTE.

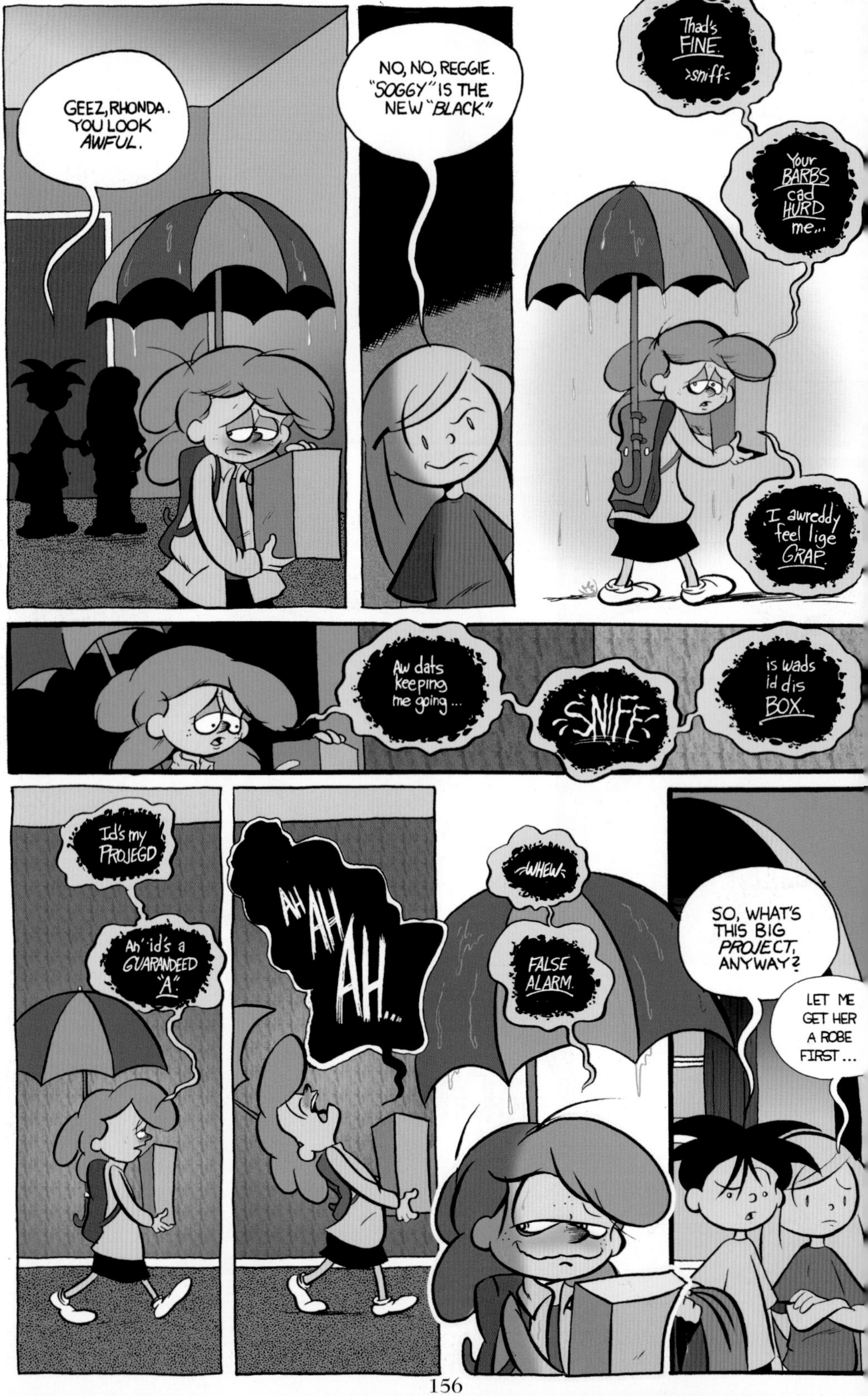
GEEZ, RHONDA. YOU LOOK AWFUL.
NO, NO, REGGIE. "SOGGY" IS THE NEW "BLACK."
Thad's FINE. >sniff<
Your BARBS cad HURD me...
I awreddy feel lige GRAP.
Aw dats keeping me going...
SNIFF
is wads id dis BOX.
Id's my PROJEGD
An' id's a GUARANDEED "A".
AH AH AH...
WHEW
FALSE ALARM.
SO, WHAT'S THIS BIG PROJECT, ANYWAY?
LET ME GET HER A ROBE FIRST...

"SHE'S DRIPPIER THAN YOU ARE."

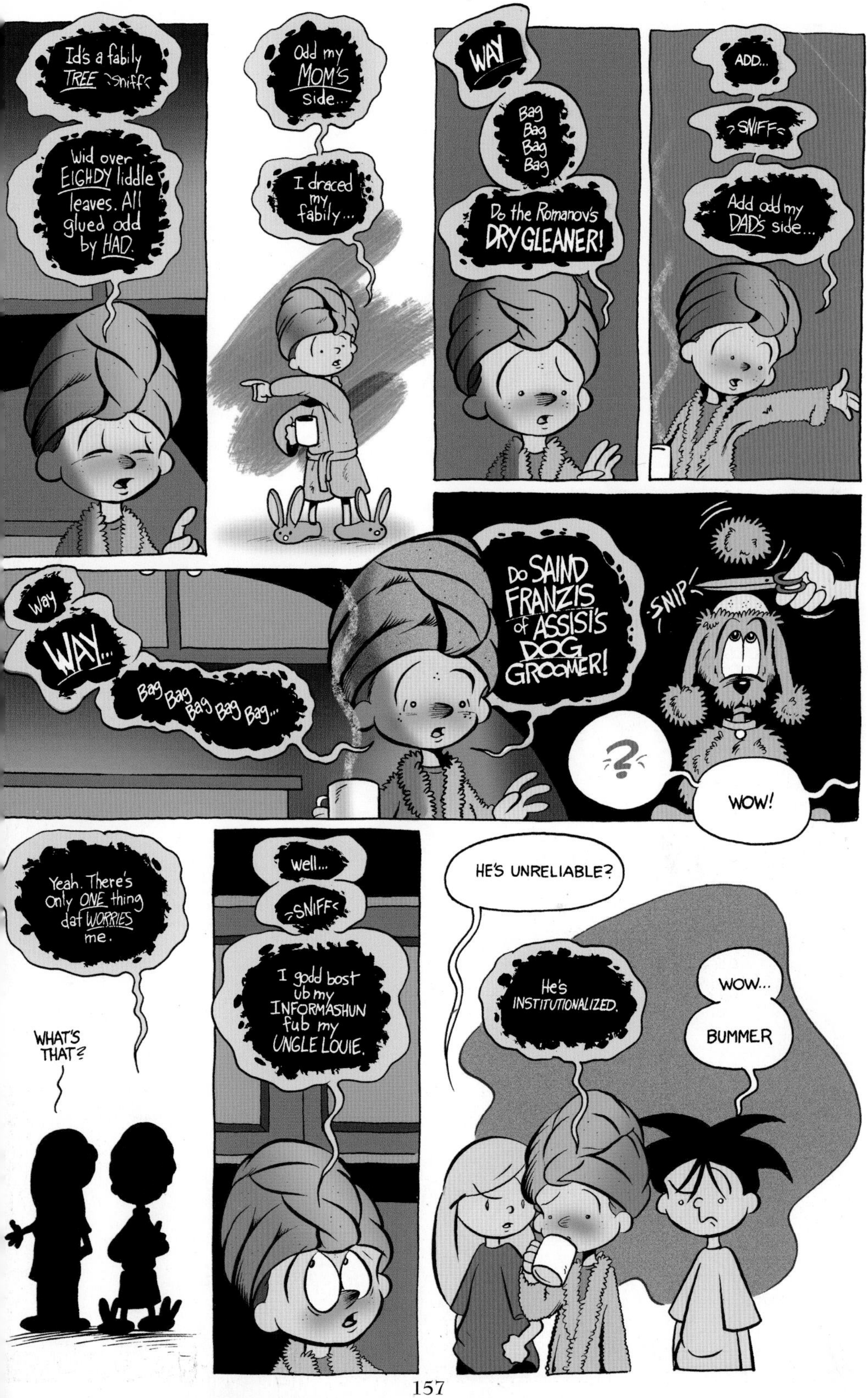

Id's a fabily TREE >sniff<
Wid over EIGHDY liddle leaves. All glued odd by HAD.
Odd my MOM'S side...
I draced my fabily...
WAY
Bag Bag Bag Bag
Do the Romanov's DRY GLEANER!
ADD...
>SNIFF<
Add odd my DAD'S side...
Way
WAY...
Bag Bag Bag Bag Bag...
Do SAIND FRANZIS of ASSISI'S DOG GROOMER!
SNIP
?
WOW!
Yeah. There's only ONE thing dat WORRIES me.
WHAT'S THAT?
Well...
>SNIFF<
I godd bost ub my INFORMASHUN fub my UNGLE LOUIE.
HE'S UNRELIABLE?
He's INSTITUTIONALIZED.
WOW...
BUMMER

158

159

Hangin' Out

Hangtavious Outacus–More commonly known as "Hanging Out"–is a 20th Century American invention, in the vein of "Bummin' Around," or "Chillin'." Although Hanging Out at first appea rather simple, in fact, its rules are myriad.

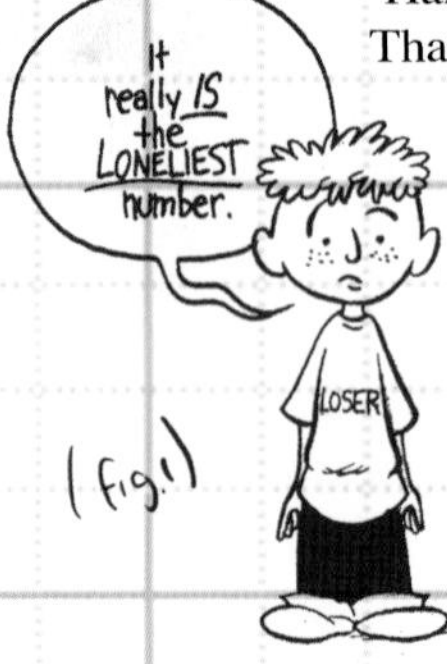
It really IS the LONELIEST number.
LOSER
(fig.1)

Hanging out cannot be done alone. That is called "moping" or "Being a Pariah," and neither one is particularly attractive. (fig. 1)

Any group containing two to five people may engage in Hanging Out, so long as doing nothing is the primary activity. For example, "Hanging Out and talking" is acceptable, while "Hanging Out and building shelters for Habitat for Humanity" is not. Snacks are not required, but are highly recommended. (fig. 2)

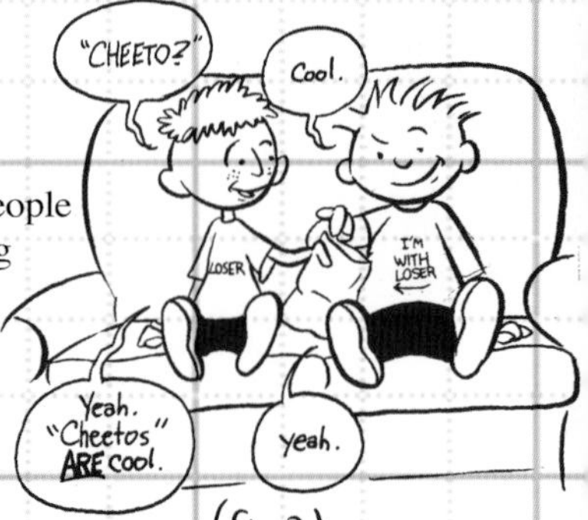
"CHEETO?"
Cool.
LOSER
I'M WITH LOSER
Yeah. "Cheetos" ARE cool.
yeah.
(fig.2)

There are strict restrictions on how many people may Hang Out, and how often the hanging may occur. For example, more than five people is now a Party, and while it may seem like you can Hang Out at a Party, you can't because the music is too loud, and let's face it, there's no way you like more than five people anyway. (fig. 3)

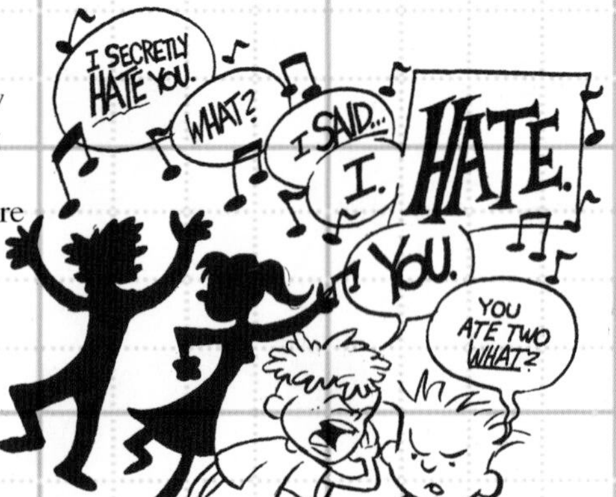
I SECRETLY HATE YOU.
WHAT?
I SAID...
I.
HATE.
YOU.
YOU ATE TWO WHAT?
(fig.3)

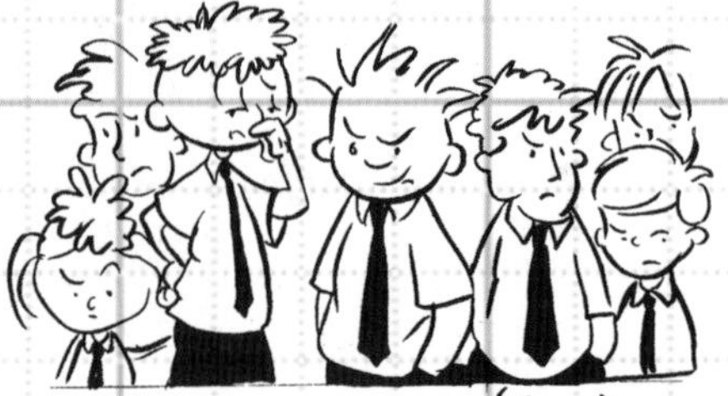
(fig.4)

Here is where the slippery slope gets even slipperier.

More than five people more than once a month is no longer a party, but a club (fig. 4). This is fine, but you may be expected to pay dues or pretend to be interested in other people's boats and/or record collections. More than once a WEEK and it becomes a cult. It is definitely advisable NOT to join a cult, but if you feel you must, remember that it is better to be the leader than the guy who collects the fingers. (fig. 5)

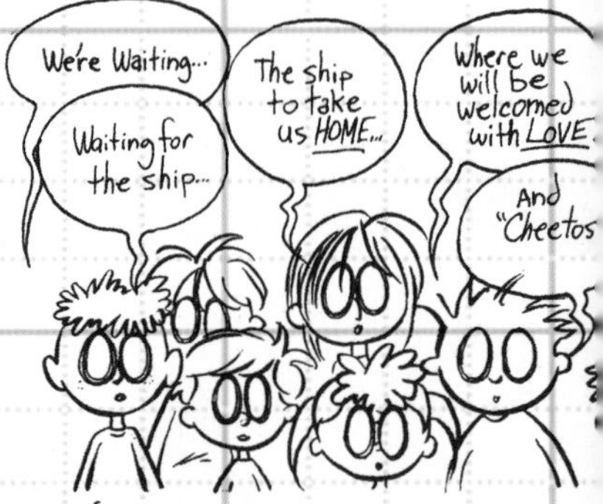
We're Waiting...
Waiting for the ship...
The ship to take us HOME...
Where we will be welcomed with LOVE.
And "Cheetos"
(fig5)

161

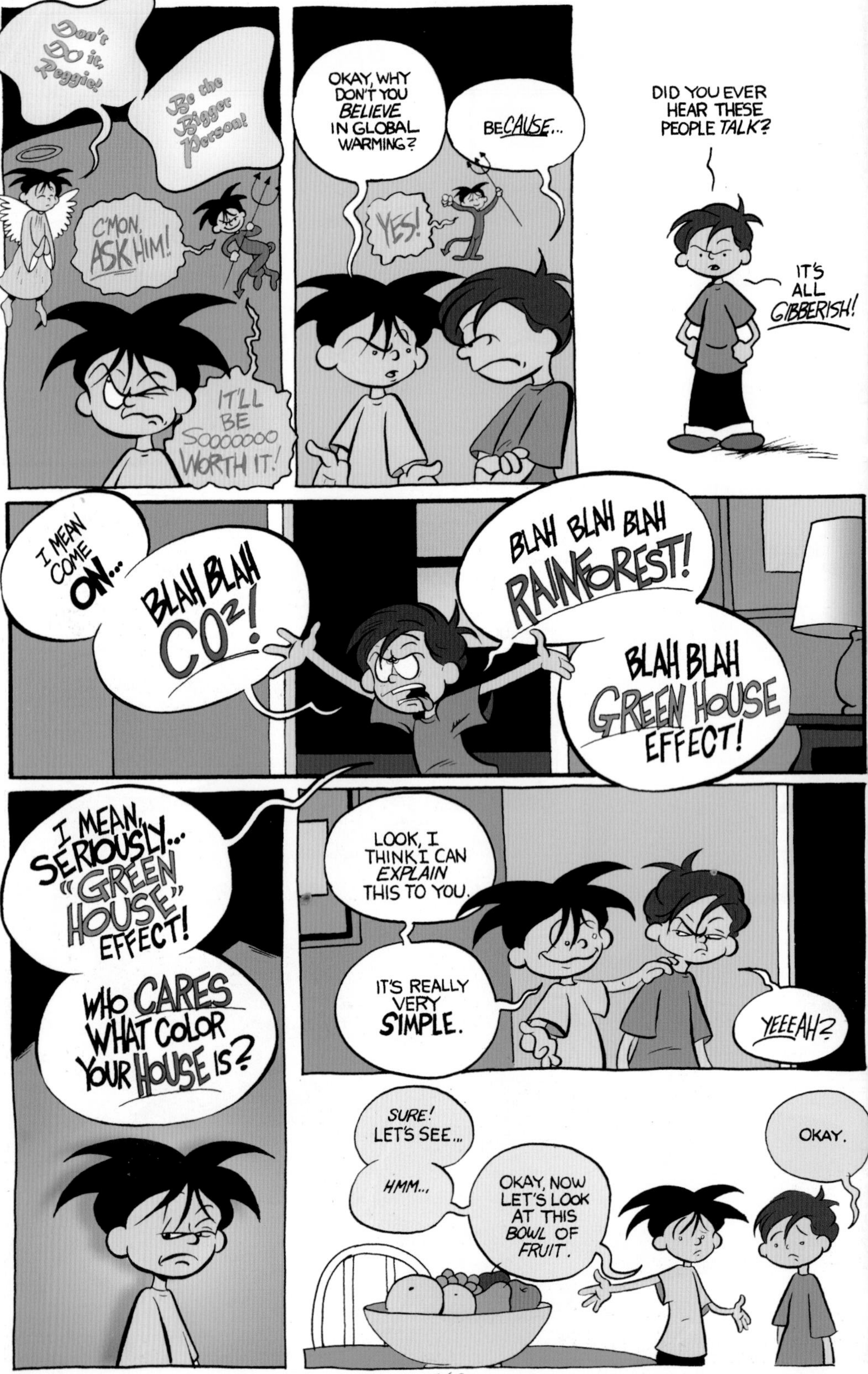
Don't DO it, Reggie!
Be the Bigger Person!
C'MON, ASK HIM!
IT'LL BE SOOOOOOO WORTH IT!
OKAY, WHY DON'T YOU BELIEVE IN GLOBAL WARMING?
YES!
BECAUSE...
DID YOU EVER HEAR THESE PEOPLE TALK?
IT'S ALL GIBBERISH!
I MEAN COME ON...
BLAH BLAH CO2!
BLAH BLAH BLAH RAINFOREST!
BLAH BLAH GREEN HOUSE EFFECT!
I MEAN, SERIOUSLY... "GREEN HOUSE" EFFECT!
WHO CARES WHAT COLOR YOUR HOUSE IS?
LOOK, I THINK I CAN EXPLAIN THIS TO YOU.
IT'S REALLY VERY SIMPLE.
YEEEAH?
SURE! LET'S SEE...
HMM...
OKAY, NOW LET'S LOOK AT THIS BOWL OF FRUIT.
OKAY.

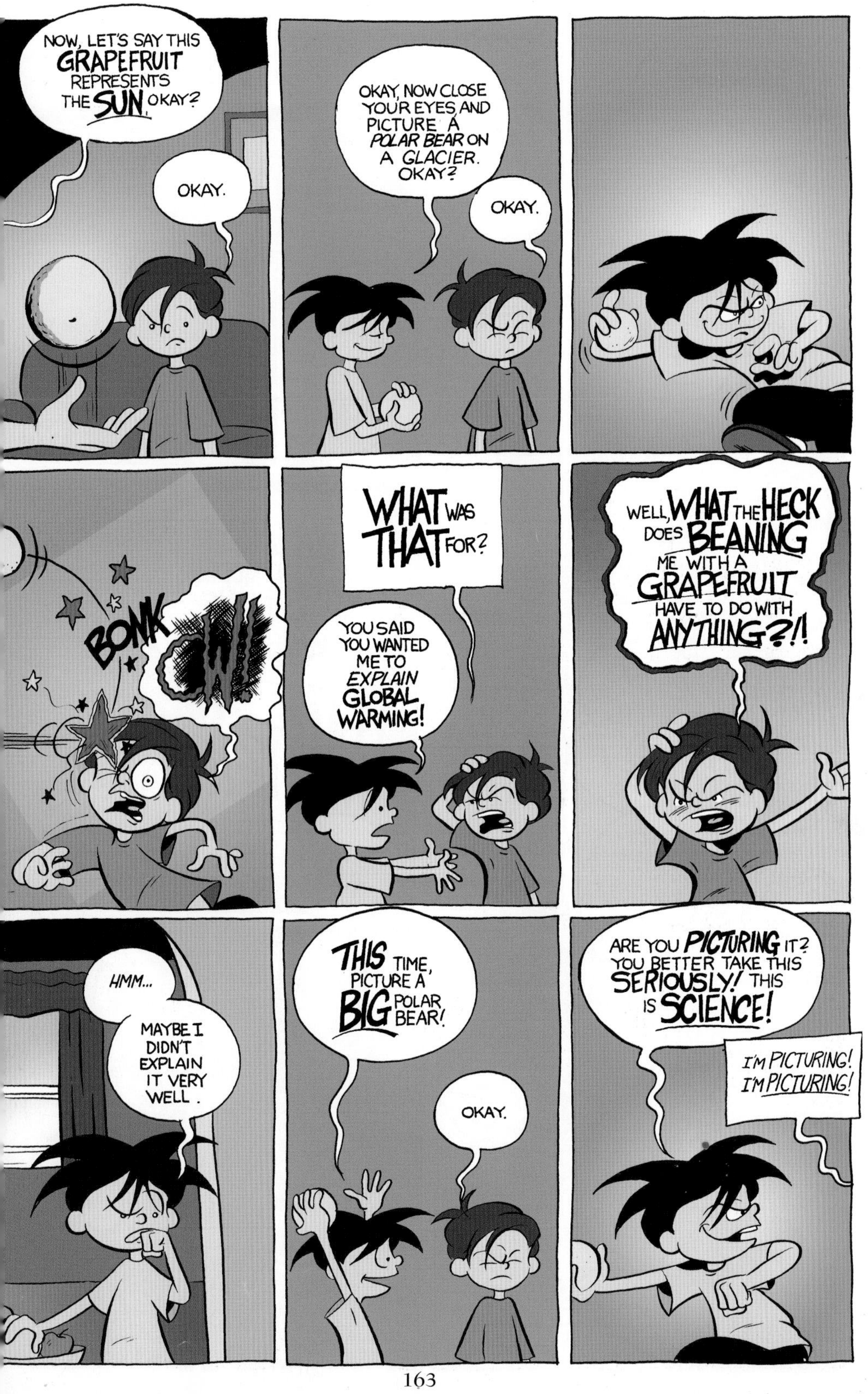
NOW, LET'S SAY THIS GRAPEFRUIT REPRESENTS THE SUN, OKAY?
OKAY.
OKAY, NOW CLOSE YOUR EYES AND PICTURE A POLAR BEAR ON A GLACIER. OKAY?
OKAY.
BONK
OW!!
WHAT WAS THAT FOR?
YOU SAID YOU WANTED ME TO EXPLAIN GLOBAL WARMING!
WELL, WHAT THE HECK DOES BEANING ME WITH A GRAPEFRUIT HAVE TO DO WITH ANYTHING?!!
HMM...
MAYBE I DIDN'T EXPLAIN IT VERY WELL.
THIS TIME, PICTURE A BIG POLAR BEAR!
OKAY.
ARE YOU PICTURING IT? YOU BETTER TAKE THIS SERIOUSLY! THIS IS SCIENCE!
I'M PICTURING! I'M PICTURING!

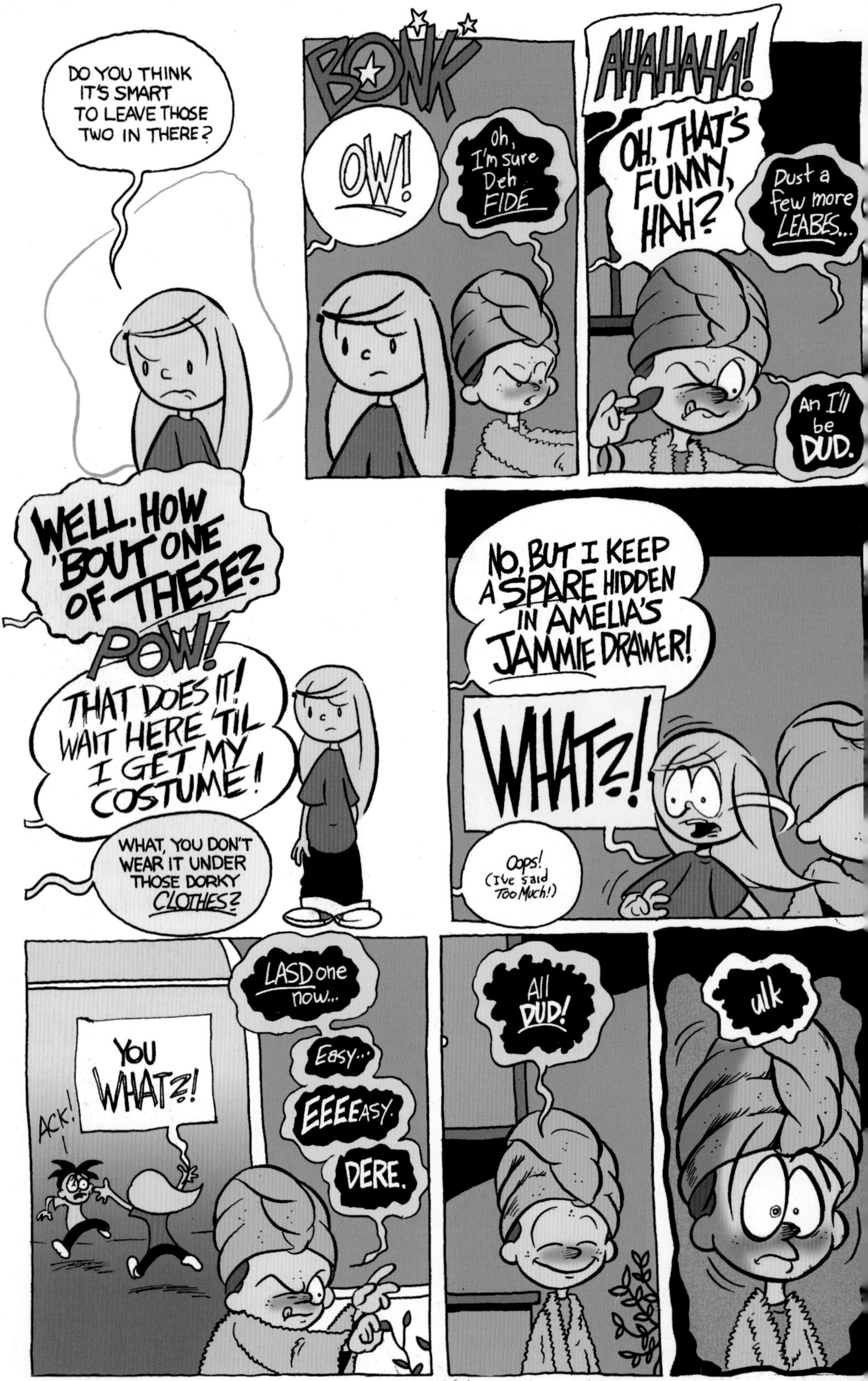

DO YOU THINK IT'S SMART TO LEAVE THOSE TWO IN THERE?
BONK
OW!
Oh, I'm sure Deh FIDE
AHAHAHA!
OH, THAT'S FUNNY, HAH?
Dust a few more LEABES...
An I'll be DUD.
WELL, HOW 'BOUT ONE OF THESE?
POW!
THAT DOES IT! WAIT HERE TIL I GET MY COSTUME!
WHAT, YOU DON'T WEAR IT UNDER THOSE DORKY CLOTHES?
NO, BUT I KEEP A SPARE HIDDEN IN AMELIA'S JAMMIE DRAWER!
WHAT?!
Oops! (I've said Too Much!)
YOU WHAT?!
ACK!
LASD one now...
Easy...
EEEEasy.
DERE.
All DUD!
ulk

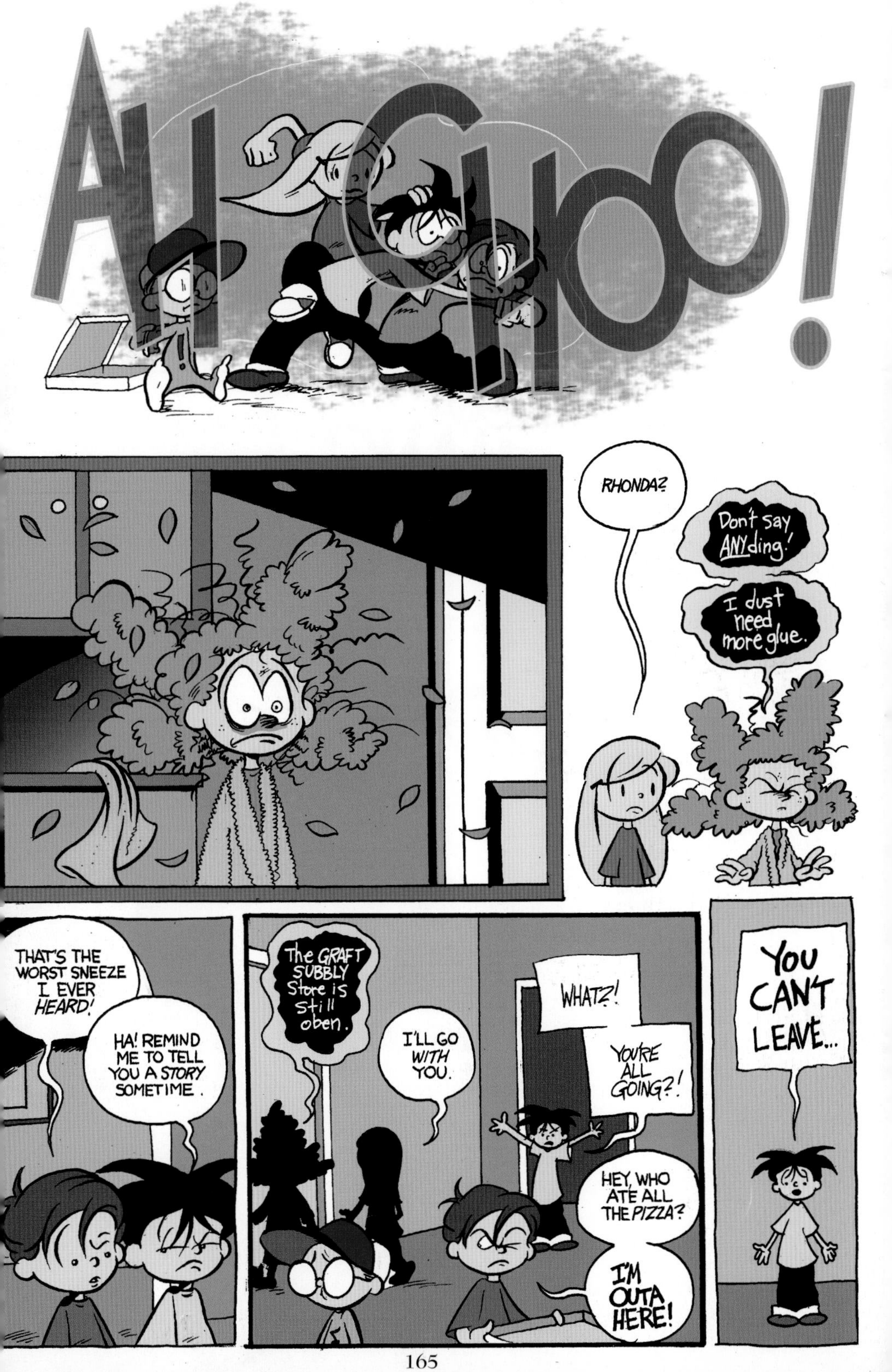
AH CHOO!
RHONDA?
Don't say ANYding!
I dust need more glue.
THAT'S THE WORST SNEEZE I EVER HEARD!
HA! REMIND ME TO TELL YOU A STORY SOMETIME.
The GRAFT SUBBLY Store is still oben.
I'LL GO WITH YOU.
WHAT?!
YOU'RE ALL GOING?!
HEY, WHO ATE ALL THE PIZZA?
I'M OUTA HERE!
YOU CAN'T LEAVE...

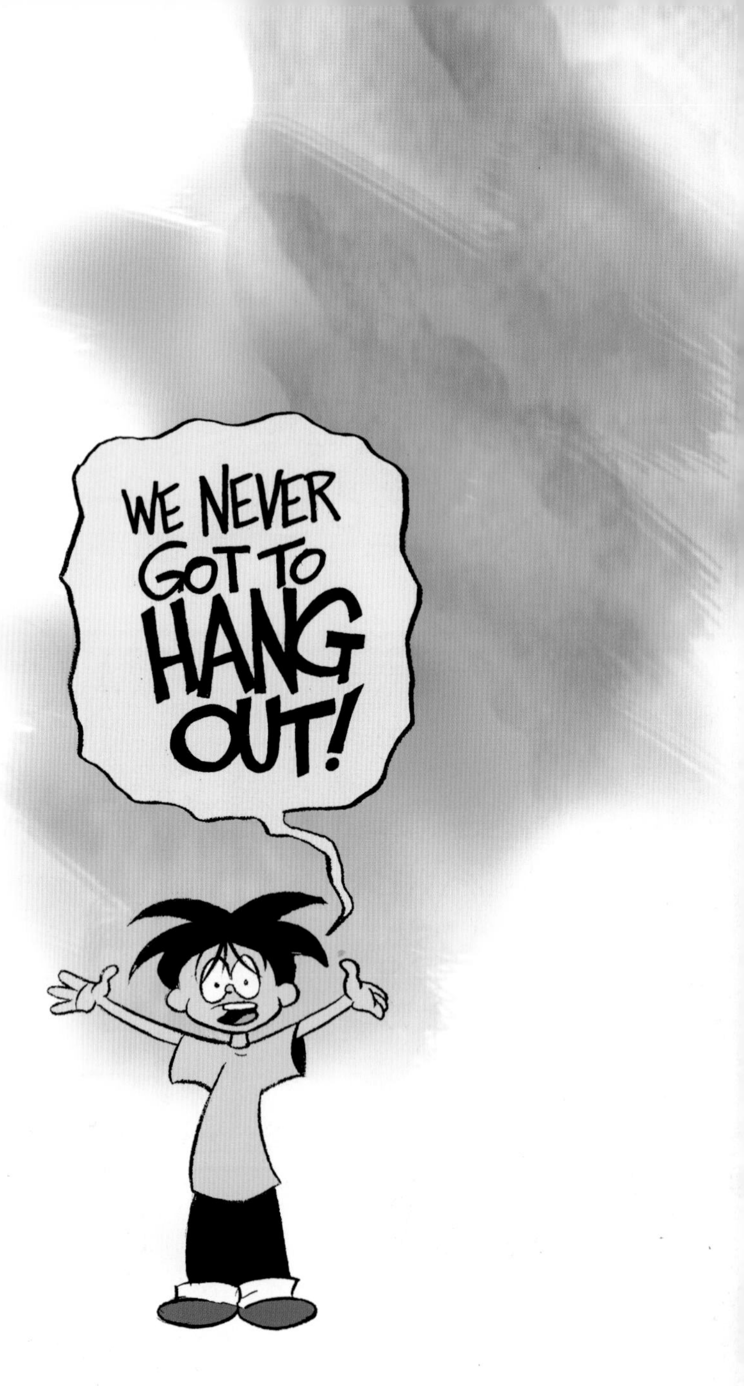
WE NEVER GOT TO HANG OUT!

Cartoonist Jimmy Gownley developed a love of comics at an early age when his mother read *Peanuts* collections to him. Not long after, he discovered comic books (via his dad) and developed a voracious appetite for reading any and all things comic-related.

By the age of 15, Gownley was self-publishing his first book, **Shades of Gray Comics and Stories**. The black & white slice-of-life series ran 16 issues and was recently collected by **Century Comics**.

The idea for *Amelia Rules!* came about several years ago while Gownley was still working on **Shades of Gray**. The goal was to create a comic book with comic strip sensibilities that both traditional and nontraditional comic book fans could enjoy. He also wanted to provide good, solid entertainment for kids that didn't talk down to them.

Since its debut in June 2001, *Amelia Rules!* has become a critical and fan favorite. It has been nominated for several awards, including the *Howard Eugene Day Memorial Prize*, the *Harvey Award* and the *Eisner Award*, and in 2006, the third volume of the series, *Amelia Rules! Superheroes*, received the *Cybil Award* for *Best Graphic Novel: Ages 12 and Under*.

Gownley lives in Harrisburg, Pennsylvania with his wife Karen and twin daughters Stella and Anna.